They've Left Us Behind

A social history
of the Carroll and McGlinn families
in Western Australia

Maureen Francesconi/Carroll

 A catalogue record for this book is available from the National Library of Australia

For queries regarding this book, please contact the author at:
<u>mfrances97@gmail.com</u>

Copyright © 2023 Maureen Francesconi/Carroll
All rights reserved.
ISBN-13: 978-1-922727-81-7

Linellen Press
265 Boomerang Road
Oldbury, Western Australia
www.linellenpress.com.au

Dedication

This book is dedicated to my four grandchildren, Emily, Amy, Braden and Kira, and my great-grandson Ren, who hopefully will have that important family history they may want to know.

Contents

Dedication	iii
Contents	v
Introduction	vii
Acknowledgements and Thanks	x
Family Origins Map	1
Part 1	3
The Carrolls – The Carroll Family Line	5
The Kemps – Kemp Family Line	45
The McGlinns – McGlinn Family Line	115
The Ashworths – Ashworth Family Line	171
The Pollards – Pollard Family Line	189
The Gawneds – Gawned Family Line	197
The Williams – Williams Family Line	203
Part 2 – World War and Beyond	243
The end of WWII and getting back to a 'normal' life	355
About the Author	400

Introduction

It is usually not until later in life when all the things that consume our time and energy finally ease that an interest is taken in our heritage. However, when that time comes and answers to our questions are needed there is often no one left to ask. This is frustrating in the extreme. We would like to know what it was like in our parents' and grandparents' time, what their grandparents were like and what they did and what their story was. Unfortunately, those early members of our families have died and their story has ended as though they had never existed. They say after three generations you might as well have never lived; all you become is a name, birth date, and death date in a family tree There is no other history, and while it is nice to see a name and a line going back in our ancestral family tree it is not enough to have just a birth and death date. Because of this I have tried to give a bigger picture of the lives and times of our recent ancestors, particularly those who came to Australia, and what life was like for them.

Stanley Lawrence Carroll's and Doreen McGlinn's family lines in Australia go back to early colonial days and each has an interesting family history. No one has reached where they are in life without their varied background influences and this may be evident in their daily lives, and the manifestation of their personalities. The main family lines are Irish, English and a touch of Manx (Isle of Man). Included are some of the earlier family members, parents and grandparents of those who left their homeland to come to Australia. It is not meant to be a family tree but is mainly the story of the people who arrived in Australia and the reasons they left their homes to forge a new life in a new land. By research and deduction this account gives an accurate a picture of their lives as possible.

The experiences in their lives which, for the most part, were hard lessons in survival with a life full of grit, determination and sometimes poverty, tragedy, sadness and loss. Most of those in the years before coming to Australia were burdened with famine and unimaginable hardship. This must have forged a certain toughness that helped them to endure and cope with the harsh colonial life in Australia, and brought a closeness to family and community that was displayed throughout their lives. If their home lives were comfortable and prosperous, few would have been likely to embark on the unknown. Most were working people but terrible circumstances forced a change. Unfortunately, their personalities can't be guessed at but their moulding was a result of their extremely difficult backgrounds. Their past family histories in the United Kingdom were fraught with invasions and wars for millennia. The fortress castles and high walls across the lands were testament to many traumatic times.

The people discussed include the Carroll, Walsh, Mahon families from the Goulburn area of New South Wales; the Kemp and Buckley families from Geraldton and Greenough; the Ashworth and Pollard family from (Van Dieman's Land (Tasmania), Guildford and York; the McGlinn and Walker family from Guildford and York, Western Australia; the Gawned and Lannan family from Victoria, and the Williams from South Australia. For various reasons all of these people made their way to Western Australia to settle. Some information is included about the recent ancestors of those who migrated to Australia. For the most part, their frugal and hard lives led to a resilience and self-determination not seen by many today.

There were transported convicts in our past and it is sad to think that they were looked down upon by their families for a couple of generations and many denied having a convict in the family. These convicts came from extremely harsh environments filled with hardship. Many at that time had to steal just to survive and to feed their families, and it is difficult to imagine the terrible times in which they lived. Stealing just a loaf of bread could lead to a conviction that resulted in transportation to the colonies. The death sentence could be imposed for stealing things no more valuable than a few shillings. Conditions were so bad that some stole just enough to get a conviction to be transported to escape it all.

Others who left their homelands during these same hard times to go to a better place came as free settlers who felt they needed to make a new life for themselves and their families. Others were in the military and were sent to the colonies to transport convicts and to guard the colonists.

There were single women and girls, who experienced such extreme poverty and wretchedness that they were forced to go into the Poor Houses in their home country just to survive. Some of these women and girls were selected to be sent to Australia to be servants to the colonists.

None of our ancestors came to Australia as gentry; most were ordinary citizens who had very little. Some were literate, which was quite uncommon in those times, and indicated that they were the better off members of their community. Literacy came later to the 'common' people when educational facilities were provided and laws enacted to force children into schooling.

The Pollard/Witherell family was the first to arrive in Australia. They were shipwrecked on the shores of Western Australia in 1830, only a few months after the first colonists arrived, but it was only a few years before others in the family made their way to Australia to make a new life in a new country. The last of the original families arrived in 1871. Some of their stories are brief, others more complete.

Throughout the generations in Australia changes can be seen in the mores of society and as time went by a modernisation took place, both in technology and fashions and life's expectations.

When the two world wars broke out, some of the McGlinn and Carroll men joined the army and fought, mostly for Mother England, as was the patriotism of the day. A detailed record of each of those who served is included, particularly the extraordinary braveness of Stanley Lawrence Carroll during WW2.

As time marched on, domesticity and providing for a family in the modern era became the priority of the day until eventually retirement and a more sedentary lifestyle could occur.

The stories begin with the Carroll and Kemp families and their forebears, and then the McGlinn and Gawned families. Each go back by earlier generations to give a reasonably complete story of their families since arrival, including the women. Part 1 contains the families' histories up until the start of World War 2.

Stanley Lawrence Carroll and Doreen McGlinn have gone now – they've left us behind, and we cannot ask those very important questions of them …

Acknowledgements and Thanks

I would like to give my sincere thanks to my cousin Max Carroll, son of Norman George Carroll, who researched the <u>male</u> Carroll line that I now have permission to use. He also provided much information on the military aspects of WW2. To Gaye Carroll, daughter-in-law of Francis Peter Carroll and Joan Irene McGlinn, for the extraordinary amount of work she put into compiling family trees and for interviewing John McGlinn, all of which she has given permission to use. To my brothers Lindsay and Glentyn for dredging their memories to find information from our past. My cousin, Kaye McCallum, daughter of Joan Irene McGlinn and Francis Peter Carroll, for proof reading sections of this book and supplying some photographs and information. Also, my cousin Lesley Watson, daughter of William Kevin Carroll and Patricia O'Donnell, who also proof-read sections of the book and who provided photos and information on the Kemp family, Stanley Lawrence's mother's line. Lesley obtained that information from a relative, Lynn Sharpe, of the Kemp family in England, who researched the family history of Joshua Kemp. Mary Ellen (Molly) Thorley/Carroll, Stanley Lawrence's eldest sister, who wrote of her life in Nannine during their childhood, her statements about their life there, and her later life, have been used in this book. Edmund Ashworth, Doreen's great-grandfather, wrote a diary that included his whole life up until he built a house at York, WA after he was married.

Thank you to my friend and colleague Greg Harold for taking me to the Holland Track and beyond. I would like to thank my other cousins for providing information not easily gained, and Julie Johns, a pupil of Stanley Lawrence Carroll, at Floreat Park Primary School. All have saved me an inordinate amount of time and I am grateful to them all. Also, my publisher, Helen Iles, for her patience and guidance.

Finally, I would like to thank Mr Arthur Leggett, OAM, who was in Stanley Lawrence Carroll's Signals Division, 2/11th Battalion, during WW2. He told me of Stanley Lawrence's participation and how Signals were carried out during battles. Arthur was 104 years old at the time of giving me this information, he is an amazing man.

I would especially like to thank my granddaughter Emily for providing the illustration in this book. She is a very talented person.

Family Origins - Map

The map below shows where the Carrolls and McGlinns and their respective in-laws and families originated.

Original map from (www.bing.com/images)

The Family lines, for those *prior* to coming to Australia, have not been verified. These dates were taken from online documentation and by individuals doing their respective family trees.

Further sources

The Australian War Memorial, Canberra for online information and online photos.

The National Archives of Australia for providing the war records of those who served.

Part 1 contains the family histories and the family involvement in WW1. It includes the early part of Stanley Lawrence Carroll's and Doreen McGlinn's young lives up until the outbreak of WW2.

Part 2 continues from the outbreak of World War 2 when Stanley Lawrence and his brothers enlist. His marriage to Doreen McGlinn and her life during wartime. His career choices and retirement to modern times ending in 2013.

*** Please note – all the men in this document with the name of John were known as Jack. The name John wasn't commonly used until after WW2 when the name Jack was no longer commonly used.

Part 1

The Carrolls

Carroll Family Line

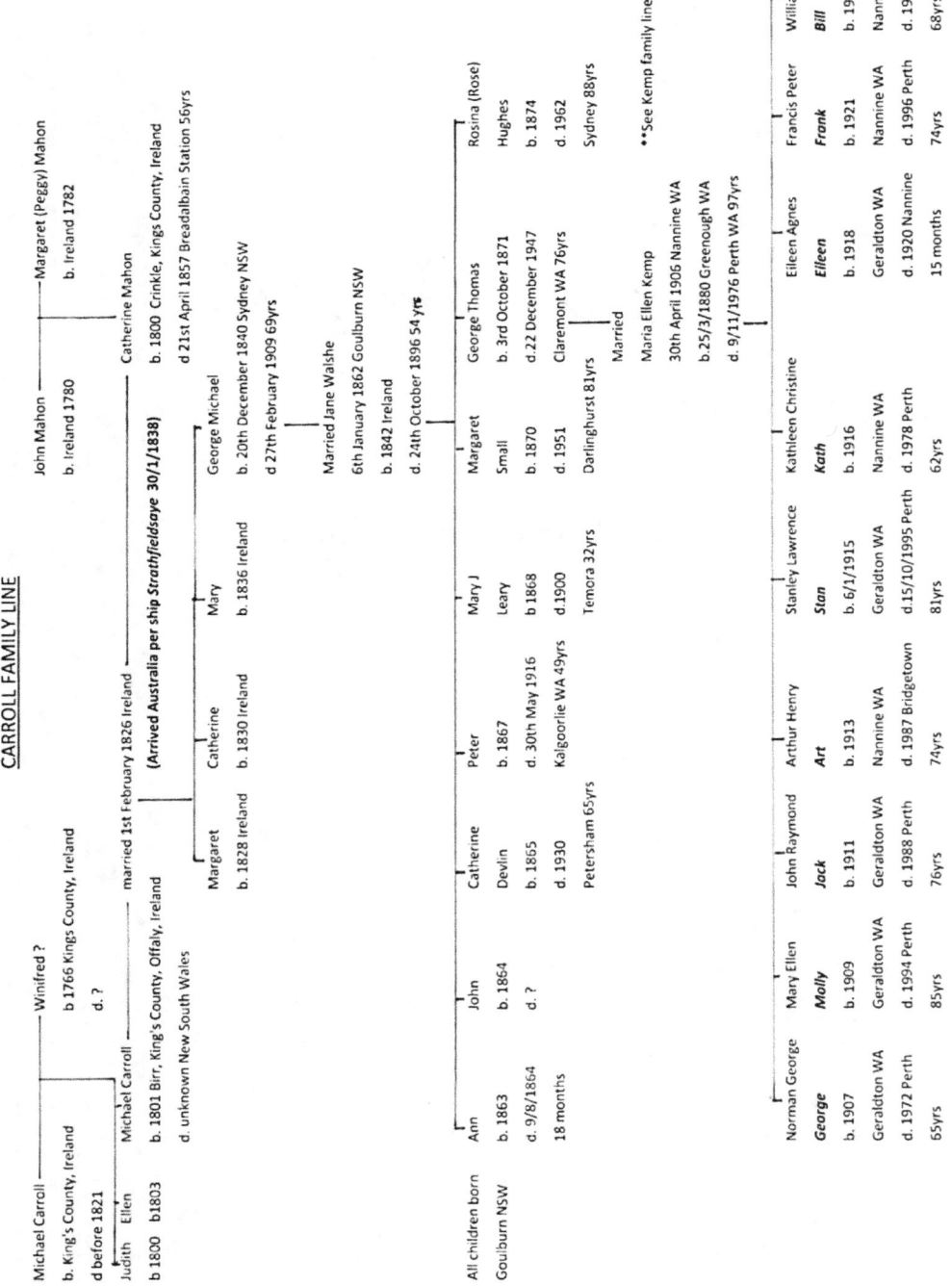

Stanley Lawrence Carroll's father
George Thomas Carroll

George Thomas Carroll was born in the rural town of Goulburn, New South Wales (NSW), Australia on the 3rd October 1871 and died from pulmonary fibrosis and congestive heart failure in Claremont, Western Australia on 22nd December, 1947, aged 76.

As a child, he lived with his parents, George Michael and Jane, on their farm in the Parish of Mutmutbilly in the locality of Muttbilly, on the Breadalbane Plains, not far from Goulburn NSW. Mutmutbilly was the Aboriginal name for the Breadalbane Plains area. It was an agricultural area in the Southern Tablelands, about 250 kilometres south-west from Sydney, and is located on the Lachlan River headwaters. Mutmutbilly was approximately nine kilometres north-west of the Breadalbane township and it is possible their farm was out along Mutmutbilly Road, a few kilometres west of Breadalbane. Breadalbane was situated on the Hume Highway on the way to Goulburn from Sydney but, in modern times, the highway was re-routed and Breadalbane was bypassed, causing its demise. Goulburn was 'discovered' in 1820 and soon became a large and prosperous town that was the centre for a large rural community. Allotments of farmland in the hinterlands and wider areas of Goulburn were granted free to the early colonists but these grants ceased in 1831, prior to the arrival in Australia of the Carrolls. The gentry had claimed a good proportion of the land and probably leased plots to tenant farmers. The Goulburn and Breadalbane Plains districts became rich agricultural areas and was prime sheep country.

George Thomas was brought up on the farm along with his four sisters and two brothers. It is known he was literate, so it is likely his parents made sure he had, at least, a rudimentary education. George Thomas's father could read and write but his mother was illiterate. His father may have given his children a basic education. In many cases, in those days there was no school close by and children who lived on farms were expected to work from an early age, especially boys. The girls were to work in the house and kitchen garden, but when they were needed to do farm work they pitched in and helped. School was unimportant to most families who preferred their children to work and contribute to the household finances. The older Carroll children probably didn't attend school because it wasn't until 1875 that formal education in the district was provided. LAMBERT, Tracey Jennifer. *Upper Lachlan shire community heritage study 2007-2008*. (Upper Lachlan Shire Council and Heritage Branch, NSW Department of Planning, 2008) p. 68

That same year, a school was planned for Muttbilly but whether George Thomas attended or not would probably have been dependent on the distance to travel to that school. Report of the Council of Education upon the condition of the public schools *1874*, p. 97 (www.trove.com.au)

George Thomas's father probably began his farming career on a farm that had to be cleared and prepared for cultivation. *"Due to lack of assistance from the British Government, primitive implements were invented and produced in Australia to help in the process of seedbed preparation. For over 100 years, until the 1930s, the horse was the chief source of farm power."* PRATLEY, J. and ROWELL, L. Evolution of Australian agriculture: from cultivation to no-till (www.csu.edu.au 2020)

Crop preparation on their farm was likely to have been done by using the newly invented 'Stump Jump Plough' that would have been pulled by a draught horse, a boon for difficult land that had rocks and stumps left after clearing. *"In 1876 a special plough was invented by agricultural machinery apprentice Richard Bowyer Smith, and later developed and perfected by his brother, Clarence Herbert Smith, on the Yorke Peninsula, (South Australia) … The plough consisted of any number of hinged shares: when the blade encountered an underground obstacle like a mallee stump, it would rise out of the ground. Attached weights forced the blade back into the ground after the root was passed, allowing as much of the ground to be furrowed as possible. Although a little unorthodox, the plough … proved remarkably effective, and was dubbed the "stump-jump" plough."* (https://en.wikipedia.org/wiki/Stump-jump_plough)

Crops were sewn, probably harvested with a horse-drawn hay cutter, stacked and processed by hand. Sheep would have been shorn by hand using big shearing scissors or, if the family was wealthy, they may have had a rudimentary mechanical shearing stand. The Carroll family would have had their work cut out for them, this labour-intensive farming was back-breaking work that went from dawn until dusk during the busy periods and they would have worked long hours six days a week.

Religion was important to most people and Sundays were sacred, so no one worked on a Sunday. These early pioneer farmers were made of tough stuff; many succeeded and made a success of their farms, especially in prime farming lands like those of the Breadalbane Plains district. On George Thomas's Marriage Certificate, he stated that his father was a 'Grazier', a sheep farmer.

When George Thomas was a child and young man there would have been days off from the grind of work to attend social gatherings and they would have had a good social life, as most rural people did. Then, as he grew older, there would have been dances, sporting events, and social gatherings and many group picnics such as that shown in the photo below of the Carroll family. Perhaps the picnic is to celebrate a birthday or part of a church picnic. The all-important water barrel is on the cart behind them.

A Family picnic: George Thomas Carroll, centre rear, pouring a glass of beer.
(Family photo)

This 'Irish' family was Roman Catholic, so they would have regularly attended the local Catholic Church, and many social gatherings would have taken place with the church parishioners. In small communities such as this, the people would have all known each other and supported each other – it would have been a tight-knit community.

Whatever the reason for the picnic, it certainly looks as though the Carrolls were enjoying the celebration with lots of booze and food. All were dressed in their best 'outing' or 'church' clothes and, by the prosperous look of the family, all was going very well. George Thomas looks as though he was having a great time and has a cheeky look about him!

Unfortunately, unknown to them, the rural sector was on the cusp of a huge downturn in the farming economy in Australia. Things soon began to go bad financially and, by 1890, when George Thomas was nineteen years old, a serious depression had hit the whole of Australia and things got very tough indeed.

"*There were many factors that led to the 1890s depression, including a fall in the price of wool which, at the time, made up around half of Australia's exports. During the boom years of the 1880s, overseas capital had poured into Australia, with much of the investment going into pastoral industries"* (www.australianfoodtimeline.com.au/1890s-depression)

Being farmers, sheep, wool, and a small amount of cropping were probably the Carroll's main sources of income and they would have been very comfortable. However, they were soon to experience extreme hardship.

***George Thomas Carroll before he left NSW for the WA goldfields.
(Family photo)***

By the end of the century, George Thomas and his older brothers, Peter and John, may have had little hope of a prosperous future in the area and there was unlikely to be any decent employment in rural NSW. Work on other farms would have been non-existent with many other farmers trying to eke out an existence just to survive. George Thomas and his brothers only had farming skills so they would have struggled to get work. Their life of reasonable affluence was over. The family farm may have been sold. However, during those hard times, many farmers were financially ruined and walked off their land – they lost everything. This may have been the case for the Carrolls.

Before 1883 when George Thomas was a teenager the family left the farm at Mutmutbilly and moved to Sebastopol, just south of Temora NSW.

The Lure of Western Australian Gold

The goldfields of Western Australia were discovered in Southern Cross in 1887, then in Coolgardie in 1892 and Kalgoorlie in 1893; they were thriving and very rich fields. Now that their mother had died and their father had moved in with their married sister Margaret Small, the family unit was fragmented. The brothers, Peter and George Thomas, decided they would have a go at finding gold in Western Australia. Their struggle to be financially well off may have been too great and they wanted easier wealth in those tough times. Gold may have been the hope for their future and they may have dreamed of striking it rich. Unlike their older brother John, they were still unmarried so their future decisions were made easier.

The gold rush had been on for several years but they may have thought it was still worth a try. News from the Western Australian goldfields was still full of stories about rich finds, and the brothers had nothing to lose and everything to gain ... so they thought.

George Thomas and Peter farewelled the family and *"travelled from ... NSW by Cobb and Co coach to Melbourne, Victoria, then by ship to Albany WA. They then walked to Coolgardie."* CARROLL, Max. *Memoir*

From early shipping records, there is an entry for Messrs Carroll (meaning more than one male Carroll) arriving in Albany on 22nd January, 1899 on the ship *Adelaide*. This was highly likely to be them because there were no other Carroll males noted as travelling together during the correct time period. George Thomas was now twenty-seven years old and Peter was thirty-two.

The problem was thousands and thousands of other men from eastern Australia decided on the same thing and they poured into Western Australia with the same dreams of striking it rich. A passenger on one of those ships who travelled to Albany from Melbourne during that same period wrote a letter explaining the situation at that time. He said: *"the whole country is in a panic ... with Melbourne "nearly ruined" as "over ten thousand men have cleared out to the Western Australian goldfields". In Albany the "ship put down several passengers, and I can assure you they were like raving mad men, so great was their ambition and excitement of gold, for they believed it was to be picked up in the streets ..."* DOWSON, John. *Old Albany, photographs 1850-1950*. (Albany Chamber of Commerce, 2008) p. 80

The brothers immediately set out for the Eastern Goldfields where gold was still being found in large quantities, perfect timing coinciding with the downturn in agricultural prices. They would have travelled via the Holland Track which was cut through from Broomhill to Coolgardie by John Holland, Rudolph and David Krakouer, and John Carmody in 1893. These men *"left Broomehill with five ponies, a light dray, a 100-gallon (450 litres) water tank and provisions for 5-6 months. Using a small compass, they aimed for Gnarlbine Rock, the goldfield's main water supply which they reached in June. Holland would go ahead each day and scout for water and horse feed, while the others cut the track. They reached Bayley's Find at Fly Flat on June 18th, having covered nearly 330 miles (538 km) in 2 months and 4 days, cutting the longest cart road ever made in one stretch in Western Australia. Prospectors could now land in Albany and make their way to Broomehill and on up the Holland Track to the goldfields, cutting off more than a fortnight to their journey. Some 18,000 fortune seekers used the track and teams laden with food, general stores and mining equipment made regular use of the track when gold was first discovered in Kalgoorlie."* (https://www.monumentaustralia.org.au) 2020

The wheel tracks at the bottom right of the photo are part of the Holland track
(Personal photo)

The track went through virgin eucalypt woodland and areas of low heathland and, for the most part, was waterless. It was a rough dirt track but, with much use, it became suitable for carts, camel teams and men on horseback as well as those who walked the distance pushing their wheeled carts. Water would have been carted along the track and it is probable enterprising men would have had lucrative businesses carting and selling water to the travellers. It was the only track from the south on which to travel for the many thousands of men, and a few women, who had come by ship to Albany.

At that time, Albany was the main port in Western Australia and, until the end of the 19th century, the only port of call for the many mail ships heading to England from Sydney and Melbourne. Fremantle was not on these ships' routes and was bypassed. This is the reason so many from eastern Australia travelled to the goldfields via Albany and the Holland Track.

In 1892, the trip from Melbourne to Albany via ship cost £5 *and prior to the opening of the Holland Track travel would have been a complicated affair. The main option was, after arriving in Albany, catch the train to Narrogin which was 178 miles at a cost of £1/2s/3d then walk via the Perth to Coolgardie road (sections of which is now Great Eastern Highway) from Narrogin to Coolgardie, a distance of 328 miles, with the cost of having their gear transported by team (horse or bullock), not exceeding 100lb, was £2.* Australian Gold Magazine (July 2020) p. 30.

At that time, if you had work, the average wage was approximately £2 - £3 a week so the cost of travelling to the goldfields was quite expensive. The costs would have been approximately the same, perhaps a bit cheaper by the time George Thomas and Peter travelled in early 1899. The Holland track was a very attractive option for them.

The Kalgoorlie pipeline wasn't yet completed so water was at a premium in those hot dry areas. A huge effort was applied to get and store water. Large granite outcrops were used to dam water and long low walls were built to guide rainwater into large tanks or dams at the base of the outcrop. The water was then carted to the growing towns, of which there were many, and sold to the people. Water was expensive and was not wasted; it was used very frugally. To supplement this dammed water, condensers were built in some of the little goldfield towns. The brothers would soon learn the value of water. Their home in Muttbilly and Temora had no problems with water as the rainfall was reliable and plentiful.

An example of these long low walls is on this granite outcrop is near Norseman, Western Australia. The wall to guide the water went for over a kilometre.
(Fifty Mile Rocks. Personal photo 2021)

Here, a large 'bowl' approximately 40m wide and 5m deep was built to catch the guided water.
(Fifty Mile Rocks. Personal photo 2021)

The brothers would have bought some prospecting supplies and non-perishable foods, particularly flour, tea, and very likely sugar, in Albany before heading off overland to the head of the Holland Track at Broomhill. Any meat along the track would have been what they could catch or shoot, if they were lucky. The area would have been wiped out of wildlife by then, and often damper and dried salted meat were the popular staples for prospectors. To transport their gear, many men would only have a type of push cart, as shown in the photo below, to get their supplies and equipment to the goldfields. Others who were financially better off would have had their gear carted. Whatever choice they made there was a great deal of walking to do. The Carrolls would have experienced a very hard slog in the blistering hot, dry summer during their walk!

Typical mode of transport when George Thomas and his brother walked to the eastern goldfields from Albany (http://museum.wa.gov.au)

They would probably have used a shaker/dryblower similar to this to find gold after they arrived in the goldfields. (http://museum.wa.gov.au)

When they arrived in the eastern goldfields, they would have had to kit themselves out with the tools they needed. A prospector needed a pick and shovel, a dolly pot to crush rock, and a dry-blower - an ingenious contraption that could sort gold from dirt without the use of water. Plus, they needed a tent, bedding and eating implements. The shopkeepers of the goldfields were the ones who 'struck gold' and many made a fortune selling their wares.

Dry-blowers and shakers were common and would have been used on many of the smaller claims and to test areas for alluvial gold George Thomas and Peter would have had a difficult job ahead of them to strike it rich. They could have simply been extremely lucky to chance on a good patch but, unfortunately, it seems they didn't make their fortune. Some prospectors did hit a good strike but the vast majority did not even make enough to pay for their food! Thousands of men had descended on Coolgardie and surrounding areas and available gold leases or land to peg would have been few and far between. To find new ground, prospectors travelled all over the greater area looking for likely patches and many spread out for hundreds of kilometres, well beyond the known alluvial gold. Most of them would have had no luck, or very little luck, and the work was extremely hard, arduous, risky, boring, hot and dusty. A lot of men perished during their search for wealth, often alone, dying from thirst or disease, and many were left in unmarked, or crudely made graves out in the bush, some of which can still be found out there. Things were so tough that suicide was common. Their families may have never been notified, or even knew where they were; they just disappeared and were never heard from again.

From Coolgardie, George Thomas and Peter went on to Kalgoorlie where the famous Golden Mile had been discovered in 1893 by Paddy Hannan, Dan Shea and Tom Flanagan. It was a very rich find and had a massive deposit containing greater than 1500 tonnes of gold, much of it underground. For a short time, the streets of Kalgoorlie-Boulder had indeed been paved with gold!

By the time George Thomas and Peter arrived and tried to find ground to work, the gold leases would have been scarce and it seems their luck wasn't in. Their finances may have dwindled to such an extent that they may have been forced to stay close to Kalgoorlie. Gold had been found several years before in Kanowna, an area just north-east about 20 kilometres from Kalgoorlie, and was still a rich gold-bearing area so George Thomas and Peter moved there. A couple of years before they arrived in Kanowna, there had been a major gold rush to a new rich find.

On *"the 3rd of December 1897 by 2pm nearly 3000 people had gathered to witness the rush and to peg a big portion of the action in the hope of making their fortune. Sergeant of Police at Kanowna was in charge of the event and at 2.30 he raised his hand and dropped his handkerchief as the signal to start pegging could begin ... all the ground was pegged without any serious injury to anyone. A claim for each individual miner was only 25 square yards and 25x50 yards for 2 mining partners ..."* (www.outbackfamilyhistory.com.au)

Whether the brothers struck gold is unknown, but apparently they ended up staying in Kanowna.

During his life, George Thomas told the story that his brother had died of typhoid in Kanowna. No record can be found about a Peter Carroll and his death from typhoid even though good records were kept during that period. The only Peter Carroll with records of having lived in Kanowna at that time were census, marriage, and death records. It is suspected that George Thomas's story was fabricated. Peter Carroll's death certificate had all the correct dates for his birth and the periods he had lived in both NSW and WA. The only Peter Carroll living in Kanowna found romance and married in 1903 and became a miner. Sadly, he died, aged 50, on 30th May, 1916. He had injured his arm somehow and it had become badly infected. His death was registered in East Coolgardie (that is Kalgoorlie) and he is buried in the Roman Catholic section in Kalgoorlie Cemetery. He died of a Suppurated arm (infection) and poison in the glands (that probably led to sepsis). (The Registry of Births, Deaths and Marriages Online Index Search Tool (www.wa.gov.au))

There were no antibiotics then – penicillin wasn't discovered by Alexander Fleming until 1928 – so infections were extremely dangerous and life-threatening and the home remedies of the day weren't always successful.

His death was noted in the *Family Notices.* (Kalgoorlie Miner. WA: 1895 – 1954. Wed 31 May 1916) P. 4

> *"CARROLL. -- The friends of the late Peter Carroll, late of Kanowna, are respectfully informed that his remains will be removed from Messrs. Mannion and Cruse's private mortuary, Hannan Street, at 12 o clock this day (Wednesday), May 31, for interment in the Catholic portion of the Kalgoorlie Cemetery -- Mannion and Cruse, Undertaker. Kalgoorlie and Boulder".*

At the time Peter married in 1903, George Thomas probably felt he was either in the way of the romance or there could have been some friction between the brothers. It is suspected that George Thomas either had not been pulling his weight or had become 'interested' in Peter's wife.

The story of Peter's death by typhoid could have been very plausible. At that time, there was a very real danger of contracting typhoid and there was a general fear throughout the area. Typhoid was a very real threat to the mining communities of Western Australia.

In 1895, only two years after the big Kalgoorlie discovery, a typhoid epidemic hit Kalgoorlie and surrounding areas, including Kanowna, *"and … reached epidemic proportions. An infectious food and water-borne disease, typhoid was linked to poor sanitation, often combined with overcrowding. Instant crowded tent towns, unsanitary conditions, and a limited fouled water supply combined with basic health amenities, (i.e. no toilets) provided ideal conditions for the spread of the disease. Its greatest impact was during the long hot summer months. In the early years of the epidemic, up to twenty percent of - mostly - healthy young men, died. Nearly 2000 people in Western Australia were officially recorded as dying of the disease, though the actual number was far greater. Most deaths occurred on the goldfields. An estimated ten times more people suffered from the disease. It was the largest episode of epidemic typhoid in Australia's history".* (http://museum.wa.gov.au/explore/wa-goldfields/dangerous-life/typhoid-fever-raging-epidemic)

The Carroll brothers' time in the eastern goldfields coincided with the epidemic that had spread to most of the greater goldfields, including the Murchison goldfields, and even to Perth and lasted until 1910 when better sewage management was introduced and 'night soil' began to be collected. Prior to that, open cesspits were used to dispose of human waste – most people only had a hole in the ground. Typhoid is a very unpleasant condition that can take several weeks to kill the person. Its symptoms include a high temperature, fatigue, headache, rattly cough, constipation or diarrhoea, distended and very painful abdomen, and intestinal haemorrhage. It is caused by faeces to mouth contamination, usually through fouled water. (www.cdc.gov/typhoid-fever/symptoms.html)

George Thomas made plans to leave for other fields. He was now at a crossroads in life: go home to New South Wales or stay in Western Australia. He decided to stay in Western Australia but must have felt the need to move on to other fields. Perhaps he had friends who wanted to go to the Murchison goldfields and so decided to accompany them.

It is not likely he was interested in the hard work of mining; more likely he was looking for easier work and eventually made his way to the township of Nannine. Nannine was the first proclaimed town in the Murchison. *"John Connolly discovered gold at the site in 1890, prompting a gold rush to the area. A town was proclaimed in September 1891 and gazetted in 1893. It is claimed that it was the first town in the region. By 1894 the town was large enough to be given its own electoral district, and in 1896 construction began on a Northern Railway between Nannine and Cue, Western Australia, which was completed in 1903".* (www.australiaforeveryone.com.au)

It is not known how long it took George Thomas to get to Nannine or whether he had the funds to travel on commercial transport. The railway had reached Kalgoorlie from Perth in 1895 so he may have taken the train to Perth. To get to the Murchison most people travelled from Perth to the coastal town of Geraldton and out via Mullewa to Mount Magnet and elsewhere. There is a shipping record for a George Carroll who travelled to Geraldton in March 1904 on the ship *Bunningyong*. This is probably him: the timing is right.

Depending on just when George Thomas travelled to Nannine from Geraldton, he either walked the distance, which many men did, or went on one of the many teams of horses pulling the stage coaches, or maybe he took the train. If he had the funds, he may have then taken the train to Cue and on to Nannine.

It is not known just where in the northern goldfields George Thomas began. It may have been Cue, or nearby Daydawn that he first tried his luck at getting a job or doing some prospecting but it wasn't long before he headed to Nannine where he stayed. He must have arrived there sometime between 1904 and early 1906, and wasn't there long before he met his future wife, Maria Ellen Kemp, and ended up staying there. He may have obtained work contacts along his journey to Nannine, and at some time was a 'carter', a person who did deliveries to mines and around the town. After he was married, he became employed as a Mail Coach Driver to the outer regions of the Murchison goldfields, including Meekatharra and Peak Hill where there were no rail lines. He obviously wasn't a successful prospector so would have struggled to make a living at it, especially if he wasn't keen on the very hard, dirty work involved.

In Nannine, George Thomas would have lived in a boarding house or hotel. In those days, it was very common for single men to live in these places where they had their meals provided and their laundry etc. done for them, otherwise he could have joined the men on the alluvial flats and the unsanitary and unhygienic conditions where there were no such things as toilets etc. – just an open cesspit. Hygiene was lacking and typhoid was prevalent in these areas as well so there was no escape. Probably not to George Thomas's liking, and who could blame him.

On the early Australian Electoral Rolls, George Thomas was stated as being a "Mail Driver" from at least 1910 until 1922. Mail was very important to people because it was the only form of communication apart from a very expensive telegram. There would often be over a tonne of mail on each coach. He may have continued as a Mail Driver for longer than that time but perhaps in a reduced way. There were no records kept prior to 1910 but it is known he was a general goods delivery person before he became a Mail Driver. He was not employed when he married in 1906 and there is no record of employment on his Marriage Certificate. His wife was stated as being a Domestic; she may have been the main source of income for the couple. Perhaps he became a Mail Coach Driver after their marriage.

Being a Mail Coach Driver, George Thomas would have worked with a team of horses to pull the coach that would travel between localities that had passenger "stations" which consisted of a hotel and or accommodation and restaurant of sorts, where the passengers would either have a meal and a break or stay overnight. The coach would then have a fresh team of horses to continue the journey; the tired horses would be left to rest, be watered and fed, and wait until they were required for the next coach swap over. These passenger stations were not like today's hotels and motels. Sometimes the passengers stayed for the night and they would very often have to share a room with a stranger – or two! At times there were no available beds so sleeping on the floor was common. BLAINEY, Geoffrey. *Black kettle and full moon.* (Penguin books, 2003) p. 340.

It is known the coach to Peak Hill went through a gap, known as Connelly's Gap, in a rocky ridge on Norie Station, a short distance from Nannine. This must have been a very busy track because the rocks through the gap were painted with large advertising slogans that were still faintly visible during the 1980s.

It is here, it should be added, that in the book *Nannine by the Lake* by P.R. Heydon, there is a mention on page 95 of an "*informer Carroll*". This is not George Thomas – it is a man named John Carroll and from all accounts he was a rogue and a scoundrel of the largest order. He was described in a newspaper article as a *"Putrescent police pimp menacing the Murchison"*. The Truth. (Sunday March 3 1907)

The mail and passenger Cobb & Co coach similar to the one George Thomas Carroll would have driven in the Murchison. (Photo - Battye Library number 000696D)

As the railways began to spread throughout the northern goldfields and progressed from Cue to Nannine in 1903 and then to Meekatharra in 1910, the trains carried all the goods and passengers in a much more comfortable and reliable manner. As a result, the horse-drawn coach-lines came to an end along these rail routes. George Thomas would have been limited in his coach line job to driving out to areas where no trains went. These deliveries too would have come to an end eventually because the Murchison Goldfields were worked out and coming to an end and people were leaving in big numbers. Now that there were not as many people out in those areas, the size of the mail deliveries would be very much smaller. Private carriers may have taken over from the larger coach lines. Also, the new trucks and cars, which were a lot faster though a lot less reliable, began to arrive in the goldfields and they too would have eventually taken over the transport along these outer routes. The era of horse-drawn transport was now nearing the end.

With reduced work opportunities, it was fortunate he was good with horses and was familiar with farm work so it was probably at this stage George Thomas was *"contracted to bring the wool bales down from some of the stations, conveying them on large drays drawn by four draught horses"*. CARROLL, Max. *Memoir*

Wool wagon similar to the one George Thomas Carroll used.
The brand on his coat. Ed. R. Erikson (UWA press, 1983) p. 309

However, this employment was precarious because the wool carting business would have only been seasonal work so he would have needed other work to support the family. The horse was not really suited to that part of the country and camels soon became the main transport to and from the stations and other outposts. The problem with horses was that they required feed and water and this was often too difficult to provide in those dry areas. Stage coach routes would have had feed delivered to the 'stopovers' so there was not a problem but out in the bush it would be very difficult to provide and they would have to cart feed and water as well as their load. Camels on the other hand can go across that country for long periods without water and they don't need feed carted for them – they can graze very well on the local vegetation. They persist as feral animals in the dry country today.

It is known that George Thomas was familiar with the camel-drawn wagons because Stanley Lawrence talked of his father almost being killed by a camel that was about to bite the top of his head (off?) and was saved by the Afghan cameleer. Another story Stanley Lawrence recalled was a time during summer when George Thomas rode his bicycle to some far-off destination, got two flat tyres, and ran out of water – an extremely dangerous situation in those remote, baking hot areas. He was in a bad way when an Afghan cameleer found him and gave him water, hoisted George Thomas and his bicycle up onto the wagon and gave him a lift. The cameleer once again saved George Thomas's life.

In order to provide better for his large family George Thomas needed to change to a more reliable and regular job. He would have found it difficult to get another job because he had no trade and no particular skills apart from farming, which wasn't an option in that remote area. Fortunately, he was able to secure part-time casual employment as a Length Runner with the Government Railways *"operating a hand propelled tricycle ... between Nannine and Meekatharra, in advance of the trains, to clear the line of obstacles."* CARROLL, Max. *Memoir*. The train only went to Meekatharra twice a week so his wages from that job would have been minimal in the extreme.

Hand propelled railway tricycle
similar to that used by George Thomas Carroll at Nannine
Photo – (www.bing.com/images). 2020

This was the last of the jobs he had in Nannine and, even though the train ran well into the 1970s, it no longer required a Length Runner because a 'clearer' was built onto the front of the trains. The dying town meant there was no longer any opportunities for employment and it was time for the family to leave Nannine and go south to work and live.

He was now approximately fifty-four years old and was fortunate enough to get another casual job with the railways in Sawyers Valley, a small town situated in the hills east of Perth. From 1926 until 1936, while they were living in Mt Helena and then in Claremont, it stated on the Australian Electoral Roll as him having the occupation of a "Repairer" with the Western Australian Government Railways (WAGR).

"A 'Repairer' was a member of the track gang. There were usually about 5-6 men in a gang, with 4-5 'repairers', overseen by the 'ganger'. These men were also referred to as fettlers or platelayers. The WAGR system had track gangs all along the network, with the gang working either side of their home station or camp. These gang sections were all numbered and the WAGR encouraged competition between gangs to maintain high standards of track repair. The best sections were rewarded with pay bonuses.

In the late 1920's the WAGR was engaged in a major project to upgrade the rails on the Eastern Railway from Fremantle-Northam. (George Thomas) may have been engaged in this work while based at Mt Helena. After the railway from Meekatharra-Wiluna was opened in 1932 the railway from Mullewa-Cue was progressively upgraded to handle the increased train traffic. This was a long project and went through to about 1937. Again, (George Thomas) may have been engaged in this work while based at Mt Magnet". The photo below shows a typical 'gang' on their motorised trolley. Information from Jeff Austin, Railway Heritage WA, 2021.

These Repairers travelled on their trollies until they found a problem with the track. They would repair the track then continue on their trolley. This work was not like the hard and constant work of track layers. The team was likely to have been a cohesive social group and they probably enjoyed working together.

*Railway Gang on their motorised trolley with Repairers and a Ganger on board.
(Photo – RHWA P13604, Courtesy - Railway Heritage WA, 2021)*

After moving to Claremont to live, George Thomas, once again, went away for long periods to work as a Repairer in Mt Magnet, probably on the Mt Magnet line as stated above, and stayed with John and Mary Bald. He probably carried out this occupation away from home until he retired when the work on the line was finished. He was now sixty-five years old and could retire on a pension.

It seems George Thomas always liked to dress well and to always look well groomed – and he liked to have nice shiny shoes! He stood straight and tall and didn't have the stooped appearance of a man who worked hard physically.

It seems George Thomas was the one in the family who was the nice guy with his children. He could come home for short periods and spend time with them, but he was away a lot trying to provide for his large family. His wife, Maria Ellen, had to take the children in hand alone and she became the tyrant to maintain control and was the one who had to discipline their eight surviving children and care for their upbringing. His eldest son, Norman George, followed in his father's footsteps and spent most of his time working in the Pilbara away from his family, leaving his wife Dorothy to bring up their three boys alone. He must have thought it was normal. It seems working away would be a lot easier than staying home, going to work, and having the responsibility of family on a daily basis!

George Thomas's father
George Michael Carroll

George Michael was the first of the Carroll line to be born in Australia. He was born at Pyrmont NSW on 20th December 1840 and died in Temora NSW on 27th February, 1909, aged 69. At some stage along the way he added the middle name of Michael, making his name George Michael Carroll. On his burial details his mother is stated as 'Mary'. His mother's name, however, was Catherine but there were strange circumstances that involved his mother.

The newly-arrived Carrolls had been in Australia almost three years before George Michael was born. His parents, Michael and Catherine, and his older sisters probably doted over this child, because he was the first and only son to carry on the Carroll name. George Michael's three older sisters, Margaret, Catherine, and Mary, were all born in Ireland. He named his daughters after his sisters.

His father, Michael Carroll, bought a farm at Grabben Gullen, northwest of Goulburn, NSW in 1855. George Michael was fifteen years old and it is highly likely he worked for his father on their farm. His mother Catherine died in 1857, only a couple of years after they arrived at Grabben Gullen. George Michael may have left the farm soon afterwards to go elsewhere to live. The circumstances surrounding him leaving the farm are not known but, by the age of twenty-one, he had moved to Breadalbane near Goulburn, NSW, to live and work. Records show that, during 1862 to 1864, he was living in the Breadalbane Hotel and would have worked in the area. He married Jane Walshe in 1862 so it is likely they met each other there and lived in the hotel together. She may have been a domestic servant in the hotel. Sometime after 1864, they decided to leave the hotel to give farming a go.

Marriage in those days may not necessarily have been because of romantic love. Marriages of convenience were common with both the woman and the man agreeing to 'partner up'. The man needed a woman to care for him and his daily needs and the woman often married to get out of a job of servitude.

There is a record on the 1865 Electoral Roll stating that George Michael lived on a block of freehold land in the Parish of Mutmutbilly at the locality of Muttbilly which is part of the Breadalbane Plains district and about forty kilometres south of his father's farm in Grabben Gullen. (Goulburn Historical Society, 2022)

Well before 1883, the family went to live at Sebastopol just south of Temora, NSW and ran a sheep farm there. Unfortunately, George Michael went bankrupt – he may not have owned the farm because he was listed as a 'Labourer' in the insolvency case that was written about in the newspapers of the day.

> "INSOLVENCY COURT In re insolvency of George Carroll, of Sebastopol.
>
> Mr. Healy severely cross-examined in solvent for over an hour, and the evidence elicited was of a conflicting nature. It was shown that, in spite of the existence of a lien to Goldsbrough and Co. over his wool clip, he sold the sheep to one Denis Kavanagh, of Sebastopol ; that he treated correspondence with reference to his affairs with indifference, insolvent admitting that he took no notice of certain letters when he received them ; but that there was a possibility of the creditors obtaining payment in full from insolvent s estate by realising on property, the ownership of which they have to prove remains with him in spite of his allegations to the contrary. It was further elicited that he had been pressed by only one of his creditors for the sum of £9 odd, which he alleged was the cause of his insolvency."
>
> *(Cootamundra Herald. Sat 4 Aug 1883 Page 4).*
> *https://trove.nla.gov.au/search*

Jane died in Temora in 1896, aged only fifty-four, not long before George Thomas and Peter left for Western Australia. It was then that George Michael moved in with his daughter Margaret. It seems George Michael became one of Temora's highly regarded citizens.

There was a write-up about him in *The Catholic Press*, (Thu 11 Mar 1909) p. 26 which stated:

> "Mr. G. M. Carroll.
>
> Another of the old pioneers passed away on Saturday morning, 27th. At Temora, in the person of Mr. George Michael Carroll, aged 72 years. The deceased, who was a native of Sydney, first

went to the Temora district about 30 years ago, where he followed farming pursuits. His wife predeceased him about 12 years ago. Since that sad event the deceased had resided with his daughter Mrs. W. Small, of the Royal Hotel. Deceased leaves three sons and three daughters. The funeral took place on Sunday, 28th ult., the cortege being one of the largest ever witnessed in Temora, thus demonstrating the respect and esteem in which he was held. The Rev, Father G. Shannon officiated at the graveside, -- R.I.P."

There is some mystery about the above information. Firstly, the dates are incorrect for his age, and the years he was in Temora are wrong. There is no mention in the article that the family lived in the Goulburn district. For some reason, the Carrolls may have tried to hide that fact and perhaps kept it a secret from the Temora community. Scandal in these small communities would have been very uncomfortable and it may have been that they tried to distance themselves from his parents' problems that had reached the newspapers of the day. George Michael may have been a native of Sydney but a lot had happened between the time he left there and the move to Temora.

Official records for this Carroll family are almost non-existent.

George Michael Carroll (Family photo)

George Thomas's mother
Jane Walshe

Jane Walshe was born in Ireland in about 1842 and died in Temora NSW on 24th October, 1896, aged only fifty-four.

It is not clear what her surname name was – there were various spellings – but George Michael signed her name as Walshe on their marriage certificate. Jane was illiterate and signed her name with her mark; marks were usually an 'X'. They were married in Goulburn, NSW, on 6 January 1862. He was twenty-one and she was twenty.

On their marriage certificate, they are both noted as being "Servants" living at Breadalbane Plains. However, because George Michael was literate, he may have been a Public (government) Servant or doing some sort of administrative work rather than a Domestic Servant, as Jane probably was.

It can be seen from the photo of Jane that she was not considered as important as the men in her family and a lower-quality photo was taken. This sentiment was not unusual at that time.

Jane Walshe. (Family photo)

Copy of marriage certificate for George Michael Carroll and Jane Walshe. Her mark, an 'X', can be seen between Jane and Walshe in the right of the document. George Michael has signed her name for her.

They had two children, Ann and John, while living at the Breadalbane Hotel before buying and moving to the farm at Muttbilly.

Jane's background in Ireland was terribly hard and she was brought to Australia to satisfy the growing needs of the colony. *"In the 1850s-1860s there were boat loads of orphaned or single young Irish women, post (potato) famine, brought to Australia. There was a shortage of women in the colonies! A large number of them ended up in South Western NSW. To this day, Yass has a festival to commemorate the contribution these women made to the district. Jane was one of them."* CARROLL, Max. Memoir

"The Great Famine, also known as the Great Hunger … was a period of starvation and disease in Ireland from 1845 to 1849, which constituted a historical social crisis which had a major impact on Irish society and history as a whole". (https://en.wikipedia.org/wiki/Great Famine (Ireland))

The Great Famine (Potato Famine) killed more than a million people from starvation and disease in Ireland and forced two million to emigrate; mainly to America. Many of the Irish in Northern Ireland were tenant farmers to the rich English who had taken over their plots of land for their own. When the potato blight hit Ireland, the Irish couldn't get money from their potatoes, which was their main source of income, and could not pay the rent to their English landlords. They were forced off their farms and were basically forced to emigrate; they had nothing and they were starving. This famine was all across Europe, not only the British Isles. Many people in Ireland and other places lived in absolutely wretched conditions; millions were starving, homeless and desperate. Many starved to death, particularly children. Young female orphans and single women were hard hit and, with no family to support them, they had to go into the infamous workhouses (Poorhouses). At that time, the Australian colony desperately needed women so requested these women and girls to be sent to Australia to fill the need. Over four thousand young females from these Irish workhouses were shipped out to eastern Australia between 1848 and 1850, and later to Western Australia, to meet the demand for domestic servants. It would have been such a very traumatic time for these girls having to leave their familiar surroundings, as bad as they were, to travel a great distance on a small cramped sailing ship to a country so very different to theirs. A certain toughness would have resulted after such a hard and harsh life.

These girls had an important, and still widely unknown, role in the Australian story, and one which countless Australians can claim in their own family story. Many of these women worked as servants for their keep and many others married and had families, as was the case for both the Carroll and McGlinn families. (www.irishtimes.com/life-and-style/abroad/the-story-of-the-irish-famine-orphan-girls-shipped-to-australia)

Jane Walshe must have had a very difficult time in Ireland to be included in this part of the Irish/Australian history. To have to leave Ireland under such dire circumstances would have been exceedingly hard and frightening for her. Even though her life in Ireland would have been destitute and desperate and she would have struggled to survive, the move would still have been quite daunting.

In the photo of Jane, on page 31, it can be seen that she has no teeth which makes her look rather hawkish. Her teeth probably fell out years earlier because of the dreadful conditions in which she lived and the meagre and very poor quality of the food she ate. If her teeth fell out some time after she was married dentures would have been too expensive and, for a woman with a large family, it was unlikely she would ever have had them, in fact, many women were encouraged to have their teeth removed before marriage so as to not cause expense to their husbands! Men may have been lucky to be able to disguise their toothless look by the big mustachioed fashion of the day!

Jane would have had a complete change when she came to Australia and now had opportunities that were impossible for her to imagine in Ireland – from almost no hope to a good and prosperous future. It is likely she would have been given employment as a domestic servant immediately after she arrived; the Breadalbane Hotel probably requested a servant and she was sent there.

Poor Jane's time was right in the Victorian era when women's fashions were severe and very bulky, with metres of heavy fabric in the dresses, under which they wore a very restrictive corset to keep their waists narrow. There were ample petticoats as well but, shock horror, no underpants, just leggings with a split at the crotch. Of course, there were no underpants – how could you get to them? The woman just squatted and the split opened and the skirts hid everything … It must have been hellish to cope with, especially during the hot Australian summer.

Because of the strangling corsets which deformed the chest cavity making breathing difficult, women were prone to fainting attacks. They carried with them 'smelling salts' (ammonia-based) that was placed under the nose to bring them round after a fainting attack. Prim and very formal behaviour was also expected during that time. In the photo of Jane, her clothes show the pouted puffed-up pigeon look of these severe clothes under which there was the restrictive corset that pushed her bosoms up high. Her hairdo is plastered down in the typical very severe Victorian style. Queen Victoria had something to answer for, making this a fashion of the day – but unfortunately, like today, they too were victims of fashion …

Queen Victoria and the fashion of the day – similar to the clothes and hairstyle Jane and other women wore in that era. (www.bing.com/images)

George Michael and Jane had eight children, five girls and three boys. On the birth certificate of George Thomas, it stated that George Michael and Jane had two boys and three girls at that time with one girl deceased. The deceased girl was their first child Ann, who was born in 1863 and died in 1864, the same year their next child, John, was born. Infant mortality was common and, sadly, George Michael and Jane suffered the heartbreaking loss of a child. George Thomas was the seventh of their eight children and the youngest boy. Presumably, he was doted over and pampered by his older sisters.

George Michael's parents
Michael Carroll and Catherine Mahon

Michael Carroll was born in 1801 in Birr, King's County, Ireland. His death date is unknown; he probably died in the Goulburn region of NSW, Australia. Catherine Mahon, was born in 1800 in Crinkle, (also spelt Crinkell), a small town in King's County, not far from Birr, Ireland. She died on 21st April, 1857 on the Breadalbane Plains, aged 58.

Michael Carroll's father was a tenant farmer in Ireland until his death. Michael, his mother, and his two sisters, Judith and Ellen, moved to Crinkle into a housing complex that boarded the local police.

Michael Carroll and Catherine Mahon would have met and married there. The reasons for Michael and Catherine leaving Ireland are lost – it was before the Potato famine so that wasn't the reason. They probably knew that Australia urgently needed new settlers to work the land and contribute to the growing society by doing all sorts of jobs. Australia sent advertisements to England and Ireland to attract such skilled people. Michael's occupation was 'Farmer and Clerk', whilst Catherine was a 'Dairymaid'. Being literate and a clerk as well as a farmer, Michael Carroll was in a prime position to fulfil the colony's needs and he could see new opportunities to settle and own a farm in a new land. At that time, free or subsidised passages were available to these skilled settlers: the Carrolls were subsidised passengers so had to pay part of their fair. This indicates that they were reasonably well off in Ireland.

Catherine Mahon was also literate, which was very unusual for a female in those times. If she was a dairymaid on a larger property in Ireland, she would have been responsible for the record keeping of milk quotas, sales of milk and butter and their quantities, the customers' records, and other record-keeping duties. She too would be a valuable asset in the fledgling colony.

Michael and Catherine were married in Crinkle on 1st February, 1826. He was twenty-five and she was twenty-six. They had been married for eleven years and had three daughters by the time they decided to leave Ireland and migrate to Australia. They had put their ages down by several years for some reason before they left, perhaps there was an age limit on entry to Australia and they were considered too old. In late 1837, they packed up, boarded the tiny sailing ship *Strathfieldsaye*, and left their home and their families to begin a new life in Australia. They were about thirty-seven and thirty-eight years old respectively when they arrived. On their immigration list they were stated as Michael being thirty and Catherine twenty-eight years old.

It had only been fifty years since the first fleet of settlers arrived in Australia in 1788. The Carrolls left during the freezing Irish winter and sailed into Sydney Cove, New South Wales, on 30th January 1838 into the middle of the baking Australian summer, certainly a stark contrast. They brought with them their three young daughters, Margaret, aged ten, Catherine, eight, and Mary, two years. Their only son, George Michael, was born in Australia almost three years later. The family moved into a house in Pyrmont where Michael may have been a farm labourer and Catherine a domestic servant. At ten years old, Margaret was of working age and she may have worked as a "teeny maid" to supplement the family income. This was certainly a new and very different life for them all. At some stage, Catherine's brother, John Mahon, also came to Australia and lived on Breadalbane Plains Station which was close to the Carrolls and south of Grabben Gullen.

Immigrant record of the ship "Strathfieldsaye" Michael Carroll is number 9 on the list. It gives the ages of Michael and his wife and states they were both literate, also that they had three children with them and that Michael was a farm servant (not a labourer). (https://slwa.wa.gov.au/eresources)

> Michael Carroll
>
> MARRIED MALE IMMIGRANT.
>
> Arrived by the Ship
>
> Brought out by
>
> A Native of — Ireland, County of King Parish of Birr — son of Michael Carroll a Clerk in the service of John Welsh
>
> Calling — Farmer and Clerk — Miller there and Winifred wife of Carroll —
>
> Age on Embarkation — about Thirty —
>
> Person certifying registry of Baptism
>
> Character, and person certifying the same — The Revd Marcus McLeiveslani Rector of Birr, and Simon Brown and John Colburn certify that Carroll is an honest and industrious man
>
> State of bodily health, strength, and probable usefulness
>
> Religion — Roman Catholic
>
> Remarks — Can read and write

Immigrant document for Michael Carroll – note in 'remarks' that Michael Carroll can "read and write". Also that "Carroll is an honest and industrious man"
(https://slwa.wa.gov.au/eresources)

At some stage after their son George Michael was born in 1840, they left their work in Pyrmont and moved to the Goulburn district to live. There is an historical map showing that Michael Carroll bought two blocks of land, numbers 22 and 25, in the Grabben Gullen area not far from Goulburn. He purchased the two blocks for a total of £32 on 10th April, 1855. One was a block of 32 acres and one 35 acres, small holdings compared to other landholders in the area. His land was quite close to the town site of Grabben Gullen and had a road easement that dissected his land and went from Grabben Gullen to Wheeo. Transport by horse and wagon may have been much easier if the road was constructed before he went there. Michael Carroll would highly likely have had to clear his land and begin farming as soon as he could. He probably had help from a workforce that may have accompanied him, there was likely to be a shepherd and a labourer and possibly a housekeeper servant. Perhaps Catherine's brother John Mahon helped them out.

Their son, George Michael, who was now fifteen years old would have had to work on the farm. Certainly back breaking toil with very little equipment. Winters would have been bitterly cold and the area would have had snowfalls during the colder months.

Grabben Gullen is in the Upper Lachlan Shire, approximately thirty-eight kilometres north-west of Goulburn, NSW. There is plenty of water and the land is gentle undulating farmland. He made a good choice. This area may have been newly released virgin bush when Michael Carroll arrived. Most of the lands to the east and the spread from Sydney had been taken up by the rich land owners who, prior to 1831, had been granted huge tracts of land free by the government.

Within a year their lives were to turn sour. It appears that Catherine may have had some sort of mental breakdown or illness (or Michael was not the type of man you would want to know). It is suspected that Catherine may have had some form of dementia and her health was failing.

Only about eighteen months after they arrived at Grabben Gullen, Michael put an advertisement in the local newspaper cautioning the people in the area about Catherine's behaviour. The advertisement follows.

> "Caution.
>
> THIS is to Caution the public against giving any Credit to my Wife, Catherine Carroll, as I will not be responsible for any debts she may contract; and I further caution all parties from purchasing any property belonging to me without my consent.
>
> MICHAEL CARROLL. Grabben Gullen; 3rd Oct., 1856."
>
> *The Goulburn Herald and County of Argyle Advertiser* (Sat 11 Oct 1856) p.8
> (https://trove.nla.gov.au/search)

This is explanation enough that something was terribly amiss.

Only a short time later, circumstances had changed dramatically. Catherine was dead. An inquest was held into her death and the following was the result.

> "SUDDEN DEATH.--An inquest was held before R. Waugh, Esq., Coroner, on Thursday last, at the house of Mr. John Mahon, Breadalbane Plains, on the body of Mrs. Catherine Carroll, who expired suddenly on the 21st instant. Mr. John Mahon, being duly sworn, deposed : I am overseer to Mr. John William Chisholm, of Wollogorang, and reside at this place, which is called the Breadalbane Station. I have seen the body of the late Mrs. Catherine Carroll, on which this inquest

is now sitting. Deceased was a married woman, but for the last six months had been separated from her husband and lived with me, I being her brother. The deceased for a long time back had been in a delicate state of health, but never confined to bed. I last saw her alive on the night of Tuesday last. I came home shortly after dark, and found the deceased sitting near the fire, and not complaining of anything, but appearing more delicate than usual. In the course of the evening I assisted her daughter to place her on her bed, and then retired to my own. After being absent for a few minutes the deceased's daughter called out to me that her mother was choking, on which I instantly got up and went to see her, and found that she was just dying. This was about two o'clock. She made no noise nor did she struggle at all before her death. There are no marks of violence or injury on her person, except two ulcers of twenty years standing. This concluded the evidence, and a verdict was returned of Died by the visitation of God.

Empire (Sat 2 May 1857) p. 2. https://trove.nla.gov.au/search)

Because Michael Carroll was literate, he would have known the value of literacy and how important it was to get employment other than as a labourer or servant. He may not have educated his daughters which was not unusual in those days because girls and women didn't need an education to be a wife! However, it is highly likely he ensured his son, George Michael, got an education and Catherine, more than likely, gave her girls a basic education.

When Michael had died, George Michael may have inherited the farm. In those times, the eldest son usually became the beneficiary. He may have sold Michael's farm because he did not go back to his old home at Grabben Gullen to live and work the farm there.

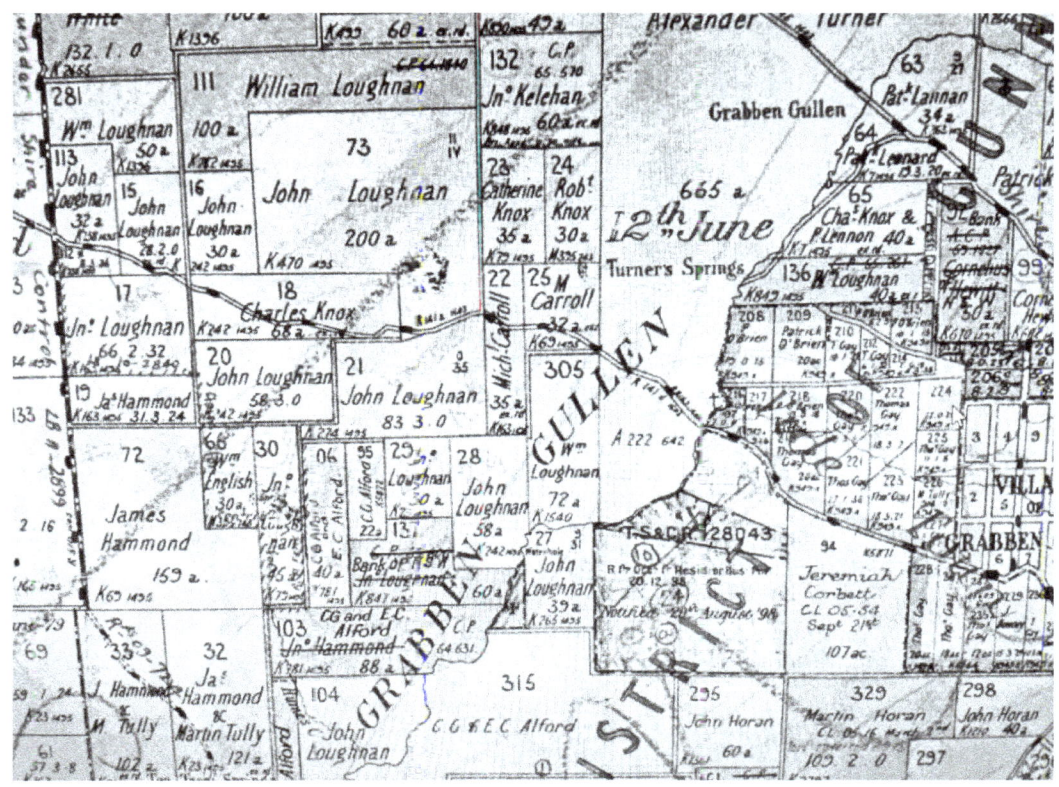

Michael Carroll's land is shown in the centre of the map (www.nswlrs.com.au)

NEW SOUTH WALES.
LAND PURCHASE.

VICTORIA, by the Grace of God, of the United Kingdom of Great Britain and Ireland, Queen, Defender of the Faith, and so forth:—

TO ALL to whom these Presents shall come, Greeting:—

WHEREAS in conformity with the Laws now in force for the Sale of Crown Lands in Our Territory of NEW SOUTH WALES, and Our Royal Instructions under Our Signet and Sign Manual, issued in pursuance thereof, *Michael Carroll* of *Grabben Gullen* has become the Purchaser of the Land hereinafter described, for the Sum of *Thirty two Pounds* Sterling; **Now Know Ye,** THAT for and in consideration of the said Sum for and on Our behalf, well and truly paid into the Colonial Treasury of Our said Territory before these Presents are issued, And in further consideration of the Quit-Rent hereinafter Reserved, WE HAVE GRANTED, and for Us, Our Heirs and Successors, Do HEREBY GRANT unto the said *Michael Carroll* his Heirs and Assigns, Subject to the several and respective Reservations hereinafter mentioned, ALL THAT Piece or Parcel of Land in Our said Territory, containing by Admeasurement *Thirty two* Acres, be the same more or less, situated in the County of *King* and Parish of *— at Grabben Gullen. Commencing at the South East corner of Knox's Thirty Acres at the West boundary of Turner's Six hundred and sixty five acres and bounded on the East by part of that boundary bearing South twenty chains; on the South by a line bearing West seventeen chains; on the West by a line bearing North twenty chains to the West a prolongation of the South boundary of Knox's Thirty Acres aforesaid; and on the North by that line ... and the South boundary of Turner's Six hundred and sixty five Acres aforesaid. Reserving for Public use a Road one chain wide which passes through this land from Nechro to Goulburn, the Area of which is deducted from the Total Area. Being the Land sold as Lot 19 in pursuance of the Proclamation of 23rd March 1855.—*

with all the Rights and Appurtenances whatsoever thereto belonging: **To Hold** unto the said *Michael Carroll* his Heirs and Assigns for ever, YIELDING and Paying therefore Yearly unto Us, Our Heirs and Successors, the Quit-Rent of One Peppercorn for ever, if demanded; **Provided Nevertheless,** AND WE DO HEREBY RESERVE Unto Us, Our Heirs and Successors, all such parts and so much of the said Land as may hereafter be required for making Public Ways, Canals, or Railroads, in, over, and through the same, to be set out by Our Governor for the time-being of Our said Territory, or some person by him authorised in that respect; AND ALSO, all Sand, Clay, Stone, Gravel, and Indigenous Timber, and all other Materials, the natural produce of the said Land, which may be required at any time or times hereafter, for the construction and repair of any Public Ways, Bridges, Canals, and Railroads, or any Fences, Embankments, Dams, Sewers, or Drains, necessary for the same, together with the right of taking and removing all such Materials; AND WE DO HEREBY FURTHER RESERVE unto Us, Our Heirs and Successors, the right of full and free ingress, egress, and regress, into, out of, and upon the said Land, for the several purposes aforesaid: **In Testimony Whereof,** We have caused this Our Grant to be Sealed with the Seal of Our said Territory.

WITNESS Our Trusty and Well-beloved SIR WILLIAM THOMAS DENISON, Knight, Governor-General in and over all Our Colonies of NEW SOUTH WALES, VAN DIEMEN'S LAND, VICTORIA, SOUTH AUSTRALIA, and WESTERN AUSTRALIA, and Captain-General and Governor-in-Chief of Our Territory of NEW SOUTH WALES and its Dependencies, at Government House, Sydney, in NEW SOUTH WALES aforesaid, this *Second* day of *April* in the *Eighteenth* Year of Our Reign; And in the Year of Our Lord One Thousand eight hundred and fifty-*five*.

L.S. (Signed) *W Denison*

ENTERED on Record by me, this *Tenth* day of *April* One Thousand eight hundred and fifty-five No 166. 195

C. Riddell
COLONIAL SECRETARY AND REGISTRAR.

Michael Carroll's land purchase papers 1855. (https://slwa.wa.gov.au/eresources)

Probably Michael Carroll at his original cottage in Grabben Gullen. Approx. 1870
(Family photo)

Michael Carroll's parents
Michael (snr) and Winifred

Michael Carroll's father, also named Michael (snr), was born in the mid to late 1700s in Kings County, Ireland, and he had died before 1821. He was literate and employed as a clerk in the services of John Welsh, a farmer and miller. Michael (snr) would have kept the records for the mill and John Welsh's business.

Michael's (snr) wife was named Winifred – her surname is not known – and she too was born in King's County, Ireland. She was born in 1766. The date of her death is also unknown.

It seems literacy was common back through the Carroll family line, and because of this they must have been respected members of their community. Literacy was very uncommon among many communities in those days.

In 1821, after Michael (snr) had died, Winifred was living with three of her children in Crinkle, Ireland and had become 'head' of the family. It is likely she ran the local police housing complex where the police of Crinkle lived. There were six police officers living there along with her son Michael and her two daughters, Judith and Ellen. *The Ireland Census Fragments*, 1821-1851. (https://slwa.wa.gov.au/eresources)

Catherine Mahon's Parents.

Catherine's parents were John and Margaret (Peggy) Mahon. Both were born in Ireland. They had seven children: five girls and two boys. Catherine was their eldest.

The Kemps

Kemp Family Line

KEMP FAMILY LINE

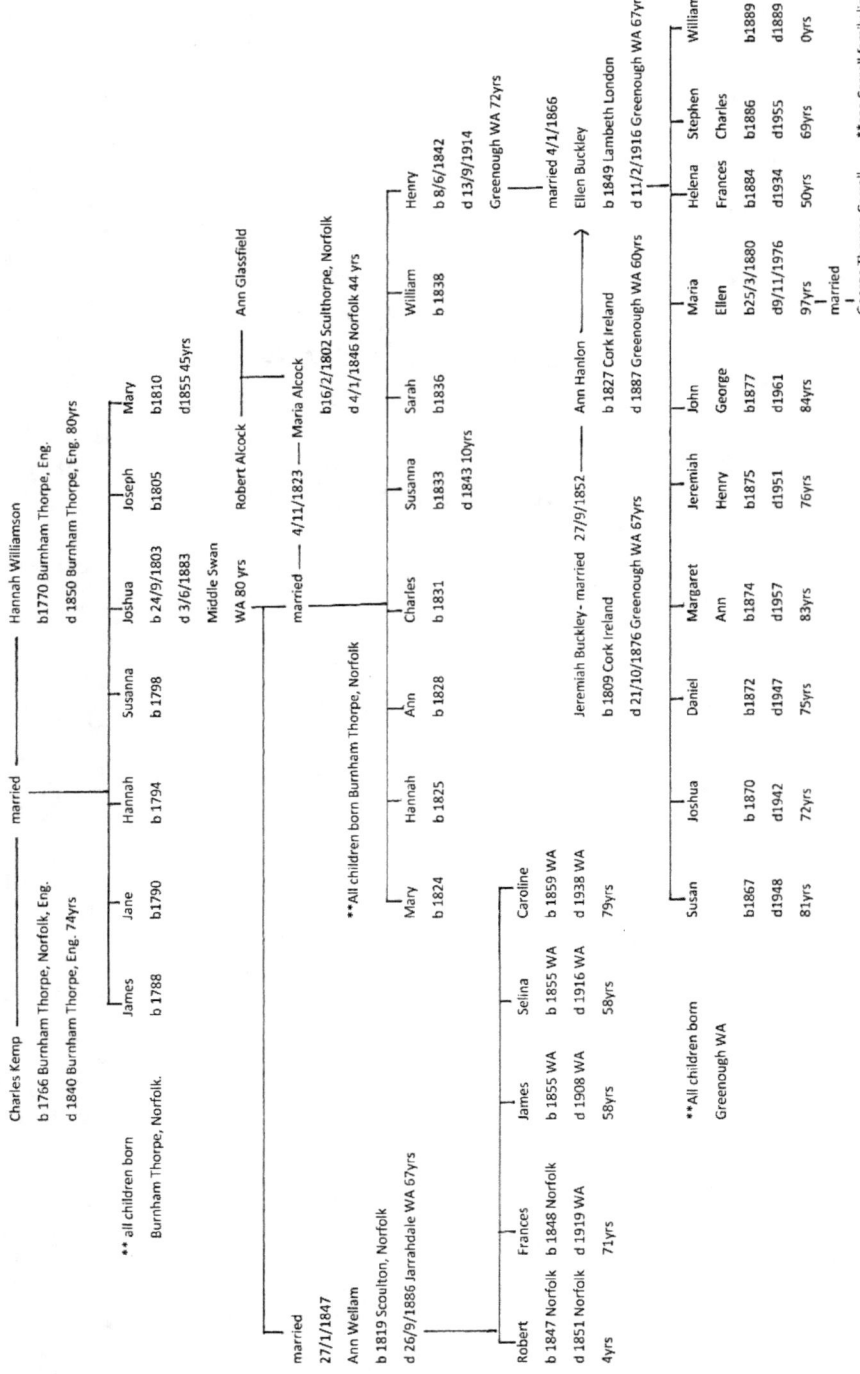

Stanley Lawrence Carroll's mother
Maria Ellen Kemp

Maria Ellen (also known as May) was born 25th March, 1880 in Greenough, Western Australia and died in Perth, Western Australia on 9th November 1976, aged 97. She was born only fifty years after the colony of Western Australia began.

Maria spent her early childhood on her parents' farm in Back Flats, Greenough, Western Australia. Life was very tough for those living in Greenough, where the *"farmers and their wives were a tenacious, hard-working people living in the most frugal circumstances, especially the women bearing child after child and with only the crudest household equipment."* (CARROLL, Mary Ellen (Molly) *Memoir*).

Schooling in those years for Maria Ellen had just changed from optional education to compulsory education for children living up to three miles from a school. It was up to the parents of children outside that distance to see to their own children's education. Some hired tutors and some, who were literate and capable, taught their own children and sometimes the children of their neighbours. Prior to Maria Ellen's time, children were schooled from the age of four to ten. At the age of nine boys could be employed as shepherds and girls "teeny maids". Then the colonial government changed the age for schooling from six to fourteen years of age and education became compulsory. Many schools were run either by the Catholic Church or the Church of England and the Colonial Government paid a fee per child to these institutions.

Many parents resisted the new law of making children stay at school until they were fourteen years old because now they did not have any income from their working children. (*The brand on his coat*. Ed. R. Erikson (UWA Press, 1983) p. 301-311). Three schools were built along Back Flats and Maria Ellen may have attended one of these for a short while, but it is more likely she attended a school at Bootenal, Greenough, after her family had to leave their farm at Back Flats. Maria Ellen's family were strict Roman Catholics so it is likely she would have gone to one of their schools.

Not much is known about her childhood but it can be deduced that it was a hard existence. They were very poor after her father went bankrupt. He was not alone; many of the farms in the district failed during a particularly harsh time.

She grew up as a determined and ambitious young woman. She may have had to make her presence felt in the family and elsewhere, and she had the temperament that meant she stood her ground and was not to be pushed around. She was bright enough to see that women had it very hard, bearing child after child and slaving away at household chores and trying to please their husbands. She decided that she wasn't going to put up with it in her future. As a child, Maria Ellen would have been expected to do all sorts of household chores and to work hard in the house as well as attend school as she was legally obliged to do until she was fourteen years old. It seems she couldn't wait to escape it all.

It appears that Maria Ellen left home at a young age and went to work. She may have worked or lived in a convent boarding house, perhaps the one in Geraldton that is mentioned in the letter below from her boyfriend who was serving in the Boer War. She told the story of a priest chasing her around the beds in a dormitory and she would laugh and say how terrible it was.

She was a petite, trim, very attractive young woman with long, dark, curly hair. She kept her hair long all her life and always wore it in a chignon bun at the back of her head or in plaited rolls over her ears. She was someone who knew what she wanted and took no rot. She had little patience and would soon let someone know if she thought their behaviour wasn't to her liking.

Maria Ellen Kemp (Family photo)

At the age of twenty, Maria Ellen was living and working in Geraldton. She had a boyfriend, Samuel William Lawrence, who went off to the Boer War while they were courting. Prior to going to war, he was an Orderly at the Victoria Hospital in Geraldton. He and her father, Henry, often debated the pros and cons of the war. During his time at the Boer War, he wrote many letters to Maria Ellen about the conflict and his love for her, calling her his sweetest May. Even though the relationship didn't eventuate, she kept his letters and they exist to this day.

The Boer War was fought between 1899 and 1902. "*Australia was not yet a nation when the war broke out in 1899. The various colonies each sent troops – more than 16,000 in total – to fight alongside the British forces in South Africa in their struggle against the Dutch-Afrikaner settlers, known as Boers. During the war, Australians served in mounted units, and conditions for both soldiers and horses were harsh. During the day, the heat was often unbearable, while at night it was freezing cold. By the end of the war in 1902, approximately 600 Australians had lost their lives…*" WALKER, Charlie. *Audacity: stories of heroic Australians in wartime.* (Australian War Memorial, 2014) p. 5.

The following is one of the letters from Samuel William Lawrence to Maria Ellen during the Boer War. It gives a good description of the conditions there …

> 11th Brigade Staff
>
> Natal
>
> Jan/9/00 (January 9th 1900)
>
> My Sweetest May,
>
> I am writing a few lines Dear as we are off Boer chasing tomorrow morning in the Transvaal and I shall not be able to write for a couple of weeks, when we return. I am still on the Staff as galloper. General Hildegard who is in command of this district is coming with us this time so I expect I shall have to act as galloper to the General on the field. I wrote to you last week Dear and enclosed (?)M.G.G. for insurance. Hope you will get it in time. I had my photo taken on my horse yesterday. I will send you one when they are ready Dear. Do send me a photo of yourself a small one so that I can carry it in my tunic Pocket. I have nothing to keep your face in memory though I shall never forget it but it will be nice to pull your photo out of my pocket and look at it and think of you Dear. The people in Australia must be getting very sick of the War now. I can tell you Dear we are all heartily sick of it but it must be carried

through. The Boer will not give in although we are killing them off fast and there will be some more of them dead in another week if we get a chance. It is madness for them to stick it out, it means extermination for them. But the British are too humane for the Boer. When we advance against a Boer laagar (a circle of wagons) and the Boers get the word of the fight they clear off and leave their women and children behind as they know they will be cared for by the British Authorities. If it simply encourages the Boers and most of the Boer women are quite bitter against us as the men are, and in the earlier part of the War the Boers did not care how the British women starved in the Ladysmith Kimberly and (?) and the Boer women heaped insult upon insult upon the British women that were left in the Transvaal. I think if the British were not so generous and made the Boers look after their women and children and feed them that it would bring the war to a speedy close, they have no food to spare for their women as the fighting men all living on mealies only and the women would soon get knocked upon (for?) that food and the men would have to submit. But Lord Kitchener is in command of the troops out here now and he is a very hard man and I don't think the Boers will get much mercy from him. During the Sudan campaign at the battle of Omdurman the British killed 18,000 Dervishes in one day. The troops were under the command of Lord Kitchener so you can see Dear the kind of man that the Boers have to deal with now, so they better surrender.

What does your Father think of the war now. I expect he is wondering why we have not finished off the Boers yet but the beggars are too happy and they know the country.

Now Dear I must close. Write me a nice letter won't you pet. I have not written to Mrs Kemp for some time now, I must drop a line. Remember me to all old friends and Hospital Staff. I suppose Lizzie has left the Convent now there are so few Sisters left. Is Mr Kenny still at the Depot. Remember me to him will you.

Give my love to Mrs and Mr Kemp, Lena and Maggie and remember me to Jack. With fondest love to yourself Dear.

I am your loving

xxxxxx boy Will xxxxxxxxx

Write to the old address Dear it will be forwarded to me wherever I shall be

3rd Squadron, Volunteer Composite Regt, Natal"

Samuel William Lawrence – left - at the Boer War. (Family photo)

Staff – Geraldton Hospital. Samuel William Lawrence – left (pre-1900). (Family photo)

Some of his letters indicated he was a rather demanding young man and their relationship did not eventuate. Maria Ellen may have seen that he was a bit too demanding so ended their relationship while he was away. She didn't send him a picture of herself and he complained in another letter to her, pleading for her to send one.

She may also have worked, or at least known the staff at Geraldton Hospital because, in the letters from Samuel William Lawrence, he mentions nursing staff and the doctor of the hospital in such a way that it seems they were both well acquainted with them. Perhaps this is where they met.

Maria Ellen was an independent young woman who left Geraldton before 1904 at the age of twenty-four, and went to Perth to live for almost a year. Perhaps she left Geraldton to escape the awkwardness of the return to Geraldton of Samuel William Lawrence.

Maria Ellen Kemp's father - Henry Kemp.

Maria Ellen Kemp's father, Henry Kemp, was born on the 18th June 1842 at Burnham Thorpe, Norfolk, England and died on the 3rd September, 1914 in Greenough, Western Australia, aged 72. His grave in the Geraldton Cemetery has been chosen for the refurbishment program of some historical graves.

He came to the colony of Western Australia as a child to be reunited with his father who was sent out as a convict. Henry had a very difficult childhood in England after his mother, Maria Alcock, died and his father Joshua Kemp remarried. At the age of eight, Henry spent time in Wicklewood Workhouse in Norfolk, England with his stepmother Ann Wellam, his brother William and his two half siblings, Robert and Frances. Later, after his father Joshua was sentenced and transported to Australia, and because things were so dire, he and William had to stay in the workhouse and fend for themselves without Ann and her children. Workhouses were a place to go when all else failed in life, and for being destitute and desperate. Times were extremely hard for women with children with no man to support them. There was no charity nor government payments to help back then and often these women were charged with vagrancy instead of being helped.

Henry Kemp arrived in the colony of Western Australia on 23rd March 1854, at the age of twelve. He travelled out on the ship *Victory* with his stepmother Ann and half-sister Frances. They went to live at Blackadder Creek, Guildford, Western Australia, where his father Joshua Kemp was a tenant farmer. There, and later at Helena (Mt Helena), he would have learnt the skills of farming from his father. When it came time to leave home, he moved to Greenough, just south of

Geraldton, Western Australia, where he took up farming at Back Flats.

There he met and courted Ellen Buckley and they married on 4th January, 1866 in Greenough. They went on to have eleven children, six boys and five girls. Maria Ellen was their seventh child.

Greenough today. (www.nationaltrust.org.au/places/central-greenough)

From 1862 things were not going well in the area and times became extremely tough in Greenough and the surrounding areas. The wheat crops failed due to lack of soil nutrients and the disease Rust and there was a severe drought. It was not uncommon in those times of economic depression for farmers to abandon their farms, and just walk away and leave everything; there were no handouts. As a consequence of the years of severe hardship on the farm, Henry Kemp wasn't about to give up. Unfortunately, he went bankrupt in 1886 and appears to have lost everything due to the length of time it took for him to be discharged from bankruptcy by the court proceedings. He was hamstrung and could not trade his way out of his economic woes. If the courts had acted earlier, he may have been able to trade his way out of debt and keep the farm. He felt he was treated unfairly and complained in a letter to the courts. In addition, as with the Carrolls in NSW, the world wide depression was biting Western Australian agricultural areas as well and things became very difficult. Henry Kemp complained

> "I, Henry Kemp, of Bootenal, Greenough, in the colony of Western Australia, make oath and say as follows:
>
> That I was adjudicated a bankrupt on or about the 25th September, 1886, on the petition of Charles Crowther the elder and Edward Shenton (trading together as Shenton & Co.), signed the 24th September, 1886. That I have caused search to be made in the Local Court, Geraldton, as to the proceedings herein, and I have ascertained that the first meeting was held 20th October, 1886, when Hugh Stephens was appointed

trustee at a remuneration of £5 per centum. Isaac Walker, Thomas W. Stroud, and James Hanlon were appointed a committee of inspection. It was also resolved that the assets were to be paid into the National Bank, Geraldton, realization to be left to the trustee, but no unreasonable delay to occur.

The total liabilities amounted to (as appears from statement of affairs) £1019 3s. Id. while the assets were estimated at £977. On the 5th April, 1887, Hugh Stephens resigned trusteeship and Alfred Farrelly, of Geraldton, solicitor, was appointed trustee. I am informed and believe that the committee of inspection at the same meeting on the 5th April, 1887, resolved that in consequence of legal proceedings on the part of Mrs. Scott and Mrs. Gale, the declaration of a dividend should stand over till such proceedings terminated. The estate accounts then stood -- By amount taken over from £80 13s. 7d. Stephens, late trustee, Malcy & Sons account ... £300. 0s 0d. Amount from Henry E. Kenny for purchase of hay £9. Amount purchase Victoria Locations X4 and X5 (F. Devlin) ... £125. £514 13s 7d while there was paid out ... £126 8s 7d leaving balance in hand of trustee of, £388 5s 0d That I delivered all my property of every kind as well as all my documents to Mr. Stephens. That I made several applications to Mr. Farrelly to wind up the proceedings, but he always expressed his inability to bring the case of Scott and another v. Farrelly, trustee, to a termination, and that he could not grant me my discharge until the case had finished. That I have been advised and believe that at the time of my bankruptcy I had a good and valid title to the portion or block of land now the subject of the action Scott and another v. Farrelly, and I furthermore say and believe that Mrs. Scott and Mrs. Gale have no right or title to the said land in dispute and the said case I am informed and believe is not listed for hearing in the Supreme Court this next sittings. I say that I have not been allowed anything for my maintenance or the maintenance of my family during the continuation of the bankruptcy and I have been ruined by the protraction of the proceedings. Sworn by the said defendant Henry Kemp, at Geraldton aforesaid, this 18th day of March, 1890, before me.

Edward Shenton, J, P.   HENRY KEMP"

The Victorian Express (Saturday March 22, 1890) (https://trove.nla.gov.au/search)

It seems Henry had made good and was at least comfortable in his old age. After his death, his probate left a considerable amount of money to various people, however none of his children is mentioned. Or, perhaps he still owed money and the probate was to be paid to these people before his family got any funds. When Henry died, he was a highly respected member of the community of Greenough and Geraldton.

> *"HENRY KEMP, Probate has been granted in the will of Henry Kemp, of Bootenal, Greenough, farmer, to James Stokes and Charles O Neil Stokes, -£80. Letters of administration Charles Vennier, of Mingenew, labourer, to James Vennier, £50 15s ; Mary Connolly, of Greenough, widow, to Robert A. Wilton, Emma L. Connolly, and James Bell, £957 10s."* The Midlands Advertiser Moora, WA : 1907 - 1930 (Fri 30 Oct 1914. 4) (https://trove.nla.gov.au/search)

Maria Ellen was six years old when Henry went bankrupt and it may have been at this time they had to move to Bootenal, a locality near Greenough. It appears they may have lost the farm but perhaps they managed to get other land because Henry is stated as being a farmer in Bootenal in the Probate on his will. Small packages of land at Bootenal were made available for farming plots but it is not known whether he bought another farm. He may have been near, or lived with his in-laws, the Buckley family.

In February 1888 floods swept through The Flats (and probably nearby Back Flats) killing several people and inundating the area for some time. Back Flats and The Flats were separated by a low limestone ridge. No doubt this was another very testing time for the farmers in that area.

The Kemps were a respected family who lived in the region until both Henry Kemp and his wife Ellen Buckley died.

Maria Ellen Kemp's Mother - Ellen Buckley

Ellen Buckley, was born in 1849 in Lambeth, London, England, and died in Greenough on the 11th February, 1916, aged 67.

Ellen came to Western Australia at the age of three with her parents, Jeremiah Buckley and Ann Hanlon, along with her sister Margaret who was three months old.

Nothing is known about Ellen's life but her parent's story will give an indication of her younger life.

On the event of Ellen's death, there was the following notice in the newspaper.

> "The death took place last week at the residence of her daughter, Mrs. J. Jones, of Geraldton, of Mrs. Ellen Kemp. Deceased, with her husband, the late Mr. H. Kemp, who pre-deceased her by 17 months, were once familiar figures on the Greenough, both being highly respected, and having a wide circle of friends. Deceased was 67 years of age, and leaves one sister (Mrs. Truslove, of Midland Junction), four daughters, five sons, 32 grandchildren, and two great-grandchildren, to mourn their loss. The funeral took place on Saturday, Father Fenelon officiating. R.I.P."
>
> (www.findagrave.com/memorial/215890695/ellen-kemp)

Ellen's parents
Jeremiah Buckley and Ann Hanlon

Jeremiah Buckley was born in Cork, Ireland, in 1809 and died in Greenough, Western Australia, on 21st October, 1876, aged 67. He is buried in the Greenough Cemetery.

At some stage he moved from Cork, Ireland to England and enlisted as a Private and a Gunner in the Bombay Artillery 1st Battalion, 2nd Company in the East India Company Military. He then transferred to the Horse Brigade in January 1832. His regiment number was 273. He enlisted in 1829 at the age of nineteen and was listed as a labourer in Woolwich, Kent, England. He served in the military in India and was discharged from military duties after fifteen years' service in December 1843, due to a head injury and diseased glands in the neck, perhaps from his head injury. He was described as 5 feet 7¾ inches with a fresh complexion on enlistment and dark when discharged. He had a round face, blue eyes and sandy red hair. He left Bombay, India and returned to England and then went home to Cork Ireland. (JAMES, M.S. *A superior body of men.* (Author House, 2016) p. 81-82. He was thirty-four years old when he retired from active service and became a Pensioner Guard.

In 1849 he and his future wife, Ann Hanlon, moved from Cork, Ireland to Lambeth, London. They were married three years later in Aldgate, London on the 27th September 1852. He was forty-one and she was twenty-five. By the time they married, they already had two children, one of them was Maria Ellen's mother, Ellen, who was born in 1850, and her sister Margaret, born in 1851. Both girls were born in Lambeth, London. There is a record of another child, a boy, John who was born in 1854 in Port Gregory, Western Australia. A small family for those days.

Jeremiah Buckley and his family came to Western Australia on board the sailing ship *Dudbrook*. Jeremiah was a Pensioner Guard on this ship that was transporting convicts to the colony of Western Australia. They left Plymouth, England on the 22nd November 1852 and arrived in Western Australia on 2nd February 1853, just twenty-four years after the first fleet of free settlers arrived in 1829. After their arrival, Jeremiah was stationed as a Pensioner Guard at Lynton on the Hutt River estuary, just south of Port Gregory, Western Australia and was paid 9d (9 pence) per day. The family lived in a tent village on the salt flats, along with the other Pensioner Guards and their families. Port Gregory was a busy place. It was the site of a whaling station and a port used to export lead from a nearby lead mine.

Lynton was a convict depot and an unpleasant and unhealthy place to live and the people were exposed to all types of weather which was sometimes extreme. There were few fresh vegetables which caused health problems and some people suffered with scurvy. There was also a lack of mail services and religious instruction which were very important to the people in those times. The Pensioner Guards, who were paid a pittance, could supplement their income to support their families by collecting salt from the nearby Hutt Lagoon. Jeremiah was granted three acres of salt flat on which to farm but the land was hopelessly unproductive. In 1855, during their stay at Lynton, Jeremiah's wife, Ann Hanlon, was shot by John Brown, another Pensioner Guard, who was charged and sentenced to two years imprisonment for the shooting.

Ann survived the shooting, the circumstances surrounding the crime are not known. (https://enrolledpensionerforcewa.org.au)

In 1858, after living in the tent town for five years, Jeremiah was transferred to Champion Bay, Geraldton which was then just a small harbour town with few facilities but better than the tent town. While living there he was notified that land grants were being made available at Greenough, just south of Geraldton, and, being a Pensioner Guard, he was eligible for a free grant along with a two roomed cottage. In 1860 he was granted two blocks of land at Greenough Flats. The blocks he chose were on higher ground and this is where he eventually built his two-roomed cottage. He worked this land for thirteen years before the family moved out of Geraldton in 1873 and settled on the land. Unfortunately, they were only there for three years before Jeremiah died. His two blocks totalled just over thirty-two acres (sixteen acres and two roods each) at Locations 19 and 20 along the western side of Gregory Road, which is just east of the now Brand Highway. (State Records Office, WA. 2021)

"In December 1863 an extensive fire destroyed crops, live-stock, field fences and farming implements belonging to many Greenough Flats' settlers. The Buckley's lost 2 acres of wheat and 4 pigs (others lost much more)". (https://enrolledpensionerforcewa.org.au)

Pensioner Guards were members of the *"English military personnel who served on convict transportation ships en route to the Swan River Colony between 1850 and 1868, and were given employment and grants of land on arrival. Their initial employment lasted for six months, or the duration of the voyage, whichever was the longer time. After this they became "pensioners" and had to serve 12 days per year as well as whenever called upon. They paraded annually in Perth at the Pensioner Barracks. Many enlisted in the British Army as boys, around 15–17 years of age, and served in many parts of the world including India… for about 21 years before being pensioned off. This meant a number of guards were under 40 years of age and had young families when they came to Western Australia. As an incentive they were promised a two-roomed cottage and a plot of land sufficient to grow crops, vegetables and keep livestock. It was a chance for a new and better life and a large number of families remained as settlers."* (https://en.wikipedia.org/wiki/Pensioner_Guards)

The Pensioner Barracks 1868. Built in 1866. Only the front Arch now stands at the western end of St Georges Terrace Perth. (*museumofperth.com.au*)

Ann Hanlon

Ann Hanlon, was born in 1827 in Cork, Ireland and died in Greenough in 1887, aged 60.

Even though Anne was illiterate, she was trained as an assistant tailoress and skilled in a good trade. She would have been able to sew and make the family's clothing and, if funds were short in the household, she may have made clothing for others in their community. Even though most women could sew their own clothes, Anne would have been able to make 'fine' clothing for both men and women that would have been classed as a 'going out' or 'church' outfit. Women's and children's clothes could not be bought in shops so her skills would have been in demand. It is probable that she passed these skills on to her daughters and grand-daughters. A very valuable skill for her grand-daughter, young Maria Ellen Kemp and her family. All the sewing would have been done by hand.

Henry Kemp's father, mother, and step mother
Joshua Kemp, Maria Alcock, and Ann Wellam

Henry Kemp's father, Joshua Kemp, was born on 24th September 1803 at Burnham Thorpe, Norfolk, England and died on 3rd June 1883, aged 79, at Middle Swan, Western Australia.

He was educated and literate and was an agricultural labourer and parish clerk. *"Parish clerks were literate men since one of their roles was keeping the church records. Joshua Kemp's signature can be seen on Burnham Thorpe marriages between the years of 1824 and 1830".* (Lynn Sharpe, 2012)

He held the respected position of Parish Clerk for Burnham Thorpe – this is a position that was generally held for life. He must have travelled short distances to other districts because he met his future wife, Maria Alcock, in Sculthorpe, about fifteen kilometres from Burnham Thorpe. Joshua and Maria married on 4th November 1823 in Burnham Thorpe.

Maria Alcock was born on 16th February, 1802 and died of Consumption (Tuberculosis) on the 4th January 1846. She was forty-four years old.

They had eight children, five girls and three boys. Henry Kemp, their youngest child, was only two years old when she died.

Maria was the daughter of Robert Alcock and Anne Glassfield.

Soon after they married, England went into financial decline and was on the verge of bankruptcy and things became tough for its citizens. Following years of wars, including the Napoleonic Wars, high taxes, and bad harvests, the people were on the brink of starvation and destitution. Things were bad enough at that time but the agricultural workers, including Joshua Kemp, were then affected by changes in farming technology which caused the agricultural labourers to be thrown out of their traditional work. The introduction of mechanisation to farming across England was the final straw for these men and many were forced off the land with no hope of employment and nowhere to live. *"Unemployment and starvation in Britain, especially in the rural areas was the catalyst for many people to make a complete change in their lives. A series of riots known as the Swing Riots spread from Kent to 18 other counties with unrest lasting up to 6 months"*. (http://www.wanowandthen.com)

In desperation, Joshua Kemp joined the Swing Rioters, a nation-wide group of farm labourers who protested against the newly invented mechanised agricultural machinery. In November, 1830, at the age of twenty-seven, he was with a group of Swing Rioters who feloniously destroyed the wheel of a threshing machine. They were caught, and he was sentenced to six months imprisonment in Norwich Gaol. While Joshua was in prison, his family had no income and his wife Maria must have found it incredibly difficult to care for their young children. She may have had to get some help from the Burnham Thorpe Parish, relatives, or gone into a workhouse for some time.

Still in desperate times, in July 1840, at the age of thirty-six, Joshua once again was in trouble with the law and had to go before the courts. He was charged with Larceny (theft) in Burnham Thorpe but the evidence against him was not strong and he was acquitted of the crime.

In January, 1846, his wife Maria became ill with tuberculosis and died in the middle of a freezing winter. Joshua was left with the children to care for. Some of the younger ones stayed with his sisters and some with other family members. His older children were old enough to work and fend for themselves. Because there was no longer much agricultural work, he went further afield to work, and moved from Burnham Thorpe to Norwich, approximately sixty kilometres away, where he became a fishmonger.

While there, he met and married Ann Wellam on 27th January 1847, only a year after the death of Maria. Ann was the daughter of Robert Wellam. There is no other information about her parents.

Ann was born in 1819 at Scoulton, Norfolk and died on 26th September 1886, aged 67 years, at the Jarrahdale Inn (now Whitby Falls Coach House, built in 1873), Western Australia, which was owned by her and Joshua's daughter Frances, and their son-in-law Edward Cockram.

During their time in England, Ann and Joshua had two children, a boy Robert and a girl Frances and, in addition, Ann cared for his three younger children by Maria – Sarah, William, and Henry – but soon afterwards Sarah became old enough to work so she went to stay with one of Joshua's sisters. Times were desperate and Joshua, now aged forty-three, must have had great difficulties supporting his family because he, along with some other men, stole a quantity of wool, were caught and charged with Larceny. They were found guilty and Joshua was convicted in July 1848 and sentenced to seven years transportation to Western Australia. Even though the sentence was for seven years, it was actually for life. Transported convicts were never allowed to return to England.

His crimes were committed during the horrific time of The Great Famine when there was wide spread starvation and poverty throughout England, Ireland and Europe. Thousands of people died and many stole out of desperation just to survive. He was in prison awaiting transportation when poor Ann gave birth to their daughter Frances. Ann's life was made remarkably difficult without her husband to support her; she and the children lived in abject poverty. Her young son, Robert, died at the age of four of starvation and with no one to turn to she went into the dreaded Wicklewood Workhouse on 5th December 1850 with her daughter Frances, and Joshua's sons William, and Henry. Henry was only eight years old.

Joshua Kemp's transportation record – bottom; The notations in the columns state - Joshua Kemp - Little Walsingham Quarter Sessions – 7 July 1848 – Seven Years. Australian Convict Transport Register - Other Fleets & Ships 1791-1868 (https://slwa.wa.gov.au/eresources)

Convict Joshua was held in prison for three years before being transported from Torbay, England on 30th March 1851 on the *Pyrenees* along with 293 other convicts and ninety-six passengers. He was now forty-seven years old. Ann must have been saddened and traumatised by the thought that she would never see Joshua again. The ship arrived in Fremantle, Western Australia on 28th June 1851. Joshua's records describe him as 5 feet 7¾ inches tall with grey hair, brown eyes, an oval face and a dark complexion. All his teeth were gone from his top right side.

On board the ship convicts were directed to their quarters for the journey. We are led to believe that all of these convict ships had barbaric conditions with floggings and beatings and the convicts caged. This was not the case and was more the frivolous sensationalism of some history writers, however, some of the very early convict ships to Botany Bay were dreadful. (These stories are then referenced in future papers and so the story is perpetuated). The colony needed men (and women) who could work hard and it wasn't in the interest of the government to have them weakened by starvation and harsh treatment on their journey. For the most part, ships were run by strict but fair rules. Each prisoner was allocated a bunk bed with a mattress, pillow and two rugs. The bedding was to be packed up each morning and taken on deck to be stored for the day. The bunk was then made into a seat and an area to eat and work. Food was basic but adequate and they ate in shifts. They had salted meat, or what was caught from the ocean, oatmeal, a type of bread that had currants in it, pea soup, hot chocolate drink or tea. They also had wine, lime juice, vinegar, and mustard three times a week. After the meals, the area had to be thoroughly scrubbed ready for the next meal. There was also an educational school that convicts had to attend if they were illiterate, and a work area where they made clothes and other items that may be required in their new life. Being literate, it is a possibility that Joshua was a teacher for the convicts. At the end of the day, the bunks were remade ready for the night. Prisoners had to wash three times a week in tubs of salt water. Soap was given to those requiring a shave. Any prisoner who was disobedient was locked up for a time period suiting the 'crime'. Anyone caught smoking had the most severe punishment because it was forbidden due to the risk of fire, and, because these ships were made of wood, they were prone to burning, killing all on board. *The brand on his coat.* (Ed. R. Erikson, UWA Press, 1983) p. 22 & 23

Upon his embarkation, Joshua was to wear a jacket that was a yellowish colour with a convict brand of large black arrow shapes printed on it. This was the case for all convicts arriving in Western Australia and they had to wear this until they got their 'Ticket of Leave'. Upon leaving the ship, each convict was given a parcel of items that included *"several shirts, a smock, trousers, drawers, stockings, shoes, handkerchiefs, braces, brush and comb, towel and a cap. Some were issued with ... a sewing kit."* The brand on his coat. (Ed. R. Erikson, UWA Press, 1983) p. 19

Joshua must have been considered an honourable man because he was given a Ticket of Leave as soon as he arrived in Western Australia which meant he could find employment and fend for himself, which wasn't always easy. Being a convict always ensured food, clothing, lodgings and work. It also meant Joshua didn't have to wear the branded coat, but he couldn't go outside the district to which he was assigned unless he got permission (a Ticket of Leave) from the resident magistrate of the area.

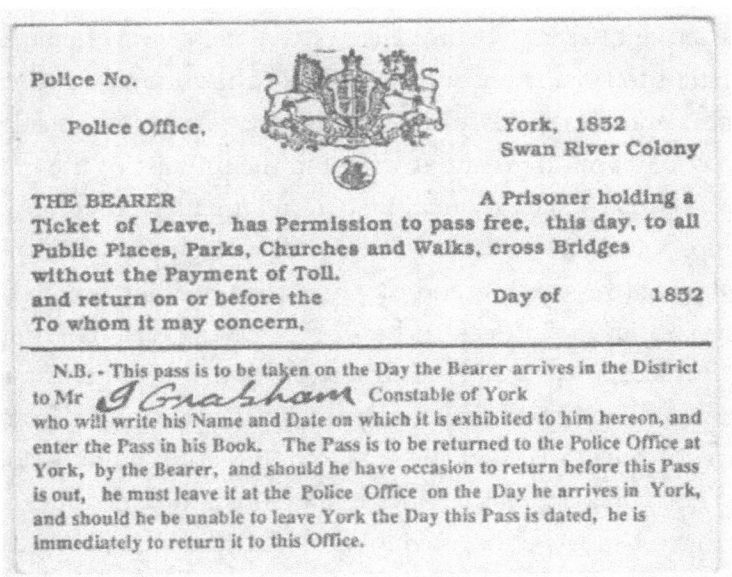

Replica Ticket of Leave from York Western Australia (National Trust Australia)

Joshua Kemp must have proven himself worthy and a trusted person and was granted a conditional pardon ten months later on 23rd April 1853. He was free but could never return to England, although he could have gone to any of the other states in Australia. His behaviour on the ship was described as exemplary. His religion was Protestant.

During the period 1862 – 1874, he went to Blackadder Creek, Guildford, Western Australia as a labourer and farmer where he employed twenty-one Ticket of Leave convicts, proving he must have been a competent farmer and a capable man. He also employed a cattle minder at Mount Helena and he became a tenant farmer, which meant he rented areas of land from a land holder. This would have been similar to the tenant system in England. All improvements done by Joshua belonged to the owner. However, what he earned from the farm he kept but had to pay rent. The work done by his Ticket of Leavers would have included shepherding the sheep, cattle and horses because at that time fences were not common, as well as work the land for food production. Most allotments of land were quite small by today's standards.

He did not forget his wife Ann and applied to have her come to Australia on an assisted passage that was available to ex-convicts' wives and children. Many wives did not want to join their husbands in the colonies and refused to come, and as a matter of fact, it was unusual for them to leave home and come to the colonies. Ann decided that she wanted to be with Joshua so she, their daughter Frances, and Henry came out to join him in Australia. All of Joshua's other children were old enough to work and support themselves and may not have wanted to go to the colony. Because Joshua was literate, he may have kept in touch by letter with his other children in England, who were more than likely literate.

Joshua and Ann went on to have another three children in Australia. James, Selena and Caroline. Their lives would have been made a lot better by the move to Australia. (Lynne Sharpe, 2012)

List of Joshua's family members, wife Ann, son Henry and daughter Frances, who came to Western Australia on an Assisted Passage on the sailing ship "Victory"
Western Australia Convict Records 1846-1930 for Joshua Kemp
(https://slwa.wa.gov.au/eresources)

Joshua Kemp's parents
Charles Kemp and Hannah Williamson

Charles Kemp was born at Burnham Thorpe, Norfolk, England in 1766. He was a farmer and illiterate and died there in 1840, aged 74.

Charles was married to Hannah Williamson, born in 1770 at Burnham Thorpe, and she died there in 1850, aged 80. Hannah was literate and educated her children. Charles and Hannah were married on 4th December 1786 at the All Saints Church, Burnham Thorpe, by Reverend Edmund Nelson, Horatio Nelson's father. They had seven children, four girls and three boys. Joshua was their fifth child. (As a point of interest, the famous naval officer Horatio Nelson joined the Royal Navy when he was twelve years old…)

George Thomas Carroll and Maria Ellen Kemp - their courtship and marriage

In 1905 at the age of twenty-five, Maria Ellen Kemp applied for and got a job as a waitress (Domestic) in a hotel in the Murchison goldfields town of Nannine. The reasons for Maria Ellen going to a gold mining town in the first place are lost to history but it is not surprising that this feisty young woman would do so. She had known poverty and hardship during her young life and probably wanted no more of it. It is obvious that she was an ambitious young woman who, in May, 1904, purchased Lots 136 and 137 in the Scarborough Estate, North Beach for £8 each. Quite a sum in those days, and she had paid them off by November, 1908. It was not common for a young single woman to buy property.

No doubt, she probably wanted a better life and more money so left Mundijong where she was living at the time and moved north to where the opportunities and riches were. While living in Geraldton, she would have been familiar with the inland goldmining areas and would have seen many prospectors and business people go through Geraldton to get to these rich goldfields.

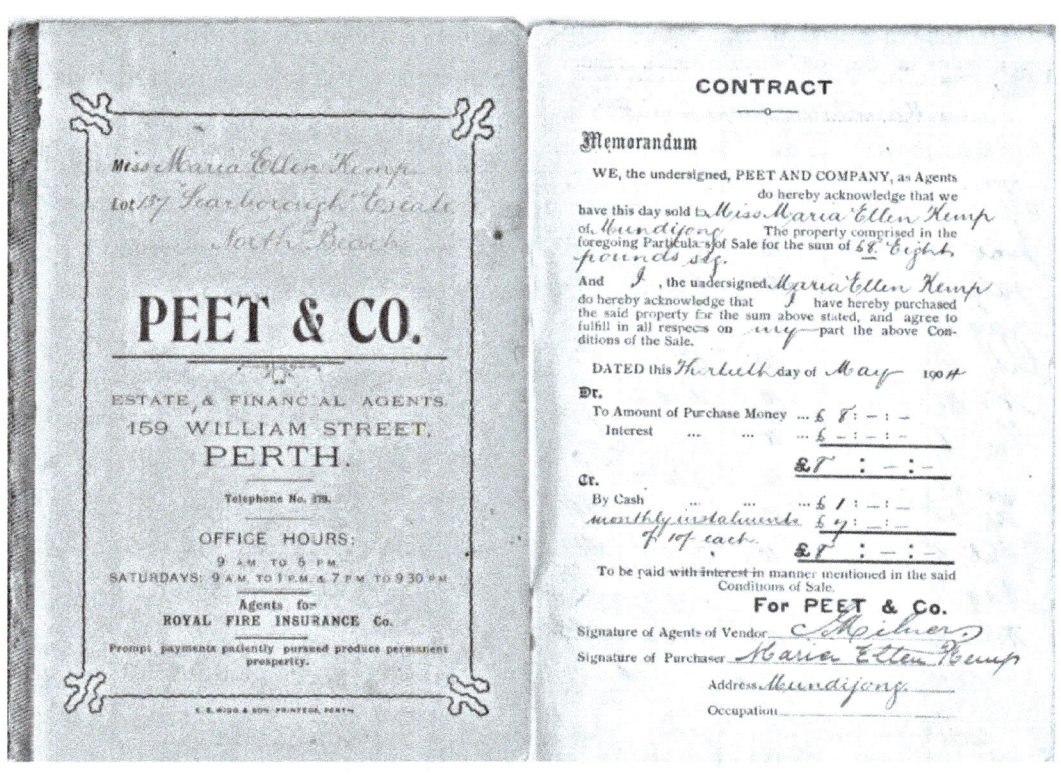

Real estate document for one of the blocks in the Scarborough Estate, North Beach. (Personal collection)

Payment book for one of the blocks in the Scarborough Estate – Paid off by November 20th 1908. (Personal collection)

Hotels in those days often had several boarding rooms for guests and permanent boarders who would eat in the tearooms or the restaurant. This is likely to have been the type of place Maria Ellen got her job as a waitress. To give some idea of what a hotel in Nannine was like, one of them was put on the market in 1899 and was typical of the larger hotels in the area at the time. A newspaper advertisement was placed for its sale. It was quite common for women to run boarding houses and hotels during those early years and *The Nannine Hotel* was run by a Mrs Willows.

It *"was described as being splendidly furnished throughout, of iron construction and containing a large bar, three parlours, a drawing room, dining room and 12 bedrooms, plus appliances. It boasted a large billiard room fitted out with a renowned 'Alcock' table, and was advertised to include stables, outhouses and a butcher's shop, and was purported to have an annual turnover of three thousand Australian pounds."* (en.wikipedia.org/wiki/Nannine)

You never know, Maria Ellen may have worked in the Nannine Hotel or one similar to that in the following advertisement.

Perhaps Maria Ellen worked in this hotel and met George Thomas in the Coach Booking Office. (www.outbackfamilyhistory.com.au)

For whatever reason, George Thomas Carroll frequented the hotel in which Maria Ellen worked, and according to their daughter, Mary Ellen (Molly), this is how they met. Maria Ellen must have been pleasantly attracted to his tall, slim frame, good looks and friendly, easy-going character and he probably gave her the impression he was well off and had come from a wealthy farming family 'over east'. He would surely have been attracted to this strong, petite beauty with a feisty manner. It must have been an instant attraction because they had a very short courtship. It appears that George Thomas may have been unemployed at the time of their marriage because on their marriage certificate he did not enter any employment. Maria Ellen's employment was as a Domestic. George Thomas stated that his father was a grazier, which might have been a bit presumptuous. Maria Ellen stated that her father was a farmer. Even though their courtship was brief they had bought their own home in Connolly Street, Nannine, before they were married. The marriage took place in the little Catholic Church in Nannine on 30th April 1906.

The little Catholic church in Nannine where George Thomas and Maria Ellen married in 1906. (www.bing.com/images) (2020)

He was now thirty-five years old and almost a veteran of the harshness of the goldfields. She was a young and determined twenty-six-year-old and new to these dry, hot, dusty and very noisy conditions. Their wedding was quite an affair with over twenty guests attending. The following is an extract from the local newspaper about the wedding.

> "A very pretty, though quiet, wedding took place at Nannine on Monday last at the Roman Catholic Church, Father Byrnes officiating. The parties were Mr. G. Carroll of New South Wales, and Miss May Kemp second eldest

daughter of G. M. Kemp, Esq., of Geraldton.

The bride wore a graceful design in Indian muslin, with bridal wreath and veil, and a large bouquet, the gift of the bridegroom. After a splendid wedding breakfast, the happy couple, accompanied by friends, drove to their own home, and the usual throwing of rice, etc., was indulged in.

A great many friends gathered at their home in the evening, and the usual toasts were gone through. A splendid wedding cake manufactured by Mr. W. Baohe, of Bond s Bakery, was on the centre of the table, and attracted much admiration.

Among the many useful and ornamental presents the following were seen: --

Messrs. Morgan, Austin and Osborne, marble clock; Mrs. H. Wright, egg cups and butter dish ; Miss M. Cleary, wall panel ; Mr. Page, breakfast cruet ; Miss McEwan, breakfast cruet ; Miss Griffin, dinner cruet; Mr. and Mrs. O Leary, liquer stand ; Miss Mulchay, biscuit barrel; Miss Terry, half a dozen serviettes; Mr. Berger, butter dish and sugar bowl; Mr. and Mrs. T. McCann, half dozen desert knives and forks ; Mrs. Bray (Stake Well) eider down quilt; Mrs. Head, set of jugs ; Miss L. Ventura, glass fruit stand and cake dish ; Mr. Doody, pair silver serviette rings ; Mrs Doody, pair piotores ; Miss Rattigan and Mr. T. Prescott, pair silver serviette rings ; Mrs. Downie, half a dozen cups, saucers, dinner and dessert plates; Mr.Goldman, set of carvers; Mrs. Duff, deck chair; Miss Head, tray and cloth."

(*Nannine Notes*. The Murchison Times and Day Dawn Gazette (Cue, WA: 1894 – 1925) Sat 5 May 1906 p. 2)

*George Thomas Carroll and Maria Ellen Kemp on their wedding day, 30th April, 1906
(Family photo)*

George Thomas and Maria Ellen looked refined and elegant on their wedding day. Maria Ellen was probably quite well off financially and, for a woman, very independent. Their wedding clothing suggests they were doing well.

Maria Ellen would not have envisaged the poverty she would once again have to endure during most of her married life and the hard work ahead having to bring up a large family for the most part, alone.

The house for them to start their new life was purchased in Meekatharra and George Thomas carted it to Nannine. "Movable' houses were common then. Perhaps, when Maria Ellen sold her Scarborough Estate properties sometime after 1908 it was to purchase a cow and some goats, and a horse and cart for the family's use. They began their married life on the outskirts of the township. The photo below explains the locality in Nannine.

George Thomas Carroll (right) and friend Mick Suliven [sic] (Sullivan)

An explanation of where their house was situated in Nannine. (Family photo)

Around that time, Nannine was a bustling gold mining town that, during its short life, had eight shops, seven hotels, a newsagent, a photographer, several veterinary surgeons, several blacksmiths and farriers, several butchers and other small businesses. A very busy little precinct.

(https://en.wikipedia.org/wiki/Nannine,_Western_Australia)

The town no longer exists but was situated near what is now Great Northern Highway approximately forty kilometres south of Meekatharra, Western Australia, and just over 700 kilometres north east of Perth. There is almost nothing left there now; everything has been cleared for a big mine. Only the remnants of the railway siding remains, and the little cemetery on the hill away to the south near the lake. However, back then it was said that *"thousands of people throng the streets. Camel teams pass through, bearing their endless loads of wood to the hungry boilers at the mine. Donkey teams, 33 or more in a string, haul supplies. Gala nights come again, with streets packed with people and three brass bands playing..."* Re-living Nannine (The West Australian Saturday 23 January 1954)

A lively and busy place indeed.

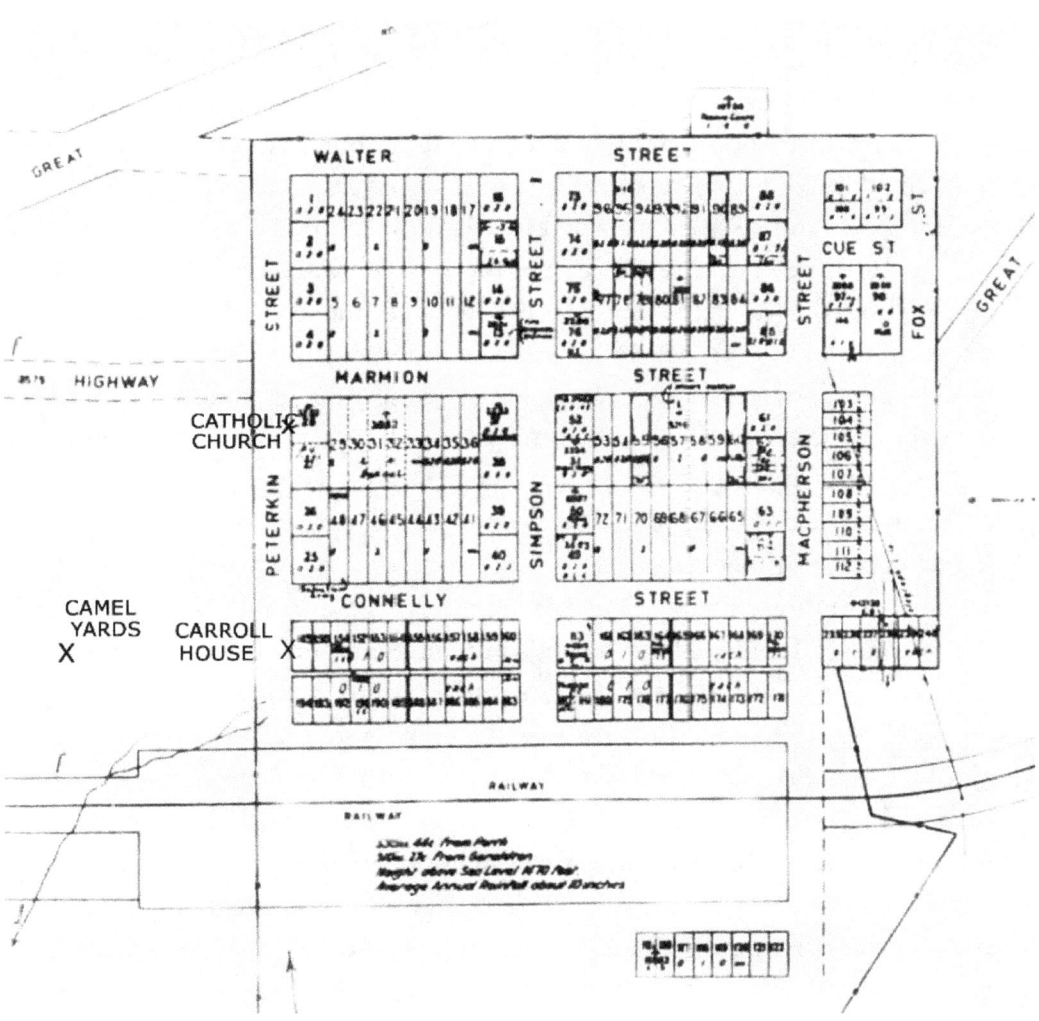

Nannine town map showing the position of the Carroll house, the Catholic Church and camel yards. (www.outbackhistory.com.au) 2021

Life was tough for Maria Ellen, she had to endure the hardship, heat, loneliness and isolation of those goldfields. George Thomas was away a considerable amount of time driving the mail coaches and the joke in the family was that he came home long enough to get her pregnant then leave to go to work again. There was a timetable for these coaches and the runs were extensive with multiple nights away; George Thomas would only have had a limited amount of time at home.

Maria Ellen was pregnant when she married and would have had a hard time with a new baby coming so soon after their marriage. It is hoped she made friends and had visits to and from her family to help her out. She had very little rest between the births of her nine children. In those days, it was not common for women to give birth in a hospital. Maria Ellen went to Geraldton for the births of some of her children and she probably spent the latter part of her confinement with her mother, Ellen Kemp (Buckley), or one of Maria Ellen's sisters. These women would then have stayed with her and helped during the convalescence period after the birth. Some of her children were born in Nannine with a midwife present. Stanley Lawrence remembered them all waiting excitedly for William Kevin, the new (and last) baby to be born after which they could go in and see him. Maria Ellen had her nine children in the short period of seventeen years. An exhausting time for her with a baby on the hip and little ones at her heel.

It was quite some time before her eldest daughter, Mary Ellen (Molly), would have been old enough to share in the caring for the younger children. She would have been only fifteen years old when the last child, William Kevin, was born but, from the age of about ten, she would have been expected to look after the younger children. She would also have had to do household chores from a much earlier age, as was common then.

Living in Nannine, or any Western Australian goldfields town, would have been extremely difficult, especially in summer. Summer in those inland areas would have been insufferable and it was quite common for the temperature to soar to between 110 and 120 degrees F (40 – 50 degrees C). Everything baked. The ground temperature would have been a lot hotter, making things extremely uncomfortable. It was quite common for prospectors to die of thirst and exposure if they strayed from their workings or went looking for new finds in these hot, desolate and mostly waterless areas. In contrast, winter was very cold especially at night when the temperature would go below 32 degrees F (0 degrees C) and the freezing easterly winds would have a high chill factor, making eyes and nose run. However, during spring, the country transformed to a beautiful place with carpets of pink, yellow, and white everlasting flowers and many other beautiful colourful flowers and shrubs. At that time, it seemed like paradise!

In those days there was no electricity, no air-conditioning, and no running water – no comforts as we know them today and definitely no phone. The only comfort would be in winter when the wood-stove would have warmed the kitchen in the little house. George Thomas and Maria Ellen's house was quite small and the roof and walls were made of corrugated iron with hessian whitewashed inner walls, and highly likely had dirt floors, which probably had a coating of ground up termite mound which went very hard and polished up to a nice shiny surface. This type of house construction was common for the times because these houses were meant to be easily shifted from one town to the next when the gold ran out. If there was a new big find a new township was established soon afterwards and these little houses moved with the family into the new town.

The photo below is taken in the old ghost town of Gwalia, north of Kalgoorlie, near Leonora, Western Australia. There is a street that remains intact and contains some of this type of small house. These tiny houses would often have housed a large family. At the time of the photo some of the houses were still complete with furnishings and accoutrements for a (semi) comfortable house. The small yard would have been a vegetable garden. It's quite dilapidated now but these houses were common in those days, and probably someone's pride and joy. (Maybe!) There is also a row of shops and boarding houses that may still be seen today.

Corrugated iron 'movable' house in Gwalia. The chimney area is the kitchen.
(Personal photo, 2006)

The Carroll's house may not have been as 'hotch potch' as the one in the photo but it was a small house that consisted of one bedroom in which the girls slept with their parents; the boys slept in a room out the back that was converted from the laundry. They all shared beds – no one had a bed to themselves – and often there would be arguments and protests when a foot was in someone's face. There was a dining room/small kitchen, and a bench outside on which to place tubs for the laundering. These metal oval shaped tubs were also used for infrequent baths, a simple wipe down with a damp cloth was usually all that was done. Good personal hygiene practices were still to come. Stanley Lawrence remembered a neighbour who had a proper bathtub and on a few occasions the kids were allowed to have a real bath – but George Thomas had to supply the water!

Metal oval tub used for laundry and bathing – there would have been no tap
(Personal photo)

Out in the yard was the 'copper', which is a large copper tub supported by a frame, under which a fire was lit to boil the water to wash the clothes and sheets etc. Ironing was done with small flat irons that were similar to the one in the photo below, however, the heavy iron base is gone. The bases were heated on the woodstove and were removable so the used iron that had cooled during the ironing process could be replaced by another one that had been re-heated. There were no synthetic materials so a hot iron could be used (except on silk).

An iron that was found at the old Nannine town site.
(Personal photo)

Washing was very labour intensive and a day a week was set aside for it to be done. Hot water from the copper was put into a tub and the clothes rubbed up and down on a corrugated washboard, an example of which can be seen below. The soap sat in the compartment in the top. The 'feet' were placed in a tub of water and washing was done by leaning over the washboard to rub the clothes up and down on the metal surface.

A common method of washing clothes by using a metal and wood washboard. (http://www.oldandinteresting.com) 2020

If the washing was to be done with boiling water from the copper, the water would be put in a tub and a 'washing dolly' would be used, an example of which is seen below. The prongs would be placed amongst the clothes and agitated by twirling the handles at the top, which were at about waist height, to move the clothes about in the water. With a big family, this was no mean feat. Poor Maria Ellen must have been exhausted by the end of the day. The women of those days would have been extremely physically fit! No need for the gym! Women had it hard and they were tough!

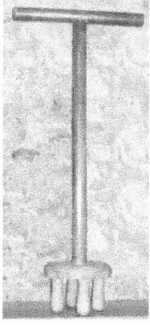

A 'washing dolly' used by women before electricity and washing machines (http://www.oldandinteresting.com) 2020

A 'washing mangle' to wring the washing (www.bing.com/images) 2021

The clothing, sheets and other items that were washed were then put through the 'wringer' or 'mangle'. The tub would be placed at the base of the mangle and the washed material was wound through the mangle to get most of the water out. This was repeated during the rinsing process.

In addition to the tough living conditions in Nannine, the loud thumping sound of the rock crusher batteries was constant and went twenty-four hours a day. No painkillers, as we know them today, for a headache, and no escape from the noise! However, it was possible to buy an opium mixture for pain if you had the money.

Mary Ellen (Molly) stated that the area around the town when the Carroll family was still living there was very desolate, no greenery at all, no trees, no grass, no gardens. Only acres of red dirt and small stones. From the photo below, it seems nothing has changed. During dry times, dust storms were common, great walls of dust that could be seen coming from far away would descend on the little town and penetrate every nook and cranny in the houses with fine red dust that would have been a nightmare to clean out. The red dust would have to be cleaned out of the furniture, drawers, cupboards, floors and even the ceilings ... everything. These dust storms were dreaded by the townsfolk, especially the women. Cleaning with water (which they didn't have enough of anyway) would have turned the dust to mud so dry wiping was done. All fabrics would have been taken outside and shaken and beaten to dislodge the dust.

Water was always in short supply because the supply to the house was rainwater that was caught in a rainwater tank during the infrequent rain events. When that supply was low, water had to be purchased and carted from the Government Well three miles away. This was achieved by carting a large iron cube shaped tank on a horse-drawn spring cart. George Thomas and the older boys would go on the horse-drawn cart that was owned by the family. The horse was named Nugget and that water tank can be seen in the photo below.

Stanley Lawrence Carroll (left) and his brother John Raymond with the family water tank at the location of their house in Nannine, about 1980. (Personal Photo)

By the time Stanley Lawrence came along in 1915, Nannine was in a serious decline. Families were leaving and the gold boom was almost at an end with just a few larger mines still operating. Some persistent prospectors remained in their little tin shacks and lived a hard and frugal life with no comforts at all. Itinerant prospectors lived in these desolate areas for many years after the demise of Nannine. New prospectors would come in and take over the abandoned prospecting patches well into the 1980s. There are none now, the big modern mines have put an end to it all.

*Nannine about 1973 with a prospector's small hut and mine with Poppet Head.
(Personal photo)*

*Nannine, 2018. No more prospectors' huts. The big modern mine is in the background.
(Personal photo)*

Stanley Lawrence's son Lindsay at the site of the old camel yards that were near the Carroll family house as mentioned in the photo of George Thomas and Mick Sullivan. (Personal photo 2020)

Remnants of the old Nannine Post Office, 1974, built in 1896/7, now demolished. (Personal photo)

Stanley Lawrence Carroll and the family during his childhood years

Stanley Lawrence Carroll was born in Geraldton, Western Australia on the 6th January 1915 and died on the 15th October, 1995, aged 80, at his home in Floreat, Western Australia. He was the middle child of George Thomas Carroll and Maria Ellen Kemp. There were four children older than him and four younger, nine children in total, three girls and six boys. It is said that the middle child is the forgotten child …

Stanley Lawrence, along with his brothers and sisters, went to school in Nannine until he was about nine years old when they left Nannine. The school had one room and all the children in the town were taught together in that one room. The teacher, usually a young man or woman in their first teaching job would be sent for a tenure of one year only and each year a new teacher came to town. There were not that many children in town at that stage because the town was slowly being abandoned as the gold ran out, the mines shut down and businesses moved away.

There was only one shop left in Nannine at that time and it only had meagre supplies, including hardware and some groceries. Mary Ellen (Molly) stated that there was no confectionery, no cool drinks, nor any other delights to tantalise the kids. Dismal.

John Raymond Carroll (left) and Stanley Lawrence about 1921, dressed in their best clothes, with the family dog "Tim" at Nannine. (Family photo)

The Carrolls had a cow and about ten goats that were used for milk. The goats were kept in a yard near the house but the cow would be allowed to wander off in search of food. Stanley Lawrence's eldest brother, Norman George, had to go and find her each day and milk her before school. Stanley Lawrence said John Raymond, Arthur Henry and he had to milk all the goats. It was quite an affair. Stanley Lawrence had to hold the horns while Arthur Henry held the back feet, and John Raymond did the milking. Sometimes while Arthur Henry was crouched down holding the legs, a goat would sometimes drop pellets of poo on his head. This infuriated him and he'd twist the goat's tail, causing it to surge forward, causing the horns to bunt into Stanley Lawrence's chest pushing him backwards. The goat would kick the bucket John Raymond was milking into and sometimes spill the milk. There would be chaos for a while and lots of cursing!

The children had no possessions of their own but a 'find' could be considered 'theirs'. For instance, the first person to see a baby goat could claim it as 'theirs'. Another instance was, if something was found in the field like a ground nesting bird's nest or a particularly beautiful flower, a ring of white stones would be placed in a circle around the item and this would denote ownership.

Christmases were pretty poor according to Stanley Lawrence. The children would get nothing, but he was quick to add that they weren't alone; many families were in the same situation. However, he was puzzled that the Policeman's children got a Christmas stocking with presents in it and he couldn't understand why Father Christmas bypassed their house. The Carroll children were a bit crooked on Father Christmas and thought they'd 'get' him next year by placing the big three-pronged prickles – Double Gees – down the chimney. They'd show him! Stanley Lawrence said one year they all got a lolly ball each, a real treat!

School was a delight to Stanley Lawrence. He and his younger sister, Kathleen Christine, before they were old enough to attend, would go and hang around the school. The teacher would allow the two of them to sit quietly in the classroom while the other pupils did their work. He said with all the grades in the one room it was a wonderful way to learn. Over time, school subjects were constantly reinforced so nothing was missed. He was a school teacher later in life and could see the benefits of this type of schooling. Being so close in age, he said he and Kathleen Christine were like twins; they were very close and did everything together. There were a few books on the shelves in the classroom, one of them was a book of coloured plates of the birds of Australia drawn by John Gould. The pictures within fascinated Stanley Lawrence and he said it was the beginning of a life-long love affair with natural history.

Mary Ellen (Molly) said the Carroll children saw their first car in Nannine, a

Buick with canvas for side windows that had a small square of "cellophane" through which to see out. Cars in the area were very uncommon in those days. Stanley Lawrence recalled the driver, a station owner, stopping and collecting the kids and taking them for a ride. He said it was the most thrilling thing he had ever experienced in Nannine. Probably because of the speed ... a real novelty.

When the nearby Lake Annean filled after good rains, duck shooting was carried out by the townspeople. Stanley Lawrence's father, George Thomas, would participate and the older kids had to go out into the deep black mud and retrieve the shot ducks from the lake. A nice feed of meat for the family and a thrilling day out. Stanley Lawrence said the main diet in their family was milk, and bread that was cooked by Maria Ellen supplemented by the meat they hunted and a few meagre vegetables if they could afford them and if they were available.

Lake Annean at Nannine after good rains in 1975. (Personal photo)

In about 1906, to the delight of the people, feral rabbits arrived in Nannine, there was now delicious and different food to put on the table. COMAN, Brian. *Tooth and nail: the history of the rabbit in Australia.* (Text Publishing, 1999) p. 30

Another source of meat was from goannas. A story recounted by Mary Ellen (Molly) and Stanley Lawrence was the time a huge goanna, probably a Perentie (*Varanus giganteus*), went into the school classroom. The teacher jumped up onto her desk and screamed loudly. The goanna ran out of the room with the kids in hot pursuit. It ran up the road and into the Council Chambers. The Town Clerk was in there at the time and he too jumped up onto his desk but was able to get a revolver out of his desk drawer and began shooting at the goanna. The kids were all milling excitedly around and it was lucky no one was shot! The Carroll kids took the dead goanna home and Maria Ellen cooked it. Delicious! The kids took some of the meat to school the next day and offered some to the teacher to eat for lunch. After she had finished, they told her it was the goanna that had come into the classroom the day before – she promptly gagged and vomited. The kids thought it was a great joke.

Outings were few and far between so any break in the normal monotony would have been a highlight in the children's lives. A favourite time for Stanley Lawrence and his brothers and sisters were the community picnics to Bond's Gardens situated about three miles from the Nannine town-site. The family and several townsfolk would get on board George Thomas's horse-drawn wagon and they'd all travel to the lush green gardens. This was the vegetable growing area that had a good seasonal supply of water from the river pools. Below are newspaper articles from the period that describe the picnics and the gardens.

> " there is also joy in visiting the gardens and walking along the paths close to where the orange trees are growing. The fruit is large and golden. Ah! If the rainfall could be relied upon the Murchison would easily provide itself with vegetables and export a little as well. The gardens owned by Mr. Jose and Mr. Bond are a credit to the owners, and at present the fruit and vegetables growing in them are simply magnificent".

Our Nannine Letter. (Geraldton Guardian Friday 26 July 1907, p. 7. (www.trove.com.au)

> "Nannine Tuesday
>
> The picnic at Bond's garden on Sunday was a success. The money cleared from the ball; amounting to £10 was given away in prizes and toys; and there was enough food in the way of cakes, biscuits and aerated waters to provide plenty for the day. A large number of children and adults were present."

(Meekatharra Miner WA : Sat 27 Sep 1913) p.2 (www.trove.com.au)

Stanley Lawrence told stories of his mother being a strict Roman Catholic and that they all had to go to church on Sundays, and say their prayers each night. Often at church they would sit behind their mother and during the Hail Mary they would say "Hail Mary full of grapes" instead of "Hail Mary full of grace", get the giggles and go almost hysterical laughing and trying to stay silent. Maria Ellen would turn around and give them a good 'cuff around the ears' (hit them) and give a dire warning of what was to come later. She was a no-nonsense woman who was *very* tough on the kids and punishment was dealt out with the strap (razor strop) or a cane. His body language said it all when he spoke of her toughness. When one of the children did something not to her liking, she would get the other children to go and get the culprit of the misdemeanour and drag him or her back to get their punishment. Stanley Lawrence said that looking back on that he felt it was highly unfair to the other children and that she shouldn't have done it. He said they felt awful having to drag the terrified child back. She had little patience. Mary Ellen (Molly) stated that Maria Ellen had told her she hadn't wanted children so I suppose the life she had was nothing like she'd dreamed of … poor Maria Ellen.

Tragedy struck the family during the baking hot summer of 1920 when baby Eileen Agnes, who was born on the 18th November 1918, died of *"Enteritis and Asthenia"* in February 1920. She was just fifteen months old.

(https://www.wa.gov.au/organisation/department-of-justice/online-index-search-tool)

The Enteritis was probably caused by bacterially contaminated food or water, or from flies, and caused her to have severe abdominal pain and probably diarrhoea. She possibly had typhoid. The Asthenia, which is physical weakness, was probably caused by a high temperature from the Enteritis and she became too weak to recover and died. Nannine Hospital, which was just a tent, was operational at that time, both Maria Ellen and George Thomas subscribed to it, but she wasn't taken to hospital and sadly, she died at home. *Nannine Hospital Records 1909 – December 1920. (State Records Office, WA).* The hospital was quite a distance away and with no transport it may not have been possible to take her. George Thomas may have been away on the coach run and not been home to help.

Maria Ellen laid the baby out on the bed and got the children to come and kiss her to say goodbye before she was taken to be buried. Stanley Lawrence remembered during summers the older children would have to take it in turns to fan the baby to keep it cool and keep the flies off. There were a few babies born in summer after Stanley Lawrence was born. Even though he was very young, he remembered Eileen Agnes dying. He said they all tried hard to keep her cool in an impossibly hot summer. He said it was heartbreaking to hear her whimpering cries. After her funeral, he remembered his mother crying in sadness for weeks. The doctor was apparently drunk and could not be found until it was too late to save her. Maria Ellen *"carried that bitterness until she died ... She loved her family and was a formidable matriarch."* (CARROLL, Max. *Memoir*) They had no money for a gravestone and only a metal number marked where she was buried.

Eileen Agnes's grave stands on the sandy hill in Nannine Cemetery. (Her name in the wood at the foot of the grave was carved by Stanley Lawrence). The wooden surrounds were replaced recently by Mary Ellen's (Molly) family. Many years after Eileen Agnes's death, her brothers, John Raymond and Arthur Henry, went to find her unmarked grave. They remembered the position and they dug down and found her small skull and the little blonde curls of her hair. They then built the wooden surrounds to mark her gravesite. (personal comment Jacqueline Carroll) Eileen Agnes's grave is still visited by many of her extended family.

Eileen Agnes Carroll's grave at Nannine. (Personal Photo 2019)

Eileen Agnes's grave with the memorials of some of her family members whose ashes have been scattered are there in the background. (Personal photo 2019)

Mary Ellen (Molly) has a plaque and her ashes within Eileen Agnes's grave surrounds. Mary Ellen (Molly) would have felt the death of Eileen Agnes keenly, she was the "minder" of all the babies and would have been very involved with her care, possibly more so than her mother. Stanley Lawrence said that John Raymond was very upset because he loved his new little sister and he tried to explain to the smaller children that Eileen Agnes would be buried in the ground and then she would go up to heaven. Stanley Lawrence said he couldn't understand how she could be buried in a hole in the ground and then get out and go to heaven. He said he puzzled over the concept for several years. Such are the thoughts of children.

Every Sunday the family would go to the cemetery to be with Eileen Agnes and take flowers if they could get them. On one occasion, a huge dust storm blew up and was headed for the town. Maria Ellen told the children to run back to the house. They were in a very big hurry to beat the storm, but the dog, 'Tim', was sniffing around after a goanna when Maria Ellen gave him a kick up the bum and told him to get out of there and get home! Stanley Lawrence laughed as he recalled the occasion. Luckily, they got back to the house in time to lock everything up. Later in Stanley Lawrence's life, he had an almost pathological hatred of dust!

Mary Ellen (Molly) and several of her brothers' ashes and memorials, including

John Raymond, Stanley Lawrence, Francis Peter, Arthur Henry and his wife Thelma (Feazey) and also their daughter Maxine are close by in the Nannine Cemetery. Such was the draw of Nannine to the Carroll children – that little town was always in their blood.

Stanley Lawrence's eldest brother Norman George (George) was an extremely bright young man. He won an educational scholarship to Geraldton High School, where he was Dux of the school two years running. There he won another scholarship to the college in New Norcia to study but unfortunately the family did not have the funds to send him so he missed out. (Probably just as well!) Such were his mechanical and engineering skills that, after World War 2, he designed and built a huge gold 'harvester' that could be moved to new ground to process and sift out gold from loads of dirt fed into it by a front-end loader. An amazing contraption!

The 'Gold Harvester' designed and built by Norman George Carroll. The design is built on military Grant and Valentine tanks. Their brother John Raymond is in the photo, date around 1950. (Photo Max Carroll)

It is not known whether the harvester was successful; no one mentioned him making a fortune but he did get some gold. Norman George's son, Max Carroll, stated *"that Dad designed and built the plant around a Grant* (military tank) *hull, using the tracks and lower assembly. The upper hull, turrets etc. were cut off and the original Radial engines in the Grant were removed as they were too heavy on petrol fuel; and the power unit he put in was a Diesel engine from a British Valentine tank. All of this came from Post WW2 Disposals".* The gold harvester was out in the Murchison for some time but scrap metal was valuable and someone might have salvaged it because no one seems to know of its whereabouts.

In 1924, Nannine was at the end of its heyday and the family decided to leave because there was no longer a future for the children there. George Thomas got a transfer to Sawyers Valley with the WAGR (Western Australian Government Railways). He sold the little house for the same sum he purchased it and it was subsequently moved to a nearby pastoral station. Stanley Lawrence was nine years old and it was the end of an era in the outback for him and his siblings as they left for greener pastures; but the outback stayed in his blood forever. He said they were heartbroken when they left; they gathered little bottles of dirt and hair from the goats and took them as reminders.

The time came to move to Sawyers Valley, situated in the hills to the east of Perth. George Thomas packed everything up and sent the family on ahead with their belongings to their new abode down south while he stayed in Nannine for a while and had a peaceful journey to Perth. William Kevin was just a small baby and Maria Ellen, with the help of the older children, was able to manage the smaller children on the long train journey. Initially, the family went to South Fremantle for a short period to stay with Maria Ellen's relatives. It was the first time the children had seen the ocean and Stanley Lawrence said he couldn't believe how big the expanse of water was and how big the waves were. He said it was a bit frightening at first.

The house in Sawyers Valley didn't eventuate so they moved into a house at Mt Helena. Stanley Lawrence told of the amazing change to see green grassy pastures, fruit trees, and tall forests. An almost overwhelming change and something he had never seen before. He was very impressed. The house too was a complete change and Mary Ellen (Molly) stated that it was of white painted weatherboard with a beautiful rose garden and other lovely flowers.

The house stood on several acres and had a small running creek and a waterfall. It was very peaceful and beautiful. What a change!

The year after they arrived, John Raymond had to go to High School in Midland Junction and he travelled the distance on the steam train. Train travel from Mt Helena was easy; regular trains serviced the people in the hills areas. Maria Ellen wanted her daughter Mary Ellen (Molly) to be a success in life and made her go to Stott's Business College in Perth. She travelled on the returning Kalgoorlie Express in the morning and returned on the Albany Express in the evening. It seems public transport was better then than today! Norman George had left home and was working and living in Claremont, a suburb of Perth. He was working as a motor mechanic for Gascoyne's Garage in Claremont.

The Carroll children at Mt Helena – back- L-R Mary Ellen (Molly), John Raymond, Arthur Henry, Stanley Lawrence. Front - Francis Peter. Centre – Kathleen Christine. Not in the photo - Norman George - had left the family to go to work in Perth, William Kevin was still a babe in arms. (Family photo)

Sawyers Valley School. (Family photo)

Sawyers Valley Railway Station. (Family photo)

A small part of Stanley Lawrence's matchbox collection that was collected along the Sawyers Valley railway line. (Personal photo)

Early in the morning before school, and after school, Stanley Lawrence and Arthur Henry had chores to do. One was to milk the newly acquired goats. They had to do this in all weathers – freezing cold, rain, or hot. Stanley Lawrence said that on cold mornings it was delightful to warm his hands on the warmth of the goat's udder and nestle his face into the groove of her hip. Cherry, the cow, had come down from Nannine with the family and she too had to be milked and that job now belonged to John Raymond. In those days, it was expected that children would share the household work and all of them would have had something to do before and after school. If it wasn't done, there would be trouble.

When these goats had kids, the first child to see the kid was the "owner". This ownership could be very handy because now they could extract payment of some kind from the other children by "selling" the kid to them but no money changed hands, more likely a favour was given. Stanley Lawrence said that the children had nothing, but he said it wasn't a problem because you didn't really realise you had nothing: it was normal for them.

To help with the family finances, George Thomas cut down dead Jarrah trees and the boys used a cross cut saw to cut it into lengths to sell for firewood. They also caught possums, probably Brushtailed Possums, to kill and sell the skins. They would also collect the 'fluffy wool' from Banksia cones to sell for the stuffing of furniture.

For fun, one of the goats was used to drag the kids around in a homemade cart. Stanley Lawrence's face would light up and he would chuckle when he told of the antics with the goat hurtling along with the kids screaming and hanging on for dear life.

Goat and cart – a bit more sophisticated than the "Carroll" cart. (www.bing.com/images)

The family was always poor and Maria Ellen must have found it difficult to make ends meet. Life was hard but they struggled on and supported each other in any way they could. George Thomas absented himself again and regularly went away for long periods to Mt Magnet. During the last year of their time in Mt Helena, probably at Maria Ellen's urging, they planned to move to Perth. No doubt she was tired of being alone and having the constant pressure of bringing up the children alone. After being in Mt Helena for three years, they decided to move out of the hills region to go and live in Perth. Maria Ellen could see that opportunities for her family were limited and they would eventually have to leave home to seek work. She probably knew work in Perth would help keep her family close by.

In 1927, when Stanley Lawrence was twelve years old, his brother, Norman George, found a house for them to live in. The house belonged to Norman George's employer and he sold his motor bike to get enough money for the deposit. The house cost £500 which was a lot of money at that time. The family moved into the house at 54 Robinson Street, Claremont. George Thomas was now fifty-six years old and still had to provide for four children under the age of twelve. To support his family, he continued his work as a Repairer with the railways in Mt Magnet. The older children were of working age and it is highly likely they helped supplement the household income.

The area of Claremont where they lived was known as Sunning Hill and was mostly bush, but there were a few scattered weatherboard houses in the area. Brick homes in the suburb were to come later. Their home was a small weatherboard house with a tin roof and was on a quarter acre block. It had two bedrooms, a lounge/sitting room where only visitors went, a large kitchen/dining room with a woodstove and a walk-in pantry. This was luxury compared to Nannine's modest home and there would have been the magic of electric lights – a newish phenomenon for the houses of Perth and certainly for the Carrolls. There was a verandah across the front and an enclosed verandah (a sleep-out) at the back where the boys slept, still in shared beds. Outside, down the back stairs in the backyard was the laundry with a copper tub under which a fire was lit to boil the clothes and bed linen etc. Further out was the toilet that had a plank seat with a hole and a large bucket underneath into which toileting was done. The "night soil" was collected each week and carted away in a truck. This was how it was for everyone in those days. They had a small garage with a mechanic's pit in the floor, probably because the house was previously owned by a mechanic. There was a large mulberry tree down near the back fence with stinging nettles underneath. (Stinging nettles are a sign of very healthy soil). The house has since been demolished. It was situated where what is now the Chelsea Village car park.

The Carroll family home at 54 Robinson Street, Claremont, WA. (Family photo)

An amusing tale told by Max Carroll describes the back yard and the 'night soil' collector …

" . the path from the back steps of the house led down to the Dunny, about 40 metres away at the end of the quarter acre block. (Most dunnys stank hence the long walk). There was also a fork in the path which led to the back door of the garage, then a second fork leading to the vegie garden and chook yard. The path to the first fork was covered by a trellised archway with grapevines. In the daytime it was quite beautiful and it was made by Popski. (George Thomas) However, at night time it was scary for small people like me, a fact which Frank (Francis Peter) and Bill (William Kevin) used to take delight in exploiting with ghost stories, as we all slept in the big double bed on the back verandah. One night during the Dunny man's weekly call, we heard him whistling as he made his way down to the dunny, where he picked up the full container, put a lid loosely on it, swung it up onto his shoulder; and still whistling made his way back up the path towards the front gate where his patient horse and Dunny Cart awaited. As he moved under the vine covered archway, his whistling stopped, followed by a bloodcurdling scream, then a crash and a lot of loud swearing profanity. Frank and Bill were delighted as they had a pet possum which used to spend the days asleep in the vines before coming out at night to forage. The little chap had dropped from the vines onto the dunny man's head, which caused him to abandon his hold on the "Honey Bucket", which burst the loose lid and the contents went everywhere over the unfortunate Dunny man, the path and wash house. The racket roused Popski (George Thomas) and Grandma (Maria Ellen) who switched the back light on to survey the scene of carnage and stench. Grandma took her ire out on the laughing Frank and Bill whilst Popski hosed the Dunny man down with the garden hose. A night still vivid in my memory. Grandma made Frank and Bill clean up the wash house and path next morning."

Dunny bucket that had to be carted away (Personal photo)

An outside dunny or Thunderbox, as they were known (Personal photo)

While George Thomas was working away in Mt Magnet, he wrote letters to Maria Ellen. There are two letters still in existence and they are shown below but unfortunately there are no dates on them. The spelling is how George Thomas wrote the letter.

Letter 1 …

"This is confidentil

My Dearest I have missed you very much since I returned. I feel the same as when we first came engaged a longing to be always with you. It must be all the old affection returned of course the Family all grown up and no babys to divide the love my be the cause for the Greater love for you the only thing that keeps me here is to try & get something so as we can live with a little comfort in our old days & always together. You can take this with all Sincearity from the Bottom of my heart.

Yours Most loving George xxxxxxxxxxxx

Anything you would like confidentil write in on a separated pice of paper as I always let Jack and Mary read your letters. Love again goodnight darling"

Letter 1 – To Maria Ellen from George Thomas.

Letter 2 …

"Well my dearest I was delighted to see by your letter that your belief in one was so true as I can honestly say the same as you there has never been another Woman in my life since I met you. I've had a few trials but I resisted them all for you as I loved you to dearly. So as I said about Frank it will help him in his time of temtations so I think honestly that when a man or woman sincearly love one another there is no need to fear of any other of this conscions happening.

Well sweetheart dear I hope it will not be long before I am back with you. I can understand how lonley you must be by yourself by the way I feel as here by myself. So dearest I'll come home to you it might brighten your life up.

So now darling I'll say Good night

With all the love of my heart

Your Loving George xxxxx

Write soon Love.

PS. Put address C/O J Bald

Box 33 Mt Magnet

So Jack can get the mail out the same night as it arrives He can send my letters out with the man that drives his van as he leaves early otherwise they will not get to me till the next day"

> Well my dearest I was delighted to see by your letter that your belief in me was so true as I can honestly say the same as you there has never been another woman in my life since I met you. I has had a few trials but I resisted them all for you as I loved you to dearly. so as I said about Frank it will help him in his time of temtations so I think honestly that when a man or woman sincearly love one another there is no dread to fear of any other conscious happining
> Well sweetheart dear, I hope it will not be long before I am back with you. I can understand how lonley you must be by yourself by the way I feel up here by myself. so dearest I'll come home to you it may brighten your life up.
> so now darling I'll say good night with all the love of my heart
> Yours loving George xxxx
> Write soon Love.
>
> P.S. Put: address
> C/o J Bald
> Box 33 Mt Magnet
> so Jack can get the mail out the same night as it arrives he can send my letters out with the man that drives his van if he leaves early other wise they will not get to me

Letter 2 - To Maria Ellen from George Thomas.

From the way the last letter was written perhaps there was a problem between them and that one of them may have thought the other unfaithful? Perhaps Maria Ellen was suspicious of his behaviour while he was away? The paper on which they are written is the same and the pen and ink writing is the same so it is expected that they were written during one period that George Thomas was away.

In 1936, at the age of sixty-five, George Thomas retired and moved home to Claremont and went on the Aged Pension.

The Carroll children grew into responsible adults and were all working even though there was a severe economic depression. The photo below was taken in the back yard of their Robinson Street home – it was taken in 1939 after Stanley Lawrence had enlisted in the army and was about to go to war. George Thomas is about sixty-eight and Maria Ellen about fifty-nine.

Left to right back row - Arthur Henry (Art), Stanley Lawrence (Stan), John Raymond (Jack), George Thomas, Maria Ellen, Norman George (George) Middle row - William Kevin (Bill)   Bottom row - Mary Ellen (Molly), Kathleen Christine (Kath), Francis Peter (Frank) (Family photo)

All of George Thomas and Maria Ellen's surviving children had successful lives and they all endured through the tough times of life in the goldfields, the Great Depression, and World War 2, to marry and produce twenty-two children between them. They were a close-knit family with a very strong bond between them all. Throughout their lives, they were always there for each other through thick and thin. Some of my cousins, who knew our grandfather George Thomas, said he was a gentle easy-going man with an even and generous temperament and they loved him.

Finally, after the retirement of George Thomas, he and Maria Ellen could spend some of their old age together. Family members, at times, would live with them during the difficult times of war and the Depression and often grandchildren would stay. George Thomas and Maria Ellen lived in the house in Robinson Street until his sudden death in 1947 from Pulmonary Fibrosis and Congenital Heart Failure.   (https://www.wa.gov.au/organisation/department-of-justice/online-index-search-tool) 2021. This disease can linger for years or can come on suddenly and kill the person quickly. It can be caused by smoking but George Thomas was not a smoker, nor a drinker to any extent. (Personal comment Max Carroll.) It may have been caused by the dusty mining environments in which they had lived. Maria Ellen continued to live in the house alone until well into her eighties and was very active. She went ballroom dancing and to many other social events. She was a bit of a flirt and had a wicked twinkle in her eye and a cheeky chuckle. Her tongue could sometimes be a bit acid and hurtful but she was a good mother and wife and right or wrong she always stuck by her children. When the house became too much for her to handle, the family urged her to move into an aged care home in Rossmoyne.

George Thomas Carroll and Maria Ellen in later life, outside their Robinson Street house. (Family photo)

She had given up on her Roman Catholic faith apparently because, during the Depression, the church asked its followers for money, something she thought was a terrible thing to do to people experiencing extreme hardship. She went to the Seventh Day Adventists religion for a while but didn't stay. However, she went into Sherwin Lodge, the Seventh Day Adventist Aged Care Home in Rossmoyne and died there in November, 1976. I visited her a few days before her death. Gastroenteritis was going through the home at that time and she had contracted it. The staff had perched her on a commode and she was flopped to one side. She was very weak and dehydrated and begged for a drink of water which I gave her, only to be told off by the staff! They said they didn't have time to clean her and if she had water she would dirty herself! She died a few days later – of a similar condition to her little girl Eileen Agnes back in 1920 in Nannine.

Maria Ellen Carroll (nee Kemp) – her later years when she could finally please herself...
(Family photo)

Stanley Lawrence Carroll – a young man

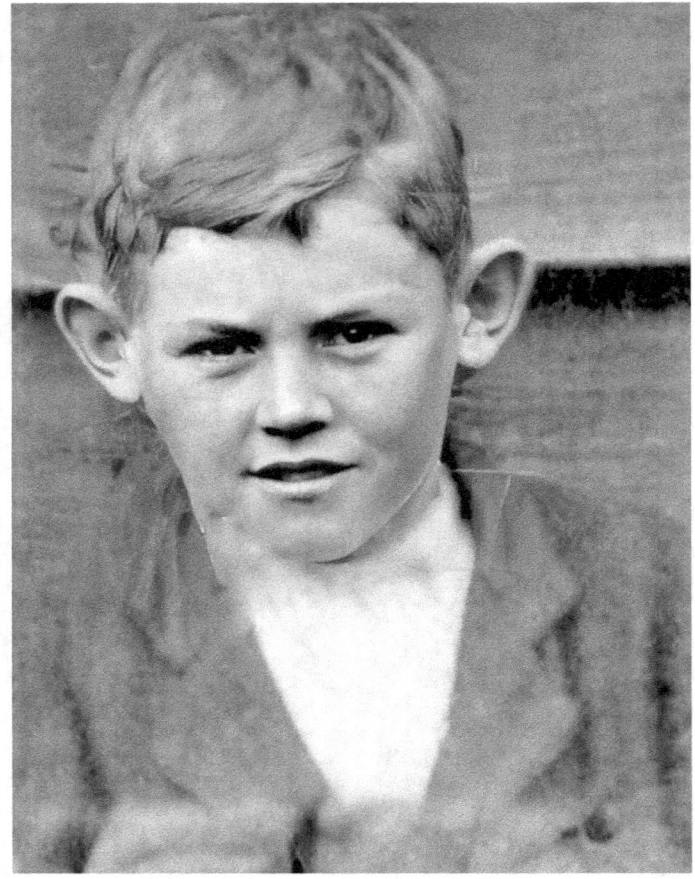

Stanley Lawrence Carroll, aged about 12, at the Robinson Street House (Family photo)

After the family moved to Perth, Stanley Lawrence went to Claremont Central School. He was a good student and liked to play many different sports including Australian Rules football, cricket and rugby and was a champion cross country runner. Later he played A Grade rugby for Nedlands, and won several trophies for best player. During their time in Nannine, the Carroll children were recognised for their sporting and running abilities; they were very athletic and Stanley Lawrence was particularly good, especially at running. He was the runt of the family so he had a lot to prove!

One afternoon, there was a great rumpus coming from the garage of their

Robinson Street home. Maria Ellen went out with the cane and belted Stanley Lawrence, Francis Peter, and William Kevin for fighting. The incident was caused when William Kevin was making a wooden pencil case with a slide on lid. He had placed it gently in the bench vice to hold it in place while he worked on it. Francis Peter came past and twirled the handle of the vice crushing the pencil case! Tempers flared and punches were thrown. Maria Ellen didn't find out what the problem was nor who the culprit was; she caned them all. Stanley Lawrence said that was her *modus operandi* – just belt them all, that way you'd get whoever the wrong doer was – the others were just collateral damage!

In his spare time, Stanley Lawrence taught himself to play the harmonica and followed in his big brother Norman George's footsteps. Norman George was an excellent harmonica player. Stanley Lawrence would climb the mulberry tree in the backyard and practice for hours. His mother would call him but he pretended not to hear her, hoping she would leave him be, but that didn't happen. She would find him and round him up with the cane! As an adult he was quite a good harmonica player and entertained anyone who would listen, especially after a bit of grog. Music was a very important part of his life and he loved to sing; he had quite a good singing voice. After he retired from his job as a school teacher, he took up playing the guitar and became quite good at it. He went around to aged care homes and played for the residents.

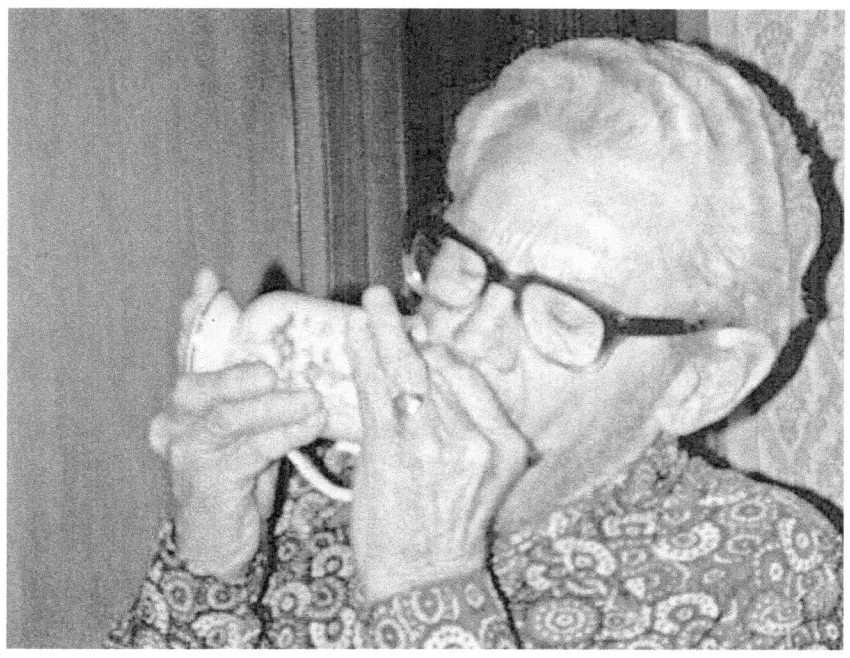

Stan playing the harmonica into a cup for that 'special' sound. (Personal photo)

His sister Mary Ellen (Molly) was an excellent pianist who went on to teach music and piano. Francis Peter played the 'squeeze box' – a smallish piano accordion – and would entertain family and friends after he'd had a bit to drink.

In 1929 when Stanley Lawrence was fourteen years old, the Great Depression began in Australia and lasted until 1939 when World War 2 began. He had to leave school and go to work. Things were very tough during this Depression and many men were out of work and a lot of people became desperate and lost everything, including their house, their furniture: everything. They became homeless and many lived in lean-tos on vacant land. Men became itinerant workers just for food and long queues were seen at soup kitchens for handouts. Women who were left to fend for themselves often had to give their children over to an orphanage or some other institution because there was no way to financially support them or even to feed them. A terrible, traumatic, and very sad time. However, in some instances, men were laid off and women were employed in their place because the employer could pay women a lot less to do the same job.

Stanley Lawrence got any job he could and, at fourteen years old, he was lucky enough to get a job as a junior 'Country Orders Clerk' at Boans Department Store in Perth city (where the current Myers store is). He was fortunate that the recently enacted law for an eight-hour day for workers was in place, meaning he didn't have to work the ten-hour day that was usual before the 1920s. The 'Labour Day' holiday, in early March each year, commemorates a hard-won victory as a result of much turmoil and strikes by workers to demand an eight-hour working day, which meant they now worked a six day, 48-hour week. It wasn't until the 1940s that the 40-hour week was made law. He did this job until he was sixteen years old when Boans ended the job because, for a fourteen-year-old, the pay was 12/6d per week (12 shillings and six pence). At sixteen, the pay went up to 16/6 per week so the sixteen-year-old had to leave and Boans would hire another fourteen-year-old.

Stanley Lawrence was then out of a job and finding work was almost impossible, until a kindly neighbour who owned the local corner shop and the Kookaburra Pet Shop asked Stanley Lawrence to find new customers to whom they could sell birdseed. He was paid £1 per week to walk the streets for miles and miles, going door to door in the suburbs of Claremont, Dalkeith, and Cottesloe. He found new customers by listening for caged birds singing in people's yards and managed to get some customers to deliver to on a regular basis. He would go in and offer his services. His 'seed book' still exists where notations were made about delivery times, customers, and their seed requirements. At that time, he didn't have shoes that fitted well – the family couldn't afford shoes so hand-me-downs had to be worn. He said it was agony because the shoes he wore didn't fit and his feet became blistered and the blisters wouldn't heal because he couldn't stop doing this job. He would wake in the morning with his feet stuck to the bedclothes!

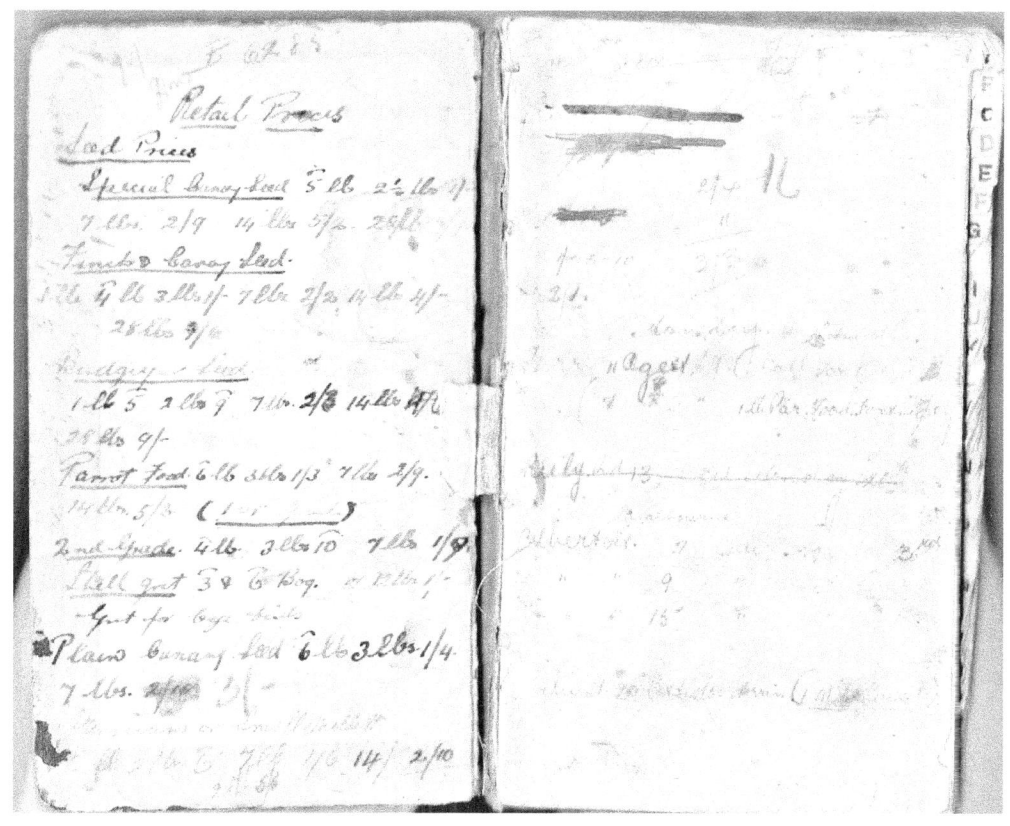

A page from Stanley Lawrence's Bird Seed Sales Book. (Personal photo)

His brother John Raymond had a job as a 'Telegraph Messenger' with the PMG (Post Master General). He would ride his bicycle delivering telegrams to the houses and businesses in the area. Telegrams were the fastest means of communication at that time. A message would come into the post office in Morse-Code, be deciphered, written out and sent to the receiving person the same day. John Raymond managed to secure a job for Stanley Lawrence as a temporary 'Telegraph Messenger' and so relieved him of his endless walking. He now rode a bicycle.

Arthur Henry got a job with Elder Smith, the agricultural business, as a transport worker driving trucks to Greenbushes and Bridgetown, taking wheat and pollard to the farms. Later, John Raymond moved from his job as 'Telegraph Messenger' to a job with the PMG as a 'Linesman', installing telegraph lines. Both he and Arthur Henry moved to Bridgetown in the south west of Western Australia where telegraph lines were being installed across the countryside, and they both worked for the PMG as linesmen. Working for the PMG became almost a right-of-passage for the Carroll boys because later Francis Peter also became a 'Telegraph Messenger'.

Francis Peter Carroll with his PMG bicycle. (Photo Kaye McCallum/Carroll)

Still in Perth, in his spare time and on Sundays, Stanley Lawrence liked to go sailing on the Swan River and eventually became quite a good sailor. It is unlikely he would have owned his own boat but was probably part of a team or just went sailing with friends. During his sailing era, Stanley Lawrence became known as 'SINNER' from the story *Sinbad the Sailor*. He kept this nickname off and on during his lifetime. He also liked swimming and often visited Nedlands Baths, a popular fenced off swimming area in the Swan River. (These skills eventually helped save his life during World War 2).

The depression was still going and his temporary job as a 'Telegraph Messenger' ended, so Stanley Lawrence, now aged about twenty, went to Bridgetown to be with his older brothers John Raymond and Arthur Henry. He hoped to get work there. The Depression was still in full swing and life was still very hard Any work he could get he did it; there were no preferences in what you could do, no picking and choosing jobs, you just took what was available.

There were many orchards in Bridgetown and apples were a big part of the fruit industry, and a lot of apple pickers were employed in the area. Stanley Lawrence supplemented his income during the picking season and, in 1937, he graded fruit for the London market. From the photo below, it can be seen that this was a very physical job with much manual handling of the heavy boxes of fruit and perhaps not a favoured job, but someone had to do it and this would have helped contribute to his strong physique. Even though he was small, he was very strong.

Stanley Lawrence grading apples in Bridgetown 1937. (Family photo)

John Raymond and Arthur Henry had girlfriends at that time. John Raymond had met Audrey Knapton, a local farmer's daughter, and Arthur Henry's girlfriend, Thelma Feazey, was from Greenbushes. Stanley Lawrence managed to get room and board in Greenbushes with Thelma's sister, Blanche, and he lived there for a short time. The Feazeys owned the bakeries in Bridgetown and Greenbushes. Stanley Lawrence enjoyed the company of his brothers and their girlfriends and probably wished he had a girlfriend too.

He was a very good Australian Rules footballer and played for the Warriors team in Bridgetown. He subsequently moved from Greenbushes to Bridgetown and began to play football there and proved he was an excellent player. In order to get him to stay in town and play football, the publican of a local hotel, a woman, and fanatical football fan, gave him a job in her hotel as barman, yardman, plus other duties. They needed him to live in Bridgetown and, because he was one of their best players, they wanted him to stay. They were keen on winning the local Premiership.

He went to the local dances and enjoyed a very active social life. He certainly knew how to 'live it up'. He travelled to dances further afield and gained a reputation for being a bit of a 'wild child' – it was a time of working hard, playing sport, dancing, and frivolity, including 'hitting the grog' after a long hard day at work. At times, he helped his brothers in the PMG in the Bridgetown area and helped in the construction of the telegraph lines in the district by digging the holes for the poles. He said his hands were so blistered that in the mornings he had to soak them to soften them so he could open them.

His sister, Mary Ellen (Molly) had married Ken Thorley not long before Stanley Lawrence went to Bridgetown. Ken had moved back to Bridgetown where he had previously lived and Mary Ellen wanted to join her husband so caught the train with their small daughter, Patti. She expected Ken to meet her at the station but he wasn't there. He was carousing with another woman! Fortunately, Stanley Lawrence was there to meet her and he got her a room in the hotel. (Mary Ellen made no secret of her husband's indiscretions and has included it in her memoir that was written later in her life).

There was much socialising and drinking in the local hotels after the football matches. Stanley Lawrence was very drunk one night and was caught by the police wheeling a motorcycle down the road. It belonged to someone else who said Stanley Lawrence didn't have permission to use it. The fellow had loaned him the bike on previous occasions so he thought he could take it once again. Stanley Lawrence was taken to the Bridgetown lockup where he put on a performance and injured his head by banging it against the wall and yelling he would kill himself if they didn't let him go! He was then charged with attempting to commit suicide! A crime then. The incident made the local paper and there was shame on the family. His two brothers spoke for him in court and said Stanley Lawrence had a horrific incident when he was fourteen years old that made him behave badly on the night. This may or may not have been true but they had to help their little brother. If it was true, no one in the family has mentioned it. The Magistrate didn't think Stanley Lawrence was a bad person, just a young drunken bloke, so he was fined a few pounds and put on a short good behaviour bond. He could be described as the quintessential Australian larrikin.

While working at the local hotel, he became a bit too friendly with the publican's daughter. She was quite young and her mother, a widow, disapproved and said she didn't want her daughter to marry an 'uneducated, insignificant waster', as Stanley Lawrence put it, so it was time for him to leave Bridgetown – in a hurry. Rumour has it that he had a daughter with this girl but there are no birth records to confirm this. Some research was done and the girl Stanley Lawrence was keen on was located. A family historian rang her – she said she didn't know a Stan Carroll and she had no children, so the search was stopped. If this was the girl, she had no children even though she married sometime later, which indicates she may not have been able to have children or perhaps she had a botched abortion. All speculation, but it is suspected the child was just rumour.

After hurriedly leaving town, Stanley Lawrence went back to the family home in Claremont and had to 'face the music'. His mother had heard of his behaviour in Bridgetown and he was given a good telling off about his irresponsible behaviour. Even at his age (now about twenty-two years) she was still the tough matriarch who kept her children in line.

Because he had left Bridgetown in a hurry, he now had no work. An advertisement came up in the newspaper for a job at a hotel in Southern Cross so he went to apply. The queue of men wanting the job went the length of Howard Street in Perth. When it came to Stanley Lawrence's turn, he told them of his hotel experience of barman/steward, yardman, killing chooks and dressing them for the dining room, and polishing guests' shoes. To his surprise, he got the job and, not long after, caught the train to Southern Cross. (He was now in the eastern goldfields district where his father, George Thomas, first came to Western Australia). The train arrived at night and no one was at the station to meet him so he slept on a bench on the platform. Next day, he met the proprietor, a woman, who told him she had sacked the yardman and so the job now was for a yardman. Stanley Lawrence was disappointed and a bit angry because he had been led to believe the job was for better work than that. Apart from yard duties, he had to drive a truck to go out and get firewood. He only had a car licence so went to the police station and got a truck driving license; it was as easy as that.

He met a fellow named Ted Argyle and they became friends. He and Ted Argyle would go out with the truck to get the firewood from the surrounding district for use in the hotel. One day, they were out getting the wood and were using a large cross cut saw. The saw slipped and the sharp barbs fell onto the top of Stanley Lawrence's foot cutting deeply into the flesh – he was only wearing sandals. They had to continue the work with his foot bleeding profusely – he just wrapped it up with a rag and kept on at the sawing. There was no stopping, he had to just get on with it! When he got back to the hotel, the publican noticed the bloodied foot. Stanley Lawrence explained what had happened and the woman told him he was an idiot for not wearing boots and to go and get some! The only problem was he didn't have the money for boots which were quite expensive so he didn't get any.

Stanley Lawrence Carroll (right) and Ted Argyle with the truck in Southern Cross. (Family photo)

They did other deliveries as required and he told of delivering bags of wheat where he would stand on the ground and the heavy bags would be slung onto his shoulders from the truck, the weight nearly breaking his back. He thinks this is where he got his bad back from – he suffered with a bad back most of his life. Another incident was when he was cranking the truck. The crank handle kicked back and took the skin off the back of his hand and then caught in his trousers and ripped them. He sewed up the trousers as best he could – there wasn't enough money for a new pair! He went to the local chemist and the girl there cleaned his hand. Her name was Nellie Wilkinson and they formed a close platonic friendship. He was able to get a tetanus vaccine, which was fortunate because not long afterwards he and a few men were in the process of moving a (movable) house from Southern Cross to Mt Palmer where there was a new gold find. They were carrying the panels when he stood on a plank that had nails facing upward. A nail went through his foot but they were unable to stop so he walked along dragging the plank that was attached to his foot! He had to put up with it afterwards and he said he couldn't go to the doctor because there was no money to pay him; he just had to deal with the pain which lasted for quite a while. It was usual then to use kerosene as a disinfectant so he probably just poured kerosene over the wound!

Stanley Lawrence had access to a Harley Davidson motorbike and went for a ride out to the nearby lake. He sped around in the mud showing off his skills and was travelling quite fast when he slid off in the mud and hit the ground, hurting his shoulder. He said he thought it was broken but once again there was no money for the doctor so he put up with it. He said it took a long time to get better.

At that time, there were a lot of dances, both in the city and the country, a very social time. He attended dances when he could and one night got a lift with some mates to a dance at Marvel Loch, several miles away, and had a great time. At the end of the evening, he told his mates he was going to walk a girl home and he wouldn't be long. When he arrived back, his mates had gone and there was only one car left there and that was heading out to the main road. The car was slowly taking off and Stanley Lawrence called out to them but they didn't hear and didn't stop. He jumped onto the back bumper as they sped off. He banged on the top of the car to get their attention to no avail. He was getting covered in that dreaded red dust, choking and hanging on for dear life as he kept banging on the roof. At the main road, they stopped the car for a pee and a smoke and discovered Stanley Lawrence all covered in dust at the back of their car. They were astonished at his story, and dusted him down and took him home!

While working at the hotel, he met an elderly man named Albert (Bert) Faulkner, who was of small stature and who claimed he was C. Y. O'Connor's Secretary and was now a prospector living just out of town.

C. Y. O'Connor was responsible for the design and construction of Fremantle Harbour, Mundaring Weir, and the Goldfields Pipeline to Kalgoorlie. These huge projects were thought to be impossible and he was crucified and ridiculed by the media and politicians. (What's changed?) In 1902, the pressure was so great that he committed suicide by riding his horse into the ocean at Robb's Jetty south of Fremantle and shot himself. Sadly, he saw none of his projects come to fruition. All of these projects have proven to be some of the greatest engineering projects in Australia. STOKES, John. *The Western State*. (Paterson Brokensha. 2nd ed, 1962) p. 143-149

If Mr Faulkner was connected with C. Y. O'Connor he must have found that time in his life extraordinarily difficult and he was probably quite affected by the bad press and C. Y. O'Connor's high stress and death to have left life behind to go and live alone in the remote goldfields. However, he would have been near and seen the successful operation the famous Goldfield's Pipeline.

He advised Stanley Lawrence to get a Prospector's Licence and stop sweeping out 'piss-houses' in the hotel. At that time, during the Depression, a Prospector's

License could be obtained easily and it allowed itinerant workers to be given a kit of tools with which to prospect and receive a small monetary allowance from the government, a bit like the dole but far less. Stanley Lawrence got his Prospector's License and kit and built a shanty out near Bert Faulkner's shack. Bert was a bit scruffy so Stanley Lawrence took him to the locomotive service area at the train station where there was water and a hose. Bert protested all the way but admitted that he felt good after a clean-up and Stanley Lawrence trimmed his hair and beard. (Perhaps this was the beginning of Stanley Lawrence's haircutting skills).

Stanley Lawrence described the time a giant of a man, a railway ganger, came to the hotel one night when Bert was there. When the Ganger came in, he saw Bert and said, "How are you going, Faulky?"

Well, tiny Bert saw red and started sparring around the huge ganger, yelling "Don't you call me, Faulky! It's Bert or Mr Faulkner to you!"

Bert Faulkner regularly wrote to Stanley Lawrence during the Second World War and, on Stanley Lawrence's return from Service, he went to Southern Cross to see him, only to find that he had died just a few months before. Stanley Lawrence spoke of this man with great respect and admiration, perhaps because his own father was absent so much from the family, Mr Faulkner may have been a father figure to him. (No records can be found about Mr Faulkner).

During Stanley Lawrence's time prospecting in the goldfields, he honed his bush skills. He often spoke of how he made his bed from upside down forked saplings with two side rails placed between them over which hessian bags were stretched, a bit like a camp stretcher; how he trapped rabbits, gutted and skinned them, and sold them to the local butcher. He would stretch the skins over a 'V' shaped piece of wire and tan the hides to sell. Life was still very difficult and any skills he had that would help earn a bit of extra money was used. He was a tough and resourceful young man who learned to read the layout of the land, how to navigate through the bush without aids, using just the sun and the stars. His sense of direction was *extraordinarily* good. He learned how to identify auriferous country and where best to locate alluvial gold. (Although he never spoke of finding a lot of gold). These skills came in handy later in his life when metal detectors were made for use by the modern prospector. Stanley Lawrence continued to work and prospect around the goldfields until the outbreak of World War II in September 1939 …

The McGlinns

McGlinn Family Line

McGLINN FAMILY LINE

Michael McGlinn — Married 1830 — **Mary Cunningham**
b. 1810 Ireland
d. ? Ireland
b. 1813 Ireland
d. 1879 Ireland 66yrs

David Walker — **Sarah Maybury**
b. Ireland
d. ?
b. Kilrea Ireland
d. ?

Thomas McGlinn (Convict) —(Married ?) 1857-58 Guildford WA— **Catherine Walker**
b. 1831 County Cavan, Ireland
d. 1919 Perth WA 88yrs
Arrived Perth 31/8/1853 per ship Phoebe Dunbar

b. 1836 Kilrea, Londonderry, Ireland
d. 1910 York WA 74yrs
Arrived Perth ?

Children:

David Patrick
b. 14/6/1859 Guildford WA
d. 3/5/1905 York 46yrs

Sarah Jane
b. 16/9/1860 Guildford WA
d. 20/9/1946 Perth 86yrs

Thomas John
b. 15/10/1862 York WA
d. 24/12/1891 York 29yrs

Roseannor
b. 23/2/1864 York WA
d. 28/11/1954 Guildford 90yrs

James
b. 26/8/1865 York WA
d. 14/1/1931 Pinjarra 65yrs

Catherine Alicia
b. 10/3/1869 York WA
d. 22/5/1956 Fremantle 87yrs

Mary
b. 25/6/1871 York WA
d. 7/10/1938 Perth 67yrs

Elizabeth Flora
26/2/1873 York WA
d. 4/3/1933 Mt Helena 60yrs

Selena Mabel
b. 14/4/1878 York WA
d. 13/4/1966 ? 88yrs

Sarah Ashworth — Married 2 March 1880 — (to James McGlinn)
b. 16/10/1860 York WA
d. 29/5/1931 York 64yrs

**see Ashworth family line

Children of James McGlinn & Sarah Ashworth:

Ada Jane Ashworth
b. 4/5/1879 York
d. 8/10/1947 York 68yrs

David
b. 3/1/1881 York
d. 30/10/1969 Darlington 88yrs

Thomas
b. 12/2/1882 York
d. 17/11/1932 Perth 50 yrs

Sophia
b. 9/4/1883 York
d. 21/1/1898 York 14 yrs

James Edmund
b.7/7/1884 York
d. 19/5/1946 Williams 62yrs

Ernest William
b. 25/10/1885 York
d. 13/8/1915 Egypt 29 yrs

Frank Robert
b. 5/5/1887 York
d. 8/1/1888 York 7 months

Ruth Charlotte
b. 27/10/1888 York
d. 26/5/1891 York 2yrs 7mths

Florence Hilda
b. 11/4/1891 York
d. 21/7/1979 Perth 88yrs

Alice May
b. 18/9/1892 York
d. 7/7/1924 Perth 31yrs

Maud Bertha
b. 22/4/1894 York
d. 9/5/1988 Beverley 94yrs

Sarah Ruby
b. 13/11/1895 York
d. 21/1/1986 Perth 90yrs

John
b. 11/1/1898 York
d. 5/11/1992 Perth 94yrs

Selina Mabel
b. 19/8/1900 York
d. 13/12/1984 Perth 84yrs

Gertrude Eva
b.7/6/1902 York
d. 1/7/1983 Perth 81yrs

Doreen McGlinn's father
John McGlinn

John McGlinn was born on the 11th January 1898 in York, Western Australia and died in Mt Lawley on 5th November, 1992, aged 94. He was the thirteenth of fifteen children. (His mother also fostered two children).

York was the first inland settlement in Western Australia after colonisation, and was founded in 1831. It is situated on the picturesque Avon River, approximately ninety-seven kilometres east of Perth and is now a historical precinct. Many of the early colonists moved there to work and farm.

The house John grew up in is at 2 Ford Street, York, approximately 100m from the Avon River and situated on the north side of the street. The house now has a red tin roof and is the second one from the corner of Avon Terrace.

John McGlinn's childhood home at 2 Ford Street, York. John's mother, Sarah, is standing, the children are her younger children. His eldest sister, Ada Jane, is sitting. John is on her lap. (Family photo)

*Now heritage listed - John McGlinn's childhood home 2019.
The extension on the right was added much later. (Personal photo)*

Prior to moving into this house, the family lived close by to the north in a converted stable which became far too small for the growing family so they moved into the Ford Street home. John's mother lived there until her death in 1931.

John told of fun times during his childhood, especially swimming in the Avon River down from the house, until a young boy jumped off Monger's Bridge, which was at the end of their street, and drowned. The bridge was destroyed sometime later in a flood and never re-built. John spoke of this tragedy with genuine sadness; perhaps the boy was a close friend.

The few McGlinn boys still living at home and the girls all slept in the one room. The girls had one section of the room and the boys another section. John said they would just fit wherever they could in a bed; no one had a bed to themselves and everybody shared. On occasions, after a night out, the older boys would come home with their friends and put him onto the floor to sleep while they took his place in the bed! John was the youngest boy. The next boy older than him, Ernest William, was thirteen years his senior. All the children around John's age were girls so he was particularly close to them.

John stayed in close contact with his sisters throughout his life; he didn't see much of his brothers, who mostly lived in the country where visits were difficult, but he spoke of them with fondness and saw them on the few occasions they visited Perth. The brothers he saw most during his life were his eldest brother

David who lived at Darlington and could be visited by train. The other brother was Thomas who lived in Perth.

John often joked about his mother serving up the food in a trough around the table because there were so many of them. (Untrue of course). He did say, however, that you had to eat what was put in front of you or you'd get nothing and, at times, there was little food to go round.

Sarah would make a big batch of alcoholic sugar beer that was made with hops and give it to the teamsters who passed by her house; they in turn would give her huge delicious watermelons for the family.

John and his sister Maud were the adventurous and enterprising ones in the family and got up to all sorts of activities and adventures and mischief. John was a bit of a practical joker and poor Maud was at the end of one particularly unsavoury joke. He told her he had caught a bird under his hat and that she was to grab the bird when he lifted his hat. He got her all excited at the possibility of catching a bird and coaxed her to be ready, her hand out and his hand on the hat. "Go!" he called. She, as quick as lightning, grabbed at the 'bird' only to find herself with a handful of his poo!!! Of course, John was hysterical at the great joke but she *never* let him live it down!!! He'd laugh at this well into his 90s and she scolded him until well into her 80s … but with a smile.

He and Maud would put a rope on the billy goat the family owned and take it around town. They would ask the people if their nanny goat would like a billy. They charged six pence a go and this was a good money earner until the poor billy goat gave up and wouldn't, or couldn't, perform any more!

He also told of the time his sisters chipped in a penny each to go and buy a bottle of aerated water (cool-drink). They all had a drink but left some of the contents in the bottle then got John to pee in it. Florence Hilda instructed young John to take it back to the shop keeper to complain it was 'off'. The shop keeper had a taste and agreed and gave him another bottle!! He said they roared with laughter as they drank the new cool drink.

When John was quite a young boy, he had an accident and got a bad cut that had to be stitched. Much to his embarrassment this was done in the window of the chemist shop in the main street where passers-by could clearly see him and he said he had to act tough and endure it without crying and without anaesthetic!

When Maud got a bit older, she had the job of 'wagon wheel expander' with the Blacksmith and Wheelwright at the bottom of their street near the river (not sure of the correct title for this job). When the wagons came to town, they were taken to a holding pen near the river. Maud and John would take the horses and the wagons into the river and walk the horses back and forth through the water to soak the wooden spoked wheels to expand them. This would keep the metal rings around the perimeter of the wheels in place. If the wood dried out, it would shrink and the rings would come off and cause a lot of problems with the integrity of the wheels. Horses were the main means of transport in those days so it was imperative to be able to handle them. They would take bullock teams with their large wagons as well. They were certainly a very industrious pair!

Still very close, John McGlinn and his sister Maud in their later years (Family photos)

Maud was tiny but she was a tough nut and very independent. As a teenager, she bred chickens for eggs to sell around the town. One person complained about the eggs being small. Maud replied that she wasn't going to 'stretch the chickens' arses for the measly sum of threepence'. So there!! (Personal comment, Maud)

The family weren't really religious but Sarah sent the children to the Wesleyan Church just up the road to attend Sunday School then, on the same day, to the Salvation Army Sunday School. The children were all baptised Wesleyan (Methodist) and later John joined the Salvation Army but he wasn't a religious man. He said religion did nothing for him and he was never a believer.

The McGlinn children went to school in York. All written schoolwork was done by using either a black slate, a bit like a small hand-held blackboard, and a type of soapstone 'chalk', or on paper using a pen with a nib and ink from an inkwell. One of the teachers was a Mrs Harkness who kept snakes for pets. The children could go and have a look at them any time, so one day Maud and John went to have a look and one of them was near the wire of its enclosure so Maud poked it with a pin. The snake twitched suddenly and Maud and John were terrified and ran for their lives; they said they didn't stop running!

Teachers were hard on pupils and if they didn't learn their subjects or weren't behaving properly the cane was dealt out liberally and often, even for the most minor misdemeanour. Students at that time were mainly taught English (mostly grammar, literature, and spelling), reading, writing, arithmetic and English history and they became very good at these subjects. They could do the maths for everyday life, write a well composed letter with correct spelling and grammar and knew about King and country and Mother England – most Australians thought of themselves as English in those days. John left school at the age of fourteen when it was legal for him to do so. The school was about a mile from their house and he would run there and back and wore no shoes. His clothes were whatever he could find on the day and sometimes it would be his older brother Thomas's football shorts and another brother's Salvation Army top with 'Blood and Fire' emblazoned on the front.

Even though he was adventurous and industrious, he was a quiet and rather shy young man and, it seems, this personality trait continued throughout his life.

After leaving school, he worked for a short time for the local newsagent, delivering newspapers around the town. He rode the Newsagent's horse and put the rolled-up newspapers, The *West Australian* and the *Eastern Chronical*, in bags that hung either side of the horse and he would throw the papers into people's yards. Following this employment, he worked in a barber's shop as a general hand. He'd clean the men's faces after their shave and clean the scissors, combs and other equipment ready for use by the barber. He swept the floor and kept the place tidy. He said he quite enjoyed that work.

As a teenager, John was a keen Australian Rules footballer and played with the Imperials and the Fire Brigade teams in York. He was a good player and was often stated as one of the best players in the local paper, *The Eastern Chronicle*. His older brother, Thomas, also played football in the same teams at the same time. His other older brothers played for the Northam Football Club. In 1916, when John was boarding in Claremont, he played for the Cottesloe Claremont Football Club which, in 1925, became Claremont Football Club.

John seemed to be quite close to his older brother, Thomas, who was sixteen years older and was a farrier before the outbreak of World War I.

*A Farrier shoeing a horse. Thomas McGlinn did a similar job.
(Underwood archives 2020).*

John helped him with the horses whenever he could. This was a valuable skill in those days, as with cars today, horses needed work done on them periodically. The family never owned a horse but the older McGlinn brothers would find strays in the bush and bring them home. John and Maud would break them in and they were sold, mainly to the Chinese for their market gardens.

Their mother, Sarah, would go to Northam on Sundays to watch the older brothers play football. While she was gone John and Maud would have a rodeo in their yard. They would use the horses their brothers brought home and the cattle that grazed near their home. This was an exciting thing to do until their mother found out and soon put a stop to it.

John's older brothers, Ernest William and Thomas, go to war

John was sixteen years old when World War I broke out, and two of his brothers were keen to join. They were of enlistment age but John's other brothers were considered too old to go to war. Both Thomas, the farrier, and Ernest William, another of John's brothers, who was a tree feller and labourer, enlisted in the army on the same day, the 20th March, 1915. After the enlistment process, Ernest William was assigned to the 11th Battalion, Sixth Reinforcements and was sent for a hurried basic military training at Blackboy Hill, Western Australia, and was soon shipped off to war on the ship *HMAT Geelong* on the 6th June, 1915.

World War I began for some Australian troops in the Dardanelles (Gallipoli) on 25th April 1915. This date has become known as ANZAC Day (Australian and New Zealand Army Corps), a day to commemorate those who served, were injured, or were killed in the defence of the mother country, England.

On 4 August 1915 Ernest William went ashore at Gallipoli as a reinforcement with the 1st Division, 11th Battalion. These reinforcements were to replace the hundreds of men already killed and injured there. He was sent to an area not far from Lone Pine, to what became known as Leane's Trench, which had been captured from the Turks by the 11th Battalion during a particularly savage battle a few days earlier with heavy casualties on both sides. The trench needed to be held and the Turks still battled to win it back. Leane's Trench was named after Captain Leane, a very courageous leader who was highly respected by his men. Only two days after Ernest William's arrival at Gallipoli, on the 6th August, he was severely wounded. His medical records stated that he had a bomb wound to the face and that he had a bullet wound penetrating his head. Mr Wesley Olsen, a war historian, stated that it was unlikely that a bullet penetrated his head and the bomb wound to his face would have been caused by shrapnel. The Turks' trench was only 20 to 30 metres away and stick bombs were thrown into the Australians' trench. The wound that penetrated Ernest William's head would have been caused by a lead ball about the size of a small marble that was part of the shrapnel. His face, no doubt, would have been horribly injured. It is not known how long he had to wait for assistance or the stretcher bearers, or whether he was conscious or not.

Horrifyingly, in some situations, particularly in *No Man's Land*, it was sometimes days until help came. Often the fighting continued non-stop and no-one was able to go to render assistance. Many men died out there after calling out for help or crying for their mothers until they fell silent. The men in the trenches couldn't leave to help these poor men because they too would be shot.

All of the trenches would have been dug by hand with just a pick and shovel! Miles of them! The photo below was taken at Lone Pine, not far from Leane's Trench and would have been similar. Dead Turkish men line the top of the trench. Often soldiers from both sides were left to rot and liquefy causing the area to be putrid and full of maggots and flies. Many soldiers, such as those in the photo below who saw and experienced the horrors of war, were known to have what is called 'the thousand-yard stare'. They would have a haunted look and stare off into the distance lost in the horror of their memories …

A trench at Lone Pine, Gallipoli. This is a typical trench that the Australian soldiers would have had to dig and defend. (Australian War Memorial number AD2025)

'Going over the top' of a trench, like the one in the photo above, was almost suicidal but orders were given to do just that. They had to get out of the relative safety of the trenches, go up over the top, and into the face of gunfire and run towards the enemy over open ground. If a soldier disobeyed, he could be court-marshalled for cowardice and in some cases executed! There was no option but to go. No Australians were executed.

Ernest William McGlinn– Service number 2263 – 11th Battalion – Died of wounds from Gallipoli 13th August, 1915, aged 29. (Family photo, enhanced)

Ernest William was evacuated from Gallipoli and died from his wounds at the military hospital in Alexandria, Egypt on the 13th August, 1915 and was buried at the Chatby Military and War Memorial Cemetery, Alexandria, Egypt. He was twenty-nine years old.

William Patrick Kett

Only a month after Ernest William died, a young man who had been living with the McGlinn family in York before the war also died. He was William Patrick Kett. At home, he and Ernest William were the best of friends and Sarah McGlinn probably thought of him as a son; he may have been one of the foster children she cared for. John McGlinn considered him a brother and said so in a television interview on ANZAC Day in 1998. Such was their closeness, John said he had two brothers die at Gallipoli.

William Patrick Kett was born in York in 1891 and enlisted in August 1914. After initial training at Blackboy Hill Military Camp, his unit, the 11th Battalion, embarked on *HMAT Ascanius* from Fremantle on 31st October, and joined the ANZAC convoy from Albany on 2 November, 1914. After training in Egypt, they were sent to Gallipoli and on 25 April 1915 (ANZAC Day), he was in one of the first units ashore and would have been one of the first Australians to see war and the huge number of men killed, wounded, and drowned that day. By June 1915, William Patrick Kett was acting as stretcher bearer, an enormous job of strength and endurance having to take the high number of wounded men back to the medical areas behind the lines. Disease and illness were rife in the trenches and he too succumbed to illness. He was one of the many soldiers who became ill with influenza and was so ill he was evacuated from Gallipoli on 6 September, 1915 and within days of being admitted to hospital in Alexandria, Egypt with pneumonia William Patrick Kett died on 14th September, 1915, only a month after Ernest! He was twenty-four years old and is buried in the same cemetery as Ernest William McGlinn. (www.bgpa.wa.gov.au/honour-avenues-plaques/2816-pte-william-kett)

He too would have been at Leane's Trench and perhaps they met up there for a very brief reunion. It would be nice to think so.

William Patrick Kett - Service number 797 - 11Th Battalion. Died as a result of illness – Gallipoli (www.vwma.org.au) (enhanced photo)

Ernest William McGlinn's and William Patrick Kett's memorial plaques recently installed side by side in a circular road off May Drive, Kings Park. 2022 (Personal photo)

Ernest William's plaque, above, was dedicated by the family of Private W. P. Kett and for this, we sincerely thank them.

Just over 8,700 Australians were to die at Gallipoli or died of wounds. A total of 61,522 Australians were killed and 17,260 were wounded during WWI – a big hit to the young male population of Australia at that time. Owing to the loss of these young men, there were many women in Australia at that time who became 'old maids', never to marry. This was simply because there were so few young men. You only need to look at the war memorials throughout the country to see all those who gave their lives.

Christopher James McGlinn

Among other members of the McGlinn family who went to war was John's 2nd cousin, Christopher James McGlinn, also a farrier, who was the illegitimate son of Elizabeth Flora McGlinn, a sister of John's father. Perhaps Christopher James was one of the foster children who lived with John's mother, Sarah. Christopher James enlisted in the 51st AIF Battalion, 4th Reinforcements in 1916. He was killed on the Western Front at Passchendaele, Belgium on 13th October, 1917, aged twenty-four, and has no known grave but is commemorated at the Ypres (Minin Gate) Memorial, Belgium, Panel 29. Tragedy had struck this close family once again.

This was so very common for the families of Australia during this terrible war. There were few families who were not affected by the tragedy of it all. Christopher James' mother, Elizabeth Flora McGlinn, married soon after Christopher James left for war. She was never notified of his death and only learnt of it when she wrote to the army saying she had not heard from her son for a long time. They finally stated he had died so she wrote many letters asking for his belongings, which she described to them, but was told there were none. Such poor communication to her, this woman would have suffered such grief and anger about his and her treatment. However, many men in the trenches were blown to pieces by artillery shells and the area all around them destroyed. Christopher James' personal belongings may have been blown to bits with him if he was killed in his dugout.

In her grief, Sarah had to contend with requesting Ernest William's belongings to be sent home to her. She also requested his Will. The form came back from the Commonwealth Government stating "… *You are registered on the records as next of kin, but, it is desired to learn whether the above-named soldier had any nearer blood relations than yourself, for instance his father*" (Australian Imperial Force, Base Office Melbourne 21st June, 1920) She sent the form back with the words "Father dead" on it. (Obviously the mother is not as close a blood relative as the father!) Sadly, Christopher James' mother, Elizabeth Flora, also had to contend with this.

Christopher James McGlinn – Service number 2208 - Killed at Passchendaele, Ypres, Belgium on 13th October, 1917. Aged 24
(Photo - Australian War Memorial)

After the war, memorial pieces were placed in the newspaper for Ernest William, Christopher James and William Patrick Kett.

> "Death of Ernest McGlinn
>
> McGLINN. -- In fond and loving memory of my dear son and brother, Private E. W. McGlinn, who died on August 13, 1915, of wounds received at the Dardanelles: also his sincere mate, Private W. P. Kett, who succumbed on September 14, 1915.
>
> Now the boys are home returning,

And the trials of war are o er;

How our hearts are sadly yearning

For the dear ones who ll come no more.

Inserted by his loving mother and step-father, sisters Selina and Gertie, and brother Jack returned (John McGlinn)

McGLINN. -- In loving memory of my brother Ernest William, who died of wounds received at Lone Pine on August 13, 1915.

My brother is sleeping his last long sleep, His grave I may never see.

But some gentle hand in that far distant land may plant a small flower for me.

Inserted by his sister Maud and brother-in-law Dan (returned), and his two little nephews". (*West Australian*, 14 August 1919)

Below, a memorial notice for Christopher James McGlinn.

"McGLINN. -- In ever loving memory of my darling son, Christopher James McGlinn, who was killed in action at Passchendaele Ridge, on October 13, 1917.

Oh for a touch of that vanished hand, And the sound of the dear voice that is still.

Inserted by his sorrowing mother and stepfather, Stanley and Elizabeth Bull, and brother Gordon"

(*The West Australian*, Sat 16 Oct 1926 page 1)

There were so many very sad death notices at the time of their deaths – too many to put here.

Thomas McGlinn's war

John's brother Thomas, who practiced the trade of Farrier, was of particular use to the armed forces because of its high dependence on horses. He was thirty-three years old when he was assigned to the Number Two Veterinary Hospital in La Havre, France. His service number was 954. He was then moved to the 4th Australian Mobile Veterinary Service. He didn't escape the effects of war. Due to the extreme cold from a particularly cold winter where everything froze, and the extremely harsh conditions, he became very ill with lung problems and after being evacuated to hospital had to be returned to Australia as unfit for war. From then on, he had continuing health issues until his premature death in 1932, aged only fifty.

After his death, in 1943, his wife was murdered in a small park on the corner of Bulwer and Brisbane Streets, Highgate. Their son was a WWII Japanese Prisoner of War at the time and only found out about his mother's fate on his return to Australia. Such tragedy.

John gets a job with the WAGR

In the same year that John's brothers enlisted, 1915, and at the age of seventeen, John managed to get a job as a Junior Porter with the Western Australian Government Railways (WAGR) and worked at Greenhills, a town twenty-three kilometres east of York. Because many men had gone to war, work was not as difficult to find and working for the railways was a good and secure job but meant work could be required anywhere there was a rail service. In November 1916, he was transferred to Claremont Station and remained there for a few months before returning to Greenhills. His pay rate at that time was between 4/6d (four shillings and six pence) to 6/6d per day. While stationed at Claremont he met his future wife, Gladys Catherine Gawned. After his time in Greenhills, he was then transferred back to York and, in June 1917, was granted leave to join the army and go to war. (WAGR Staff Records, Battye Library, State Reference Library of WA. 2021)

John McGlinn goes to war

John was only nineteen years old when he managed to convince his mother to allow him to enlist in the army, the legal enlistment age was twenty-one. She must have been very hesitant after already having two sons (and several nephews) go and losing one son and one nephew, plus her perhaps "foster" child William Patrick Kett. She signed the form and John went to the enlistment office in York.

John McGlinn - 2nd Australian Light Horse Machine Gun Squadron No 108A (19 years old) (Family photo, enhanced)

He passed his medical and the horse-riding test easily and because of his equestrian skills was placed in the Australian Light Horse. Most of the Australian Light Horsemen were from the countryside and had worked with horses. Most city men didn't have a lot to do with handling horses in such a skilled manner and, therefore, could not join.

In those days, young men would find it difficult to avoid going to war because the community expected it – it was their duty! Men who didn't go were often vilified by their community and some were sent a white feather to denote cowardice. It was time, so John enlisted in York on 5th May 1917. Prior to this, John was a member of the Senior Cadets (military) in Northam so was accepted into the army with no problems. On his enlistment form, he was described as being nineteen years and five months old, five feet seven inches tall and weighed 138 pounds. His chest measurement was 36 inches, his complexion fair and he had dark brown hair and brown eyes.

Owing to the attrition rate of men (dead, injured or ill) at the war, it became necessary to change the physical standards, making them less stringent. *"The requirements in August 1914 were 19–38 years, height of 5ft 6in and chest measurement of 34 inches. In June 1915 the age range and minimum height requirements were changed to 18–45 years and 5ft 2in, with the minimum height being lowered again to 5ft in April 1917. During the first year of the war approximately 33 percent of all volunteers were rejected. However, with relaxation of physical standards of age and height, as well as dental and ophthalmic fitness, previously ineligible men were now eligible for enlistment"*.

(https://www.awm.gov.au/articles/encyclopedia/enlistment)

As can be seen in the photo on page 133, John was a very handsome young man and cut a fine figure in his Light Horse Squadron uniform. Because of his horse handling abilities and his military training, he was assigned to the 1st Australian Light Horse Machine Gun Squadron (ALHMGS) Service Number 108. He was later transferred to the 2nd ALHMGS and because his number was 108 in the 1st ALHMGS his number could not be changed so was "adapted" to 108A. A soldier's number often could not be changed because there could be no room for confusion (in death). The 2nd ALHMGS was a unit from New South Wales and only twelve Western Australians were posted in this unit.

The structure of John's unit is explained below.

The "2nd Light Horse Brigade (Anzac Mounted Division) (was)

Formed in Australia, September 1914. Attached to New Zealand and Australian Division December 1914 to April 1915. Assigned to Anzac Mounted Division March 1916.

Subunits:

5th Light Horse Regiment September 1914 to past November 1918

6th Light Horse Regiment September 1914 to past November 1918

7th Light Horse Regiment September 1914 to past November 1918

2nd Machine Gun Squadron 3 January 1917 to past November 1918

2nd Signal Troop September 1914 to past November 1918

Commanders:

Brigadier General G. de L. Ryrie 17 September 1914 to past November 1918"

(www.lighthorse.org.au/mounted-troops)

The West Australian 10th Light Horse Regiment was in the 3rd Light Horse Brigade.

A note here about the emu feather that adorns the hats of the Light Horsemen, including John's. Only the Australian Light Horsemen wear the emu feather. It came about during the famous Shearers' Strike in the late 1800s in Clermont, Queensland. The shearers were on strike for fair pay and conditions. The land owners paid a pittance to the shearers and they banded together to force the price per sheep down. The shearers stopped work and went on strike, and mobilised themselves into a united front. This was the forerunner of the Trades and Workers Union.

To stop the shearers getting out of hand, the colonial government of Queensland sent to Clermont the Queensland Volunteer Defence Force, the Moreton Mounted Infantry. Their stay in Clermont was peaceful and they got on well with the shearers. They played cricket and had horsemanship competitions which included chasing, on horseback, one of the many emus in the area, galloping alongside and bending down to pluck a feather from the emu's chest and, as a trophy, placed it in their hat band. Following this, the Queensland government allowed the mounted infantry to wear the feathers in their hats as recognition of their service. The mounted infantry was the forerunner of the Australian Light Horse and the tradition of wearing the feather continued. HAMILTON, John. *Gallipoli sniper.* (Pan, 2008) p. 23-24

It was considered an honour to be chosen as a machine gunner and something to be very proud of. (Probably because the enemy would certainly target machine gunners in the first instance in war and it was considered very brave indeed to be one). John sailed out of Fremantle, Western Australia, on the ship *Kyarra* on the 19th September 1917, bound for Egypt. He disembarked at Suez on the 19th October 1917 and marched to Moascar where he was allocated a horse. The horse depot at Moascar was run by Major A.B. (Banjo) Patterson, the famous Australian poet. Patterson's responsibility was to *"take over the rough, uncivilised horses ... to quieten them and condition them and get them ready for being heel-roped; and finally to issue them in such a state of efficiency that a heavily accoutred trooper can get on and off under fire if need be. Breaking the horses in and perfecting their patience under stress would mean life or death for every trooper ..."* (PERRY, Rowland. *Bill the Bastard*. (Allen and Unwin, 2012) p. 84-85

Walers were horses from Australia that could go long distances in extreme heat and were perfect for use in warfare in the deserts of Egypt. These horses are now legends in Australian folklore.

John was allocated a horse and fought in the bloody battles in Gaza, Jerusalem, and the areas surrounding the Dead Sea and River Jordan and would have endured the baking heat and freezing nights of those desert areas. *"The Sinai Desert, with its sand storms and searing temperatures, had to be crossed, a test of endurance ...* (for) *the troops involved."* (www.bbc.co.uk/history/worldwars/wwone/middle_east)

John would have used a water-cooled Vickers Maxim machine gun as shown in the photo on page 137. When they reached their fighting positions, he would dismount and set up ready for battle. The tactic of most Light Horsemen was to gallop headlong into battle, jump off their horse and into the enemy trench and fight hand to hand with the bayonet and the rifle, and either kill or be killed. In some battles, John would have fought like this and, even though he was a machine gunner, he would still have to carry a .303 rifle. When he was required to do planned stationary battles that would involve headlong charges by the enemy, he and his assistant would have to be set up ready for battle. His equipment consisted of the machine gun, its very heavy-duty tripod, a water container with 3 litres of water to cool the gun, an extra gun barrel to change the over-heated one, cloth ammunition belts, and numerous boxes of ammunition that included tracer bullets for accuracy when firing. Training for all the setup would have been intense; accuracy in setup was vital and had to run like clockwork. His assistant would inspect every bullet that was put into the cloth ammunition belts, as a faulty bullet would cause a jam in the equipment and that could mean death. All this equipment was very heavy and had to be carried on a number of pack-horses which would be led in by several men, unloaded and taken quickly away out of danger. After the battle, they would be brought back and loaded up with the equipment to be taken away. In an ABC radio interview in 1990, when John was ninety years old, he talked about the enemy artillery and aircraft that concentrated their bombing on the machine gunners. He said it was very unnerving hearing the whistle of the bombs coming and not knowing where they were going to land. He said they had no cover and were out in the open. He said he was lucky, and that many others were killed or wounded. He said there were a number of troopers younger than him and the older more experienced ones would calm them down by talking to them.

2nd Light Horse Machine Gunner with assistant. This was John McGlinn's squadron. The Machine Gun is a Vickers Maxim. (Photo www.awm.gov.au/collection/C823)

The following is from an interview John did for a newspaper in 1998, about his experiences during the war.

> "We started as machine gunners to the 5th, 6th, and 7th Light Horse Battalions from Victoria, NSW and Queensland. We got all the dirt from the aeroplanes because they always picked out the machine gun positions. Then we were turned into cavalry to fight the Turks with swords, but the units didn't last long. The country didn't suit the sword but when we did come up against the Turks they were too good for us. They were trained horsemen and we were sent against them with only two or three weeks training. (using the sword) It was pretty rough.
>
> I could have lost my hand one time. Just the point of the sword did the damage. But I was fortunate -- plenty dropped beside me. I was just held down by my mates while the wound was stitched. There was nowhere else to get it done because the medical corps was far behind. There was no anaesthetic -- only cursing.

> *A victory for the mounted division was the capture of Turkish reinforcements travelling by train we captured the Turks after leaving the 10th Light Horse and the Desert Corps to do the mopping up. I was in the action for most of the two years I was away."* The Sunday Times (April 24, 1998)

His battles were very significant and he would have participated in terrifying hand to hand combat. Hand to hand sword fighting was uncommon by the time WWI began, John's swordfight was probably one of the last of that type of battle to occur and was how he got the sword wound in his wrist. Many of his fellow soldiers were killed in those battles. According to author Ion Idriesse, the battles were fierce and unforgiving and the enemy took no prisoners; they bayonetted the wounded and often stole their clothes and left them in the baking sun to rot. John is modest in his descriptions of the war and his participation should not be underestimated. He never spoke of his horrific experiences to the family. The authorities at the time told the soldiers not to mention the war to their families, just forget about it!

The Germans and Turks were allies and fought fiercely together. Some of the same Australian 11th Battalion and the same Turkish battalions that had fought against each other in the Gallipoli campaigns were again fighting against each other here too. War here was gruesome and difficult and John was lucky to have survived! The Turks had had centuries of experience in this type of desert fighting with the use of the sword and were excellent horsemen. War in this region was tough and many thousands of men and horses were killed. John witnessed the famous Light Horse charge at Beersheba – he was stationed in the hills nearby when the charge took place.

Trooper and author, Ion Idriesse, who was in the 5th Light Horse Regiment, stated in his diary that during a charge towards the enemy with the horses thundering over the sand *"all men get scared at times like these; but there comes a sort of laughing courage from deep within the heart...or from some source he never knew existed; and when he feels like that he will gallop into the most blinding death with an utterly unexplainable, don't care, shrieking laugh upon his lips."* (IDRIESSE, Ion. *The Desert Column; Ion Idriesse's greatest stories*. (Bookworld, 1993) p. 576.

During John's service in the Middle East, he wasn't always in the 2nd ALHMGS – he was transferred to several other units, including, the 1st ALHMGS, the 7th Light Horse, and as a motor transport driver for the Australian Imperial Force (AIF). John then was transferred back to the 2nd ALHMGS but this time they were either with the Desert Mounted Corps or the ANZAC Mounted Corps.

*This is probably John McGlinn's squadron entering Jerusalem.
(Australian War Memorial, 2020)*

2nd Australian Light Horse Brigade in the desert at Esdud on the Philistine Plain 1918 – John McGlinn would be here. (Australian War Memorial B01556, 2020)

Australian Light Horse. (Australian War Memorial, AO3424, 2020)

2nd Light Horse Brigade camp at Romani

The caption under the photo above states "Rows of tethered horses line one side of the 2nd Light Horse Brigade camp at Romani. Problems of sanitation and the disposal of horse litter – in order to reduce the prevalence of disease-spreading flies – were difficult to overcome in desert camps." (JONES, Ian, *The Australian Light Horse*. (Time Life Books Australia, 1987) p. 74.

These tent camps would have been very trying to live in. Any wind would whip the sand up into a stinging sand blast. Sand would be in everything, and conditions would have been very harsh, hot, and unforgiving, and John would have been there. These camps were mainly temporary and behind the fighting lines. Mostly, men were out at the front or near the fighting front lines and had to just live in the sand. Ion Idriesse stated in his diary that their general life in the desert was awful. He said *"Flies are persistent and in countless billions. The ground is crawling with insects, especially spiders, beetles, scorpions and their progeny and relations. A scorpion bite is poisonous and painful; as we know, for we live either on our horses or on the ground. We have no tents, of course, neither officers nor men. Each man has a waterproof sheet to sleep on, with his great coat to cover him…Fighting is continuous … day and night."* Ion Idriesse. *The Desert Column; in Ion Idriesse's greatest stories.* (Bookworld, 1993) p. 549.

Water was in such short supply that having a wash was impossible; water was only available for drinking. Shaving was compulsory so only a half a cup was used. Hygiene was abysmal and the men were filthy and suffered badly with lice, and disease was rife.

It seems Idriesse had no time for the British officers, both at Gallipoli when he was there, and now in the deserts of the Middle East. He felt they only wanted glory for themselves at the expense of their men. He said thousands and thousands of them died unnecessarily in infantry attacks that failed. He had the utmost respect for the Australian Officers, particularly General Sir Harry Chauvel, and felt the Australians and New Zealanders were the best fighting horsemen who were under appreciated. Because of the mistrust and the incompetence of the British officers, after the war and for most of his life John maintained that you should never trust a Pom! He too obviously held the British officers in low regard.

The 2nd Australian Light Horse Squadron at drill. John McGlinn was here at that time. Photo taken November 1918 – (Photo Australian War Memorial. 800462)

Below is a letter John sent to his mother from Egypt. It should be understood that many letters written from the war front often had a VERY positive 'spin' so as not to worry those at home. One such letter from John displays this 'positive spin'.

"Dated Jericho, April 6, 1918,

Dearest mother

We have travelled a long way since I last wrote. I have been through Jerusalem, past the Dead Sea, over the Jordan River, and several small towns not worth mentioning. On our march out we stopped the first day at a place called Latron, on account of it raining so hard. Three days in it and talk about mud. The last night we were there we all got washed out of bed about midnight and had to sit up in the rain, but still we were laughing and joking all the time.

We started off quite ignorant of our destination at about 10 a.m. the following day, and at 4 o clock (still raining) we entered the Holy City of Jerusalem. The road we travelled was very good, but very zig-zag of course! Hills higher than Mt. Bakewell have roads right down the front of them. I only entered the New City. We marched for three days and nights without a sleep, but I had plenty, being able to sleep while travelling on my horse.

The worst time I ever had in my life was standing all day in the rain and mud, and talk about cold. It was funny, chaps holding their horses when all of a sudden they would go flop in the mud. They would be sound asleep, and all the sympathy they would get from the crowd was: Wake up, your country needs you. We had a drink of tea which we boiled in a Bedouin tent, and it warmed us up a bit.

We are now camped near Jericho and a good dinner is waiting for us: boiled mutton, spuds, and onions.... We had a narrow squeak the other day. We were riding across a bit of a flat and one of Jacko s shells burst right in the middle of us, and we can thank the Lord for the ground being so muddy, or we would have been no more. But all we got was mud.

We have had a swim in the Dead Sea, which is very salty and thick, and there is no possible chance of sinking. You can lay on your stomach and not move a limb -- just float about with the wind. We have got a motor-boat and a few yachts with attachable engines. The

Turks have had an engineer's shop down there. They started to make a boat, not very large, but they were going to put twin screws in it.

Well, dearest mother, do not worry, some day we shall be together again.

Your loving son Jack"

The 'Wet' John McGlinn described in his letter to his mother (Photo Australian War Memorial, 2020)

The rain John mentioned in his letter was not expected by the military hierarchy. The Arabs advised them that the wet was coming but this advice was not understood. It was November and the heat remained with hot gusty winds, and it seemed that rain was impossible, then out of nowhere they arrived in torrents and the temperature dropped suddenly. The Philistine Plains were a quagmire, the roads broke up and icy rivers flowed. Horses and camels died and many men became ill. PERRY, Rowland. *The Australian Light Horse* (Hachette Australia, 2009) p. 338. The rains were not common: the conditions were usually blistering hot and the need for water a constant, very real problem.

Food was another big problem. The troopers had to eat a lot of tinned bully beef and hard tack biscuits that were so hard the men made graters out of the tins so they could grate the biscuits to eat them! John said in the very hot conditions in the desert the bully beef turned to grease and the men put their hard tack biscuits into the grease to soften them. Bouts of scurvy were quite common because there were no fresh vegetables for the fighting men. John remembered the men coming across an orange orchard; the men were feeling ill from the effects of scurvy but they filled their horses' nose bags with oranges then scoffed them until they were gone. The scurvy was cured and their intestines were certainly cleaned out!

In December 1917, John was appointed to the Egyptian Expeditionary Force (EEF) but still with the 2nd ALHMGS. He participated in several battles, the first of which was the battle for Jerusalem. The EEF worked its way to Jaffa and on to Jerusalem and, being such a holy city, the men rode through the gates quietly in respect for the holy place. Many were religious and in awe of this ancient place. The enemy stationed in Jerusalem were now in disarray and had given up and fled and the city was in chaos.

In February 1918, John was transferred to the 7th Light Horse to participate in the battle for Jericho. He was with the 7th Light Horse for one month before returning to his unit in the EEF. They fought in the Jordan Valley then went on to capture Jericho. The EEF then crossed the River Jordan and into the hills of Moab and on to Es Salt and the first battle for Amman which was fought during March 1918 and included the Sinai and Palestine Campaigns. It was in Amman that the terrible losses took place as described in the poem below. The EEF was defeated and was forced to retreat back to the bridgeheads they had previously captured on the Jordan River. (https://www.bing.com/search?q=battle+of+es+salt+ww1)

John sent the following poem home to his mother. It was written by a soldier in his unit and would have had a very deep meaning to him because he was there. The poem explains it all; it is heartbreaking.

The Old Brigade

The Old Brigade is battered,
Its numbers now are few,
We left them in the mountains —
Our comrades brave and true.
We left them in the mountains
In a sound unbroken sleep.
Through the silent hours of midnight
Now a phantom watch they keep:
They who crossed the Jordan Valley
When the stars were bright o'erhead,
With trigger finger ready
Keen on where their duty led.

They who faced the fiercest battle,
Dying gamely in the fight,
Faltering not when death was certain,
Glancing neither left nor right.
Lips compressed and stern eyes flashing,
Swerving not from shot or shell,
Hand to hand in mateship falling,
Fighting where their comrades fell.
Never more will cross the Jordan,
Lithe and merry, strong and gay,
Never more will face a battle
Keen and eager for the fray.
How I watched the troops go by me,
When the column passes through,
But my heart goes back to Amman,
To the graves of friends I knew.
And I look for some old comrade
Riding past me in his place,
But he is sleeping back at Amman,
And a stranger fills his place.
In those hills above the Jordan
There's a spot that e'er will be
Evergreen within my memory
Ever fresh and dear to me.
'Tis the battle-field of Amman,
Wind-swept hill-tops drenched with rain,
Where the bravest men are sleeping
Till the dead shall rise again.
Till the last Reveille sounding
Wakes us all on Judgment Day,
And we'll meet them and we'll greet them,
And together march away.

Poet - E. P. McCarthy, (KIA)

(No war records could be found in the National Archives)

The battle of which the poem is about was the "*First Battle of Amman* (which) was fought from 27 to 31 March 1918 during the First Transjordan attack on Amman of the Sinai and Palestine Campaign of the First World War. The ... Anzac Mounted Division attacked the Ottoman garrison at Amman deep in enemy occupied territory..." (www.bing.com/search?q=battle+of+amman+ww1)

Sadly, the battle for Amman was lost and many Australian soldiers were killed. John would have participated in this terrible battle and it may have been during one of these battles that John's horse was shot out from under him!

In April 1918, he was transferred to be a driver in the AIF. Presumably, he drove to transport the guns, making the gunners able to move with the battle instead of being stationary. These convoys were a target for the enemy planes and it would have been a very stressful time.

In John's ABC Radio interview in 1990, he was asked what the worst part of the war was. He said, apart from burying his mates, there was a time in Gaza when the English civilians were fleeing across the desert. The enemy attacked them and slaughtered the men, women and children. His unit had to go back to Gaza to defend these people. He spoke with emotion about this all those years later. He was ninety years old at the time of the interview.

John McGlinn may have been a driver for the machine gunners
(photo Australian War Memorial P00373,004. 2021)

After heavy fighting, chronic conditions in the baking heat, exhausting conflicts, and constant marches, John was sent to a rest camp at Jerusalem. Many men at the rest camps suffered with chronic diseases such as a form of malarial disease, dysentery, and other ailments, including festering sores that wouldn't heal in the desert conditions. John had some form of 'debility' but it was not described on his war records. Any infections from wounds were very serious and dangerous to life. Many men died from disease and infections during the desert campaigns.

While at the rest camp, John and some of his mates visited a brothel and got back to camp fifty-five minutes late and were fined a substantial amount of money. Going to a brothel was a risky thing to do because sexually transmitted diseases were rife. In the earlier days of the war, many men who contracted a sexually transmitted disease were given a Dishonourable Discharge from the army and sent home in disgrace. From then on, men were forbidden from attending brothels so it is natural that the fines would be very high.

Soon afterwards, John and the others left the rest camp and he was promoted to Corporal in the Desert Corps. He didn't return to being a driver and it wasn't long before he returned, at his own request, to being a trooper and re-joined his mates in the 2nd ALHMGS but still with the EEF. In August 1918, the final battle for Amman was won, and approximately 10,300 prisoners were captured in just nine days. Then, in September 1918, he fought in the battle of Megiddo which was a decisive Allied victory in Palestine.

On the 1st October, 1918 the Western Australian 10th Light Horse were ordered to enter Damascus, to 'clean up' the remains of the Ottoman Empire and to end its long reign of power in the Middle East. This was to allow the 10th Light Horse to get some glory after the absolute debacle at the Nek in Gallipoli where they were ordered by the British Officer, Antill, to continue the charges 'over the top' into certain death in successive waves that were tantamount to murder! The 10th Light Horse performed the last of their operations in Damascus where the enemy surrendered to them. The war in the Middle East ended with the signing of the surrender by the Turks in Mudros, Palestine, on the 30th October, 1918.

Even though the war in the Middle East had ended, World War I was finally considered over when fighting ceased on the Western Front in France and Belgium on 11th November, 1918. The Treaty of Versailles wasn't signed until 28th June, 1919 when the war was formally over. Unfortunately, it was such an unfair treaty that even though the allies had won the war, they didn't win peace. It was so harsh that it would have broken Germany financially and, because of this, it was a contributing factor to the rise of Nazism and Adolph Hitler and WWII.

In mid-February 1919, John may have been wounded somehow or became very ill because he was evacuated to a field hospital, then to two further hospitals and finally sent back to Moascar, where it had all begun for him. He was shipped back to Australia on the ship *Madras* in July 1919 and arrived in Fremantle to cheering and emotional crowds on the 24th August and received his discharge from the army a few days later.

The Australian idea of mateship was extremely strong during this war and WWII and men would rather die themselves than to leave a mate. Peacetime cannot possibly meet the same ideals of this type of mateship that was formed under horrendous and extreme conditions.

This war left not only physical scars, but also psychological scars for life. Many men on their return home felt the severe trauma for years and years afterwards – some never got over it. In modern times, this is called PTSD (Post-Traumatic Stress Disorder). This stress had no name then and men were told to "just get over it" and 'nerves' were not considered a 'condition' and no medical help was given. They were not encouraged to speak of their experiences of war and were told to keep it to themselves. There was no support from the Australian nor British Governments. Men joined the Returned Services League (RSL), a place where they could gather and talk about the war with their mates and other men who had served and who understood what they had gone through.

If an Australian soldier took part in World War I during 1914 and 1915, he got an extra medal, in addition to the two given for service. John joined after 1915 so received the two war medals he was entitled to. John's war medals are shown in the photo below. The one on the left is the British War Medal; the one on the right is the Victory Medal. The one John did not receive was the 1914-15 Star. These medals were awarded by the British government because Australia did not have its own war medals. John's 'Dog Tags' shown over the page were worn around his neck during the length of his stay in the war, however, men often wore another version around their ankle. This was to ensure at least one set could hopefully be found in the event of losing body parts or being blown to bits by artillery.

Left: John McGlinn's World War One Service Medals. (Personal collection)

John McGlinn's leather 'Dog Tags'

The following is an encouraging postcard written to John by his mother. A very touching note, and oh how difficult it would be for a mother having her youngest son at war, especially after her son Ernest William, his friend William Patrick Kett and her nephew Christopher James had died or been killed and her other son, Thomas, sent home so ill. Fortunately, the war ended a few months after this postcard was written.

Many mothers went through what Sarah had to bear. Some mothers lost several sons, some all of them, and some were lucky enough to have all their sons return home. Women felt the brunt of war. Many wives with small children saw their men go to war and a great many did not see them return. They were left to fend for themselves and many did not re-marry – there just weren't enough men – and in some cases, society felt that these women should stay alone to honour their dead. Others saw their men come home maimed, blind, battle-scarred, ill, and mentally unhinged – such a dreadful time for those who had to endure war.

Not many families went unscathed: they suffered either physically or from the mental anguish. Every few days, notices of those killed, missing or wounded were placed on the walls of the local hall or shops. In some instances, this was how someone at home found out the fate of their loved one. It would have been with dread that they waited for the lists to be put up. Most times, however, a very impersonal telegram was sent to the next of kin. A soldier from the front lines on the Western Front stated *"we did our best to exterminate each other in all sorts of horrible ways, succeeding to the grand total (us and them) of 27,530,700 killed, wounded and missing, not counting the millions of civilians who suffered the same fate"* KYLE, Roy. *An ANZAC's story.* (Penguin Books, 2003) p. 283

*This sad and hopeful post card was sent to John McGlinn by his mother Sarah
(Front of Post Card)*

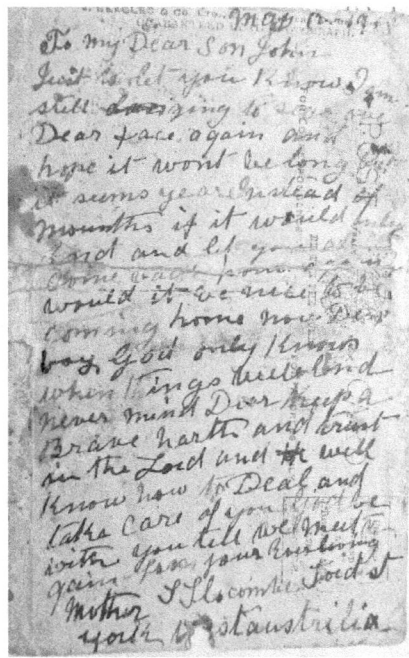

Back of the post card (Property of Kaye McCallum/Carroll)

The card is a bit difficult to read so it is interpreted here.

"May 1918

To My Dear son John

Just to let you know I am still longing to see your Dear face again and I hope it won't be long but it seems years instead of months, if it would only end and let you all come back home again. Would it be nice to be coming home now Dear boy. God only knows when things will end. Never mind Dear keep a brave (heart?) and trust in the Lord and He will know how to deal and take care of you. God be with you till we meet again. From you ever loving Mother S. Slocombe Ford Street York West Australia."

Silk Handkerchief with the British flags John sent to his mother from Egypt.
(Personal collection)

Letters from home were so very welcome and the troops really looked forward to getting them along with the parcels of goodies. The Postal Corps was the most popular section of the army!

What happened to John's war horse?

"At the end of the war the Australians in Egypt, Palestine and Syria had 9,751 horses of all types and their fate quickly became an important consideration in the AIF's demobilisation. Returning the horses to Australia was quickly ruled out ... fundamentally, returning them would cost more than the horses were worth ... In early 1919 the Australian government decided that its animals in the Middle East would be classified according to age and fitness ... The older and unfit horses would be destroyed. The surviving horses of the Australian and New Zealand Mounted Division were pooled at the imperial remount depot at Moascar in Egypt ... *"There was much sadness and a sense of injustice, which some men no doubt carried for many years."* (www.awm.gov.au/wartime/44/page54_bou)

The injustice these men felt was truly justified. Those horses that were considered too old or unfit were trotted out into the desert, lined up and machine gunned to death. (PERRY, Rowland. *Bill the Bastard.* (Allen and Unwin. 2013) p. 261 It is strongly hoped that this was not one of John's duties as a machine gunner!

John spoke with sadness at leaving his horse when the war ceased. A soldier relied heavily on his horse; they were constantly together and a great bond between them was formed. Over eight million horses perished during WWI; many of them died on the Western Front. Apart from being killed in battle, a lot of these horses had died as a result of the extreme conditions at the war front; they died of exhaustion from having to run every single day; they drowned in pooled water after rains, and they died of diseases. Many that were used to carry ammunition and supplies to the war front died from the horrors of shellfire, terrible weather, and harsh, unsustainable conditions. The destruction of the lives of horses during the First World War was so bad that Brigadier-General Frank Percy Crozier after the Battle of the Somme said, *"My heart bleeds for the horses and mules"*. According to him, it was like witnessing humans die. (www.farmanimalreport.com)

The purple poppy worn on ANZAC Day commemorates the animals that died in war.

When war ceased in November 1918, there was not enough ships to send the troops back home from their posts. Many had to wait months, some for over a year! John had to wait over seven months! He arrived in Fremantle in July 1919, right in the midst of the Spanish Flu outbreak that killed 20 to 50 million people world-wide. The first big modern pandemic that lasted three years.

> *"The West Australian newspaper reported* (on December 1st 1918) *that a troopship was approaching Fremantle carrying troops with about 100 cases of the dreaded influenza. Western Australians were already fully aware of the progress of the disease in Europe and there was great concern about the effect the arrival of a ship carrying so many cases would have on the local population. The troop ship "Boonah" arrived in Gage Roads on December 11th 1918 and dropped anchor. The ship was quarantined and anyone going aboard would have to return to the mainland via the quarantine station at Woodman Point"*

(http://www.wanowandthen.com/spanish-flu.html)

Sound familiar? It would have been so very much harder for the soldiers returning home from the horrors of war than for people returning from holiday etc … as with the 2020/2021/2022 pandemic, Novel Corona Virus - Covid 19. It seems John wasn't affected by the Flu and was able to head home without any delays. He was one of those fortunate enough to have survived 'The War to End All Wars'. (World War II started only twenty years later!) He got his final discharge from the army on 24th August 1919.

John returns to civilian life

When John returned from the war, he had to re-adjust to civilian life, a difficult thing to do after the horrors and pressures of war. Each year on ANZAC Day, the soldiers would gather to march in the parades and go to the pub afterwards to talk about their time in the war. John marched a few times but he never got to mix with the men in his squadron. They were a NSW group and the few men sent from WA with John had died. He had no one to talk to about their war and this must have been very sad and a difficult time for him.

He returned to work on the railways immediately after he arrived home. On 27th July 1920, he passed his examination for the position of 'Fireman' on the steam engines, a real skill to keep the boilers at just the right temperature for the trains to keep moving at the correct speed and not cause an explosion. He had one incident on 7th December 1920 when a 'fire bar' was burnt in a locomotive along the line between Toodyay and Clackline. A fire bar sits inside the firebox where the fire heats the water. If it has melted debris or too much ash, the bar might burn. Firing a steam train was a complicated and responsible job. No serious damage was done but he received a Caution, and was allowed to continue as a 'Fireman'. Another skill for a 'Fireman' was the amount of water on board to be monitored for the steam. There are multiple gauges and gadgets to ensure the right amount of water in the steam production line. There had to be re-watering points along the lines. (http://www.nychicagorr.org/How-to-Fire-a-Steam-Locomotive.html) In some places, water was a natural feature in the landscape, but many towns and stops had none available so dams or big tanks were erected at stations and water carted to fill them. He travelled the wheatbelt and was stationed at Northam, Toodyay and then finally at Brunswick Junction in the south. He was there from April 1921 until June 1922 when he was retrenched. His rate of pay had increased to thirteen shillings and eleven pence per day. He was offered further employment with the WAGR in November 1923 but declined the job.

A water tank erected for the steam trains. This one is at Merredin, WA. (Personal photo)

The WAGR and PMG were major employers in Western Australia. Railways were opening up the country allowing postal services to be much faster and the railway had the ability to move large numbers of people and goods around the now many country networks. The railways changed the Australian landscape. Restaurants, tearooms, accommodation, tourism, hotels and towns sprang up all along the lines. Populations in towns along the railways exploded. Railway stations and sidings were only about 10km apart so farming communities could transport their commodities more easily. This new technology caused the demise of general horse-drawn transport.

In Victorian England, the railways were the reason that "Standard Time" was introduced. Apparently, the villages throughout England had a loose time system based on the requirements of the village but, when train travel became available, a time had to be set along the line so people could know when the trains came and went. Greenwich Mean Time was adopted across England by the major railways in 1847. The same followed in Australia – and probably around the world where railways were in use. Very few people had time pieces (watches) so a flag was raised at the local Post Office to let people know the time.

At this time, postage stamps were introduced because the trains became the deliverers of mail and a set cost was introduced. Postage stamp cost was regulated depending on the distance and place to which mail was sent. Prior to this, it was the receiver who had to pay the postage. *How the Victorians Built Britain* (Television Series, 2018)

The PMG soon followed the trains, and telegraph lines were installed along the railways and reticulated out across the country to all sorts of places, making communication fast and easy.

Before John married in 1921, he had moved to Brunswick Junction with the railways but changed to work for the PMG after June 1922 where he dug trenches out through the south west of Western Australia. He was about to move from that job and work for the Road's Board. He and a mate went to work for the Roads Board near Augusta, however, before they could begin work, heavy rain fell. They couldn't work in the wet so they went for a walk in the bush. While walking through the bush, his mate fell into a hole in the ground. John was horrified and ran for help to rescue his mate, who fortunately was not seriously injured and didn't need medical help, but it scared the hell out of them! They decided that working for the Road's Board wasn't so great after all and they left in a hurry. There are several beautiful caves in the vicinity of Augusta. Which cave did they 'find'?

John's father
David Patrick McGlinn

John's father, David Patrick McGlinn, was born 14th June, 1859 in Guildford, Western Australia and died of a heart attack at the age of forty-six on 3rd June, 1905 in York, Western Australia. (His name in the Births Deaths and Marriages for WA is recorded in error as David Patrick McGlisson).

David Patrick was the eldest of nine children and was the son of a transported convict, Thomas McGlinn. Generally, free settlers looked down on the convicts and their families and this would have caused extra stress on their lives and probably made them feel inferior. The better jobs would have been more difficult to get unless they had a particular highly specialised skill that was needed at that time. Sadly, it hasn't been until modern times that people have owned up to having a convict in their family history and many denied it and were very ashamed of it. Now it has become something to be bragged about.

At some stage after David Patrick was born, his parents, who were living in Guildford, moved the family to live in the prime agricultural area of York, Western Australia.

It is highly likely that when David Patrick reached the legal age to work, he would have worked for his father, whose occupation was listed as Shoemaker on his convict records. At the age of twenty-five, in 1884, David Patrick began his own business as a Boot and Shoe Maker. He had been married for four years and had five children so it was a late start but it shows he was an ambitious and determined man.

An advertisement for his business appeared in the local newspaper stating…

> *"David McGlinn -- BOOT & SHOEMAKER, AVON TERRACE, YORK, begs to inform the public of YORK & BEVERLEY that he has commenced business in the above line, and hopes to receive the support of a generous public.*
>
> *All orders entrusted to him will be executed in a workman like manner, combined with despatch.*

SEWN WORK guaranteed." Advertisement (*Eastern Districts Chronicle* Aug 22, 1884)

The 1903 census stated he had changed his occupation from Bootmaker to Fettler with the WAGR. Fettlers are labourers on the railway lines to maintain the tracks and other equipment, a very taxing labour-intensive job that had to be done out in the open in all weathers. A certain toughness was necessary to carry out this work. David Patrick may have been forced out of his boot-making business because there was either an abundance of boot and shoemakers in York at the time and therefore competition may have been too great to make enough money for his large family – he now had twelve surviving children! More likely, shoes could now be bought 'off the shelf' from shops. He continued to be a Fettler until his premature death in 1905.

David Patrick McGlinn – York Volunteer Rifles 1878-1900. (Family photo)

On the 8th November 1878, David Patrick enlisted in the York Volunteer Rifles and would have attended military training both in York and training camps in various locations around the wheatbelt. He was initially a Private and was promoted to Corporal in November 1883. His brother James also enlisted and was a Private from 1880 until 1883. (Family History Association WA, 2021)

> "Until Australia became a Federation in 1901, each of the six colonial governments was responsible for the defence of their own colony. From 1788 until 1870 this was done with British regular forces". It was in "1872 the Metropolitan Rifle Volunteers were formed, with companies in Fremantle, Guildford, Albany, Geraldton, Northampton and York."
>
> (https://en.wikipedia.org › wiki › Colonial_forces_of_Australia)

David Patrick married Sarah Ashworth on 2nd March 1880. They had fifteen children: nine girls and six boys. John was their thirteenth child. Their eldest daughter, Ada Jane, was born out of wedlock on 4th May 1879. It was almost a year later that David Patrick and Sarah married. The reasons for the delay are lost to history but it may very well have been their fathers' backgrounds. Convict (David) and Soldier (Sarah). Social classes did not usually mix outside their class and it could be imagined that Sarah's father, Edmund Ashworth, who appeared to be somewhat of a puritan, surely did not want his daughter marrying below her class and may have made David Patrick's and Sarah's lives difficult by forbidding the marriage.

David Patrick would have been under a lot of pressure to maintain such a large family, especially during the early years when their young children were not old enough to work and help out. In the earlier photo of the house and family at Ford Street, York, the poverty can clearly be seen. Of course, as the children got older, some entered the workforce and they would have helped out financially and practically in the household.

This pressure and worry, and probably the arduous physical work, eventually took its toll and in 1905 David Patrick died suddenly at the age of forty-six. He was at home and had left the dining table and gone to sit by the fire. Seven-year-old John had just got onto his father's lap when he fell forward onto the floor, tipping John off. Poor John was terrified and stood rooted to the floor in horror.

The following newspaper article describes his death.

> "A resident of many years standing in this town, David McGlinn, died suddenly at his residence, near Monger's Bridge, at 7.30 last evening. It appears that deceased had just finished his evening meal, and after conversing a few minutes with his son Thomas respecting obtaining employment, he complained of feeling unwell, and walked into an adjoining room. He had not been absent more than five minutes when a noise of something having fallen was heard, and upon seeking the cause the deceased was found stretched out on the floor near the fireplace, quite dead. Dr Davis was immediately summoned, who pronounced life extinct. Death was doubtless due to heart disease. The deceased was a married man, forty-six years of age, and leaves a widow and twelve children -- seven daughters and five boys -- ten of whom live at home. He was a bootmaker by trade, but of late years had followed the occupation of a labourer".

(*Eastern Districts Chronicle* York: 1877 – 1927. Sat 4 Jun, 1905)

> "FUNERAL. -- The remains of the late David McGlinn were interred at the Wesleyan Cemetery on Sunday afternoon last, prior to which the Rev. Corly Butler conducted a short service at the church. The procession was a lengthy one, and included members of the Independent Order of Oddfellows, who attended in regalia to pay the last tribute of respect to their deceased brother".

(*Eastern Districts Chronicle* Saturday 1 July, 1905)

John was only seven years old when his father died and there were two sisters younger than him, the youngest being only three years old. Sarah must have been devastated, traumatised and distraught, for now she was alone and had to cope with and support all those children! She had no money to erect a gravestone on his grave.

David Patrick's father
Thomas McGlinn – convict 2368

Thomas McGlinn was born in County Cavan, Ireland, in 1831 and died of Senile Decay (Dementia or Alzheimer's as it is now known) in the Sunset Old Men's Home, Dalkeith, on 20th September, 1919, aged 78.

During Thomas's early life, he had suffered the extreme impoverished, and harsh conditions of the Irish Potato Famine that went from 1845 until 1852, its effect felt well beyond that time. In County Cavan, Ireland, where he lived, 42% of the population had died from starvation and disease. (www.bing.com/images) It is possible that some members of his family had died, but this cannot be verified. However, with such a high percentage of death in that county, it is quite possible and highly likely. He had lived to experience some of the most extreme hardship and turmoil that anyone could suffer. Not only had the people already suffered enough, now there was an extremely cold period in Europe, including Ireland, that caused further hardship and stress.

His crime occurred during a period of particularly bad winters known as The Little Ice Age *"NASA Earth Observatory notes three particularly cold intervals: one beginning about 1650, another about 1770, and the last in 1850."* (en.wikipedia.org/wiki/Little_Ice_Age). Food crops failed and the famine continued. The people of Ireland continued to live in wretched conditions and were starving. Prior to the famine, the diet of many of the Irish consisted mainly of potatoes and milk with a bit of meat on occasions. To make matters worse, the English nobility had taken over many of the small Irish farm plots of land and built large mansions in which to live and to oversee the Irish farmers who had been allowed to stay on their land but had to rent it back. When the potato famine hit Europe, the Irish were particularly hard done by. They could no longer produce the potatoes to sell and therefore could not afford to pay their rent. They were evicted from their land and their homes were destroyed so they could not return. The English wanted them out!

In 1851, at the age of twenty, Thomas was convicted of larceny (theft) by Judge (and Baron), Richard Fennefather. It is certain that Thomas was in dire straits and his crimes were caused by desperation, people *had* to steal just to survive! Because it wasn't Thomas's first offence, he was convicted of his crime in February 1851 and sentenced on the 3rd March 1851 to 10 year's transportation to Western Australia and he was given the convict number 2368.

Thomas's conviction and having to be transported to another country would have been very distressing. He did not know what was going to happen nor what it was like where he was going, but he did get used to being in prison, it was two years before he was transported, making his sentence twelve years! It was actually for life …

On Thomas's convict record, he is described as being 5 feet 7 inches tall, dark brown hair, dark grey eyes, round face, sallow complexion, slight build (highly likely starving), cut on top of finger on left hand, freckled, and a single man. His profession was stated as 'shoemaker'. Many people who were classed as shoemakers worked from home and made shoes to fit for the local people. (https://convictrecords.com.au/convicts/mcglinn/thomas/128328)

He left Ireland in June 1853 on the ship *Phoebe Dunbar* along with 295 other convicts and 93 passengers, mostly Pensioner Guards and their families, and arrived in the colony of Western Australia on 31st August 1853. *"Those (convicts) on board ranged in age from 15 to 52 and were sentenced to crimes related to the famine … These convicts, similar to many of those from other regions, committed minimal or petty crimes. Their crimes coinciding with the famine … Therefore although mistreatment or neglect of Irish convicts occurred on the ship, many were also malnourished prior to their journey and this could have contributed to the high proportion of deaths of youthful men noted in the medical journal entries. Many on the ship were evidently feeble from their experiences of Irish life in Famine times."* (www.irishaussies.wordpress.com/phoebedunbarconvictship) *"It is interesting to note that owing to the number of deaths on board this ship whilst in transit, the ship only made the one trip with convicts … from Ireland to WA."* (https://fremantleprison.com.au/history-heritage/history/the-convict-era)

The ship "Phoebe Dunbar" (www.bing.com/images) 2020

When Thomas was to leave Ireland, he was escorted, along with the other convicts, onto the little ship. It is sad to note that the conditions on this ship were very different to the other convict ships from England, including the ship *Pyrenees* on which Joshua Kemp was transported. The conditions on this ship were harsh and unforgiving and the Irish convicts on the *Phoebe Dunbar* were far more neglected and more harshly treated than the other convict ships during this late period of transportation and were more reminiscent of the much earlier convict ships. It is likely that the tension between the Irish convicts and the English guards was reflected on this voyage.

When Thomas McGlinn disembarked, he had to wear the branded convict jacket and would have worked in a convict gang building roads or carrying out construction of the colonial government buildings, or some other requirement for fifteen months before he was granted his Ticket of leave on the 17th November, 1854. Before his Ticket of Leave was granted, he was admitted to hospital on the 25th January with "Bad eyes". It was stated that he was twenty-three years old, a labourer, and his general health was good. (https://slwa.wa.gov.au/eresources) 2020. The granting of his Ticket of Leave meant he could discard the convict coat and find employment for himself. Sometimes this didn't make life easier, because once a convict was given a Ticket of Leave all benefits, like food, lodging, and work, were removed and the convict had to fend for himself. There were no more handouts and some convicts became desperate and homeless and returned to crime to get security.

The type of jacket Thomas McGlinn had to wear for 15 months

Before gaining his Ticket of Leave, he was lodging with other convicts in Guildford, Western Australia, where he had been working in the convict labour gangs, probably building roads using the new Macadam method of roadbuilding. There he met his future wife, Catherine Walker, who was most likely working as a servant. By 1858, he was self-employed, presumably as a Boot and Shoemaker in Guildford. *"Not all convicts were inherently villainous or hapless vagabonds. In time many of them commanded respect and even admiration"* The brand on his coat. Ed. R. Erikson. (UWA Press 1983) p. 224. Even though he had a Ticket of Leave, he needed permission to marry and apparently this was granted. This union may not have been for love, it may have been for convenience as was very common then.

The date of their marriage is a mystery because there are no records. It is known that some convicts and settlers had been married in their country of origin but their spouses didn't come to Australia. Consequently, defacto marriages were common. Maybe this was the case with either Thomas McGlinn or Catherine Walker, however, they lived as man and wife and assumed the 'married' status. Advice from a veteran historian (name unknown), a volunteer from Battye Library, said that in those times the Catholic Church performed the marriage ceremony and a payment of one penny was paid to the church by the couple to legally register their marriage with the government. However, in some cases, the church, apparently held onto a number of these registration monies and, as such, the marriages were not registered with the government! So, no record can be found for those particular marriages. This could be the case with Thomas and Catherine; they were Roman Catholics and probably married in the Roman Catholic Church in Guildford. If they did marry, it is likely they married in about 1858 when Thomas became self-employed and soon before the birth of their first child David Patrick who was born in 1859 in Guildford.

Sometime before 1862, Thomas, Catherine, and their now two children, David Patrick and his sister Sarah Jane, moved to the fast-growing town of York, Western Australia where there were new opportunities for work. In York, they went on to have another seven children – they had six girls and three boys.

The harsh treatment of Thomas McGlinn on the ship and his desperate background may have made this young man a bitter and resentful character, making him a prime target for victimisation by the British authorities, the police of the day. The British and the Irish had ill feelings toward each other and there was some conflict between them, the Irish sometimes treated harshly. At times, Thomas was in trouble with the law and he was never given a pardon – he became an Expiree, that is, he served his full ten-year sentence. A Ticket of Leave did not mean you were not a convict. Some years later, in 1884, when Thomas was fifty-three years old, he was reported to have stolen some money while working for the railways and living in a tent with a railway gang near Chidlow's Well. He was working there with his third child, also named Thomas, now aged twenty-two. Both were Strikers (track layers) on the railways. He was charged with stealing £5. The following is the police charge note.

> "Guildford. On the 1st inst., from the person of Robert Knightley, at Chidlow's Well, -- £15 in Union Bank notes, comprised of two £5 and five £1 notes, numbered as follows: 56102 £5, 5087, 1453, 47617, 45475, 47560, 45884; cannot say which number attaches to the second £5 note. The £5 note No. 66102 has been recovered by the Guildford Police in possession of Thomas McGlinn, Exp. late 2368." (Thomas's convict number) *Police Gazette* (Wednesday June 11 1884)

Thomas denied the money was stolen and said that he had made the £5 in his possession from making a pair of boots. The number on the £5 note that was in Thomas's possession may not have been the one that was allegedly stolen. Was he victimised? On his police report, it said that he was known to be an honourable man. *State Archives* 2022

Young Thomas McGlinn, Thomas and Catherine's third child, was a bit of larrikin who was in trouble with the law on occasions. There was a lengthy newspaper article about him and other youths getting into mischief in the Castle Hotel in York (a known gathering place for convicts). Young Thomas McGlinn died in 1891, aged only twenty-nine, from a "malignant disease" (Cancer). (https://www.wa.gov.au/organisation/department-of-justice/online-index-search-tool) 2020.

The Castle Hotel on Avon Terrace, York, at the time of John McGlinn's childhood – early 1900s. (www.bing.com/images) 2020

The same corner today, Avon Terrace. The Castle Hotel, a favourite haunt for the 'convict classes' in its early days. (Personal photo 2022)

After a few brushes with the law, Thomas McGlinn eventually settled down and returned to his boot and shoe making, and had a shop in York. He worked there probably until his wife Catherine died in 1910. He may have been suffering from mental illness for some time and eventually could only work at his old trade of boot and shoe making, something he was familiar with. After Catherine died, he may have continued to work in his shop but, as his mental health failed, it is likely he was admitted to the *Claremont Old Men's Home* where he died of Senile Decay in 1919. (https://www.wa.gov.au/organisation/department-of-justice/online-index-search-tool) The *Claremont Old Men's Home* was for destitute old men who had nothing and had no support. Prior to this, the old and destitute men were housed in the old infirmary at the base of Mt Eliza, Kings Park, near where the old Swan Brewery stands today. Thomas was a pauper when he died; he had no real estate and only £1/14/- to his name. On his death certificate, some of his children are mentioned, but not all of them. He is buried in the Roman Catholic section in Karrakatta Cemetery. In those days, there was a lot of shame about having a convict in the family and some of his family may have abandoned him. This was fairly common – many denied that their family members were convicts. It is very sad that this was the case because many of the convicts could not be blamed for their crimes. They had come from absolutely wretched conditions. No one seemed to understand and no one cared, and there was snobbery around the situation. Now there is nothing left of Thomas McGlinn to remember the hard life he had, not even a headstone in the cemetery. The area he is buried in has been "renewed" so there is no way to find his burial plot. It is unlikely Thomas would have had a headstone but the area looks nice and peaceful.

Left - Mount Eliza Poor Men's Home near the Swan Brewery at the base of King's Park and right - Claremont Old Men's Home early days (www.bing.com/images) 2020

The *Claremont Old Men's Home* later became known as *Sunset Hospital*.

Perhaps Thomas McGlinn was one of these men at the "Claremont Old Men's Home". He was there at the time. March 10th 1915 (www.abc.net.au/news/2014-11-25/perth-sunset-hospital-history/5914486)

On Thomas's death, a notice was placed in the York newspaper.

> "Death of Thomas McGlinn. The death of an old resident of this district in the person of Thomas McGlinn occurred at Perth a few days ago at the age of 88 years. Deceased left a large family of sons and daughters, and many grand and great grandchildren, some of whom reside in this district for many years the deceased carried on the business of a boot and shoe manufacturer in York, and his work was noted for its quality." Eastern Districts Chronicle. (York, WA) (Fri 26 Sep 1919) p. 3.

Thomas McGlinn's parents
Michael McGlinn and Mary Cunningham

Thomas McGlinn's father, Michael McGlinn, was born in 1810 in County Cavan, Ireland. Michael's death date is unknown and he may well have died during the famine. Thomas's mother was Mary Cunningham, born in 1813 in Ireland, and died in 1879, aged 66 years. Michael and Mary were married in 1830 and it can be presumed that Thomas was their first and perhaps their only child.

Thomas McGlinn's wife
Catherine Walker

Catherine Walker was born in Kilrea, Londonderry, Northern Ireland in about 1836 and died in York, Western Australia on 11th July, 1910. According to her death notice, she was seventy-four years old. She was the daughter of David Walker and Sarah Mayberry, both born in Ireland.

It is not clear when Catherine arrived in Western Australia and there are scant records for her, but in some private online sources, it was said she came to Western Australia in 1856 at the age of twenty. There is a record of a Catherine Walker who arrived with her widowed father and several siblings on the ship *Diadem* in 1842 bound for Leschenault. (https://www.fhwa.org.au/) She was not Catherine Walker/McGlinn. There are no other shipping records for a Catherine Walker, which indicates that she was probably one of the many single Irish women like Jane Walshe/Carroll who were brought to the colonies to bolster the female numbers to keep the men civil, and to provide the much-needed servants to the colonists. *"A good proportion of migrant girls found husbands within a year of arriving…Ticket of Leave men competed very successfully against free settlers for wives"*. (*The brand on his coat*. Ed. R. Erikson (UWA Press, 1983) p. 42.

Her baptismal papers recorded she was baptised in York, Western Australia on the 1st November, 1864 and her age was noted as about thirty years old. All dates for Catherine are confusing and are a bit loose in timing but seem to be correct to within a year or two. (https://slwa.wa.gov.au/eresources) Records were probably given via word of mouth rather than proof by documentation and in those harsh and busy times some dates provided may have been incorrect, but close to being correct.

Thomas McGlinn and Catherine had nine children (possibly ten), three boys and six girls. There is a baptismal record for a child born in 1867 but there is no birth or death record so the child may have been a still birth, or late miscarriage.

David Patrick was their first child and his name is registered in the birth registry as McGlisson, the writing on his birth certificate is difficult to read and has been interpreted wrongly. It appears Thomas may have been literate because his signature is on the birth certificate. Some of the other children were registered either as McGlinn or McGlynn, however, they all took on the name of McGlinn.

Catherine would have found it very difficult to bring up all those children, both with the meagre money Thomas was able to provide, and in the very primitive housing and conditions of those days. There would always have been pressure on households in this fledgling colony where shortages occurred with just about everything. Thomas would have been under a lot of pressure to provide for such a large family and this might have led to his alleged stealing offences. Convicts were usually last in line for any work opportunities and some of them had to steal just to get by and to stave off starvation of their family. A very difficult and frustrating time for these men. (No women convicts were sent to Western Australia).

Catherine must have been literate because she went on to be the Librarian at The Mechanic's Institute in York, Western Australia. Mechanics' Institutes were the forerunners of public libraries and adult education services in Australia. A 'Mechanic' meant artisan, tradesman or working man.

Catherine and Thomas lived in Gray Street, York.

When Catherine died, a short notice was placed in the local newspaper.

"Family Notices - Death. Catherine McGlinn

McGLINN -- At the residence of her son-in-law, Mr E. H. Trew, York, on July 11th instant -- Catherine, wife of Thomas McGlinn, and daughter of the late David Walker, of Kilrea, County Londonderry, Ireland, in her 74th year. Deeply regretted." Eastern Districts Chronicle. (York, WA: 1877 Fri 15 Jul 1910) p. 2.

The Ashworths

Ashworth Family Line

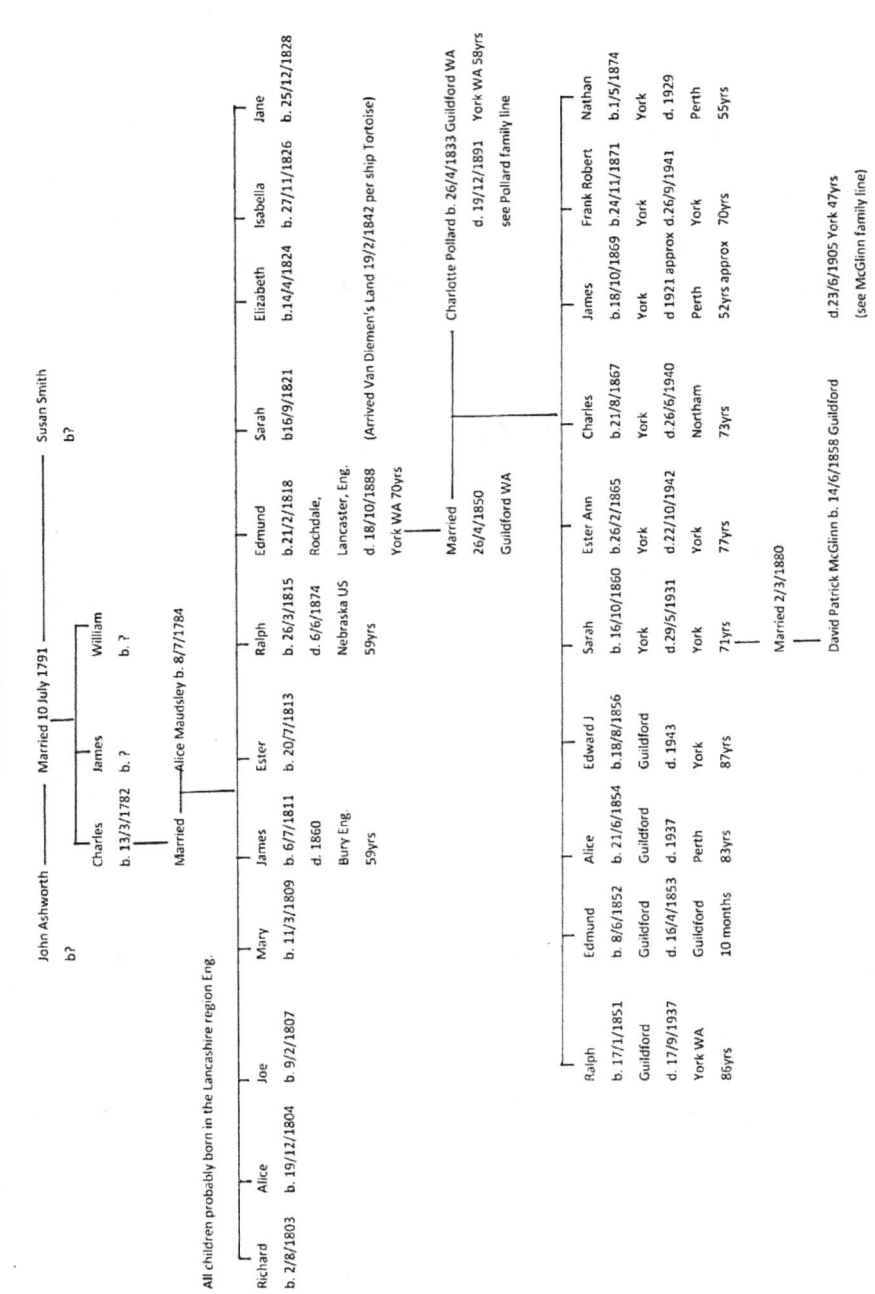

John McGlinn's mother
Sarah Ashworth

Sarah Ashworth, was born in York, Western Australia on 16th October, 1850 and died there on 29th May, 1931, aged 71 years. She was the daughter of Edmund Ashworth and Charlotte Pollard and was the fifth of their eleven children.

As a child and teenager, Sarah lived on her father's wheat farm just outside York. Her sole role in the family would have been to help her mother and, having only one older sister, she would have had a very busy life. All housework would have been done by hand; there were no modern conveniences, no running water, and electricity hadn't been invented yet. With so many children in the family, there would have been plenty of clothes, bed clothes, table linen etc. to wash and sew and mend, and a lot of food to prepare. When required, she also would have helped on the farm. Sarah would have grown into a very capable woman. With her father being a soldier, their household may have been a regimented and strict household and everyone would have had set jobs to do and he would have expected them to be done well.

Fortunately, her parents ensured she had an education because it is known she was literate. Her father, Edmund Ashworth, was literate and, as a young boy, had been very keen to ensure his own education so it would follow that he would have been very keen to educate his own children, even the girls. He may have taught them himself – he had experience in teaching children when he was stationed at Rottnest Island. Schools were very limited in colonial Western Australia and there were very few teachers. There was one small government school and a Catholic school in York and the teachers were mostly educated Ticket of Leave men. However, in the seven country schools of the Western Australian colony at that time, a total of only 219 children were taught, including York. (*The brand on his coat*. Ed. R. Erikson, (UWA Press, 1983) p.286. It can be seen that this number is very low considering the high number of children in most families.

By the time Sarah was eighteen years old, she had met David Patrick McGlinn and was probably courted by him with all the usual flirtations, giggles and love – marriages of convenience were now mainly a thing of the past. There would be no doubt that they knew each other from an early age because there would have been plenty of social gatherings etc. and, being a smallish town, everyone would have known or at least been acquainted with each other. Also, no doubt there would have been conflict because of their romance. Sarah's father was somewhat of a snob and a puritan who always did everything right; he was a tee-totaller, and always followed the rules. He held no pity for those who did wrong and here was Sarah with a boyfriend, (or 'beau' as they called them then) whose father was an ex-convict and being Irish, highly likely a drinker!

Sarah and David Patrick persisted in their relationship and it endured against the odds. When Sarah married David Patrick in 1880, the law stated that *"the married couple became one entity represented by the husband, placing him in control of all property, earnings, and money. In addition to losing money and material goods to their husbands… wives became property to their husbands, giving them rights to what their bodies produced: children, sex and domestic labor. Marriage abrogated a woman's right to consent to sexual intercourse with her husband, giving him "ownership" over her body. Their mutual matrimonial consent therefore became a contract to give herself to her husband as he desired."* (https://en.wikipedia.org/wiki/WomenintheVictorianera) The wedding band that women wore denoted ownership by her husband! This law was in place until *"The Married Women's Property Act was introduced in 1892"* (*Paupers, Poor Relief and Poor Houses in Western Australia 1829-1910.* (Hetherington, P. UWA Press, 2009) p. 123. From this time women could keep their own property and wealth, but this was more by law than practice.

Because of the norms of the day children were produced in great number and birth control was not practiced. Many were ignorant of any contraceptive methods and it required the cooperation of both the man and the woman and this was not conducive to the male dominant and chauvinistic mindset of the day. It is no wonder the high reproduction and frequency of births was common in that era. A fertile couple, such as David Patrick and Sarah, couldn't help but have numerous children during her child-bearing years. Sarah had the first of her fifteen children at the age of nineteen in 1879 and her last child at the age of forty-two in 1902. Fifteen children in twenty-three years!

A woman's sole job was to keep the house clean, prepare food for her husband, keep him happy sexually, and look after the children. However, women weren't stupid and knew they were capable of much more. Times were changing and, as women became more educated, they wanted change; they felt they were hard done by and consequently fought for their rights, both in their personal lives and politically. It must have been very frustrating to know that many men still believed that women should just focus on child rearing and doing housework. They did not want women to vote politically because they thought they were not educated enough nor intelligent enough to hold an opinion and that they were incapable of intellectual achievements! (www.nla.gov.au/Women) In 1899, one year after John was born, and when Sarah was thirty-nine years old, voting for women was introduced in Western Australia. The hard fought for rights of women gradually began to change and the Suffragette Movement for the emancipation of women was born. The groundswell for women's rights was making itself felt and Australia was the first country to allow women to stand for parliament. The amazing woman, Edith Cowan, was the first woman in Western Australia to stand in parliament. Her difficult background is very interesting.

Sadly, in most families during those times, there was a high rate of infant mortality. David Patrick and Sarah were no exception: three of their children died, two at a very young age and one teenager. The younger ones, born consecutively, were baby Frank Robert who died from diarrhoea (possibly Typhoid) in January 1888, aged seven months, and Ruth Charlotte who died from croup in May 1891 aged two years and seven months. (https://www.wa.gov.au/organisation/department-of-justice/online-index-search-tool). It may have been that these diseases were rampant in the community at those times and medical help wasn't effective, if you could afford it. Raw sewerage was carted from homes and put in open cesspits so disease spread by flies was rife.

The teenage girl who died doing domestic chores was Sophia, who died at fourteen years of age, seventeen days after John was born, in January 1898. Her clothes caught alight while she tended the fire and she died the next day from severe burns. An article in the newspaper reported her death. She died on 21st January 1898.

> *"Sophia McGlinn*
>
> *An accident having a most very serious results happened to Miss McGlinn, aged 13 (14) years, a daughter of Mr. D. McGlinn. On Friday afternoon she was engaged at the fire, and by some mischance or other her clothes ignited and were soon in flames. Prompt action to quench the fire was taken by some neighbours and her mother, which after a little while was effected. The injuries done her by the fire were so serious that she succumbed on Saturday".* (The Northam Advertiser (WA: 1895 - 1955) Sat 29 Jan 1898 York Notes).

There would have been such sadness in their household at those times and it is assumed that the community would have rallied and helped and supported them in their times of grief. The McGlinn family were poor and hard-working and the running of the household could not stop; life had to carry on.

In Sarah's day, clothes were handmade; very few items of clothing were available in shops. Cloth was bought from the Draper and the women made their own clothes and those of their children. Often the poorer families used flour bags to make clothes for their children. Hand-me-down clothing was common and the wardrobe consisted of a good outfit (usually for church) and a couple of sets for work and for around the house. This would have been the case for families such as Sarah's. However, men's clothing was available in shops but was quite expensive and so these too were usually hand made at home. Women and girls would wear a pinafore, a smock like garment that covered the clothes front and back. The pinafore protected the clothing which would be worn for a week before being washed. The pinafore would be washed more often.

Not all of life was hard work though, and there were plenty of social events and dances to attend. York was a big town by now and there were musical bands and many festivals, picnics and sporting events. It was a grand and busy place.

When David Patrick died, it would have been terribly difficult for Sarah, who was only forty-five years old, with ten children at home to care for. She took in washing and did ironing for extra money. The younger children would go out each morning and collect the washing from the wealthier people and single men around town and take it home. Sarah would then wash, dry and iron the clothes. John said his mother was often up until midnight doing the ironing with the heavy based irons that were heated on the wood stove. The next morning, the children would take the clean ironed items back to their owners and collect the next lot to be done. It was a never-ending cycle and it would have been hellishly hot during summer. At some stage, she took in two foster children. Apparently, William Patrick Kett, whose family had gone to Kurrawang near Kalgoorlie to live, moved in to Sarah's home to help out. It is known he was considered one of the family.

There was still no electricity and no running water so all household chores had to be done by hand. Water had to be carted from the nearby river for cooking, washing the clothes, bathing etc. Only fifty gallons a week was delivered by the authorities for drinking water and it had to be enough for all of them. There were several daughters, who were still quite young, but who would have had to help with domestic chores during this difficult time. No matter how small the child, they had to do something, even if it was to carry a billy full of water from the river. By now, Ada Jane had married and had children of her own but she very likely visited and helped her mother during this traumatic time. Perhaps some of the older boys were employed and could have contributed money to the household and, because of David Patrick's sudden death, there would have been huge pressure on the household finances. In those days, there were no such things as welfare or pensions for anyone, including women. Everything depended on the man of the house and, if he died or left the home, the woman just had to cope somehow. The Colonial Government did not give any money to help those who had no finances, particularly if there was a surviving relative anywhere in Western Australia who could help support the family. They were *made* to contribute to the finances of their family member and there were investigations into finding a family member to help. The Imperial Government (British) did give some money to their soldiers and pensioner guards to stave off poverty but it was a pittance. Sarah would have lived on the absolute poverty line for several years but did not need to go into a "Poor House" because she did have family members, including some of her children, and her siblings to help her. The law expected it. *Paupers, Poor Relief and Poor Houses in Western Australia 1829-1910.* (Hetherington, UWA Press, 2009).

In reality, Sarah had no time to get to know and spend time with her husband; for both it was just constant work, work, work, just to survive. It was the same for most struggling families so they wouldn't have felt alone in this. Perhaps in those times there was no such thing as 'quality' time with a spouse. The only expectation would be to work hard and survive together. There was no retirement age, and old aged pensions weren't available, so basically you worked until you died, or your family helped you out.

In 1910, five years after David Patrick died, Sarah married Arthur Ernest Slocombe. How she had the time to socialise and meet someone else is amazing. Perhaps she did his washing. The whereabouts of Arthur's birth is not known but he was born in 1867 and died at the age of eighty-one, on 18th December, 1948 in Kirup, Western Australia. At the time he married Sarah, he was living in Avon Terrace, York. Ford Street, where the McGlinns lived, ran off Avon Terrace so he could have lived close by; they may even have been neighbours for years. After they were married, he moved into her home on Ford Street.

Arthur was a bricklayer by trade and seven years Sarah's junior. He took on the family and helped Sarah to bring up the younger children. It appears he had no children of his own. By this time, there was a hoard of girls old enough to help Sarah around the house. The youngest child was now eight years old and capable of doing many household jobs. John was twelve years old and may have found this man's guidance a great help during the oncoming puberty and teenage years. Sarah and Arthur seemed to be a devoted couple and it seems Sarah's children loved him.

A notice inserted by him in the local newspaper one year after Sarah's death was very touching…

> "SLOCOMBE. -- In cherished memory of my dear wife, who passed away at York on May 29, 1931. Lonely and sad I sit at night, And think of the days gone by, When we were together, side by side, My dearest wife and I. A wonderful mother and great pal.
>
> Inserted by her loving husband, Arthur Slocombe (Kirup)".
> (*Family Notices. The West Australian* (Perth, WA: 1879 - 1954) (Sat 28 May 1932)

When Arthur Slocombe died in 1948, the McGlinn children put some very endearing death notices in the local paper. They called him "Pop".

All through Sarah's life she suffered with terrible asthma. She had a concoction that she put in a pipe and let its smoke waft up inside a towel that she held over her head while she breathed in the 'smoke' from the pipe. Sarah also suffered with 'rheumatism' (arthritis).

Sarah Ashworth/McGlinn/Slocombe in her handmade outfit. (Family photo)

Sarah McGlinn/Slocombe with her daughter Florence Hilda, and possibly Arthur Slocombe (Photo - York Residency Museum 2020)

Sarah McGlinn/Slocombe with her daughters.
Front : Left to right - Ada Jane, Sarah (mother), Gertrude Eva - extreme right.
Back : Left to Right - Selina Mabel, Maud Bertha, Sarah Ruby, Florence Hilda.
(Family photo)

**There were no photos available of the McGlinn boys.

Sarah McGlinn's father
Edmund Ashworth

Edmund Ashworth was born in Rochdale, Lancaster County, England on 21st February, 1818, and died of cancer of the liver and a tumour on his stomach, in York, Western Australia on 18th October, 1888, aged 71. The information about Edmund's death is from a letter, written in March 1889, by his son James to a cousin in America, where he described his father's death. He also stated that Edmund was a hard worker until his death. A copy of this letter can be seen at (https://purl.slwa.wa.gov.au/slwa_b1827369_2.pdf?agree).

Edmund wrote a lengthy diary during much of his life and the information given here is from that. (His diary is held at Battye Library, in the State Library of Western Australia).

His parents were Charles Ashworth and Alice Maudsley. Charles was born on 13th March, 1782 in Rochdale, Lancaster, England. "Rochdale rose to prominence in the 19th century as a mill town and centre for textile manufacture during the Industrial Revolution. It was a boomtown of the Industrial Revolution, and amongst the first industrialised towns". (www.wikipedia.org/wiki/Rochdale)

Charles' death date is unknown. Charles' father was John Ashworth and his mother was Susan Smith.

Edmund's mother, Alice Maudsley, was born in Lancaster, England on 8th July, 1784. Her death date is unknown.

Charles, and Alice, were in the wool weaving trade and they had twelve children – five boys and seven girls. Edmund was their eighth child. This family may have had a small weaving factory in their home, as some people did in those times – not all weaving was done in large factories. Unfortunately, their wool weaving business failed so they moved location to Grimble, a few kilometres away and took up the cotton weaving trade. Cotton was the new wonder fabric on the market and was favoured by customers because of its versatility and more comfortable wearing, not like the rough scratch and itch of wool.

Edmund was born in 1818 during what was known as "The Year Without Summer", when the volcano Tambora in Indonesia erupted causing the northern hemisphere to cool. Crops failed and there was great famine across Europe and over 65,000 people died – a lot of people for those times. (PLIMER, Ian. *Heaven and Earth* (Connor Court, 2009) p. 81. Times were hard and poverty and starvation were rife.

Edmund attended school until he was nine years old, then he had to leave school and go to work in the cotton weaving factory. At the age of nine, it was legal for him to go to work and it was expected that he, along with most other children of that age, would do so. At that time *"Women and children worked 12 hour days. During busy seasons, work hours could extend to 20 hours a day… In England, lawmakers enacted early labor standards in 1833. The new child labor laws mandated an 8 hour work day for 9 year olds. Younger children were no longer allowed to work in mills or factories".* (www.bellatory.com/fashion-industry/Ready-to-Wear-A-Short-History-of-the-Garment-Industry)

Edmund was too early for the reforms so he and his siblings would have worked during those times of long hours.

Children working in the textile industry (www.bing.com/images) 2020

Edmund lamented at having to leave his schooling but was able to attend school on Sundays, his day off. He stated that he cost his parents nothing for schooling and was very proud of that fact. He must have been an intelligent and determined child to want to attend school and better himself. He said his parents taught him to stay away from bad people and to always behave correctly and it seems he carried this on throughout his life.

At the age of sixteen, the family moved again, this time to Newton Moore in

Cheshire. Here he began an apprenticeship with a Cordwainer. A Cordwainer was a shoemaker who worked in fine soft colourful leathers. In those days, apprentices lived with their employer and Edmund lived with his "master" for four years and became a skilled craftsman. At the age of twenty, he fell in love and wanted to marry but there was resistance from the girl's mother. She said she needed her daughter to look after her in her old age, so out of respect he called off the romance and, to get away from the heartache, joined the army on 23rd June 1840. Obviously, a very honourable young man.

He was in the 96th Regiment of Foot, and was a 'Red Coat'. Foot was the early term for Infantry, a foot soldier. He enjoyed his new life in the army and was soon commissioned to sail on the ship *HMS Tortoise* to take 400 convicts to the penal settlement in Van Diemen's Land (Tasmania).

The *Tortoise* set sail from Plymouth, England on 26th October 1841 and almost 4 months later arrived in Van Diemen's Land on 19th February, 1842. There were 100 soldiers and 100 crew along with the 400 prisoners, certainly a cramped and crowded ship. It seems the journey was pleasant enough, though one prisoner died near the Cape of Good Hope and Edmund and a few others had to go ashore and dig his grave. Another five convicts died on the journey.

There is a copy of a letter that was written by a convict, George Reading, during this same voyage on the *Tortoise*, who stated that the voyage was very pleasant. A contrast to what we are led to believe about these voyages! An excerpt of that letter is below – perhaps Edmund helped George with his spelling etc. The letter is a bit difficult to read owing to the grammar, spelling, and lack of all punctuation. The letter is held in Battye Library, State Library of WA.

> *"Sunday 12 the fastest Sailing that we Ever had yeat thear was four hours that we went 13 knots a hour and Good Side wind The Sun rises at 5 in the morning and Sets at 7 at night and you Can See to rite a letter at halfe Past 3 in the morning and till --?-- The Sea his butifull and Plesent and I Enjoy it much I Saw Great many marble Fish and thea hear Smooth and dark Sise and thea are large and heavy. I Saw wone of them leap out of the warter 6 feet and the Sise of them his 1 hundard and halfe waight"* (George Reading, 1842, convict, letter to his relatives in England)

While sailing in the Southern Ocean, a particularly severe storm blew up and the little ship was blown off course and careered back over 200 miles. There was a very strong possibility that the ship would founder and sink or become a shipwreck with all lives lost. At that time, shipwrecks were fairly common around southern Australia (and elsewhere), and with no communication no-one would know what happened to those on board – they just wouldn't have arrived at their destination. However, search ships were sometimes sent to find survivors. Luckily, Edmund arrived safely in Hobart Town and, after a few days, disembarked and escorted the prisoners to the areas they were to be stationed to work. Hobart was declared a city in 1842, the same year Edmund arrived there.

Hobart Town, possibly some-time after 1842 when Edmund Ashworth arrived (www.bing.com/images) 2021

He was promoted to Lance Corporal soon after arriving in Van Diemen's Land and his orders were to escort convicts to various locations around the eastern side of the island. At one stage, he was stationed at Eagle Hawk Neck, the narrow neck of land at the top of the Tasman Peninsular where the penitentiary of Port Arthur is located. He was assigned to guard this area for five months to prevent convicts escaping. A row of dogs was chained across the 'neck'. (Today the Officers' Quarters and the Dog Line are preserved as a historical site). Edmund stated that only the worst of convicts were sent to Port Arthur. Most other convicts were valuable workers who were sent on work details, and they contributed greatly to the development of the colony.

Edmund also had to sail to Norfolk Island to take a consignment of the worst of the convicts there. The conditions on the ship must have been disgusting because he slept on the deck of the ship for the duration of the journey and complained of the filth he had to lie in. He went for a swim in Emily Bay and said it was the best bathe he had ever had. Emily Bay is a beautiful and picturesque place, perfect for a swim. He mentioned a prisoner who was so bad that he would be locked up and never see sunlight again!

Norfolk Island Penal Settlement to which Edmund Ashworth took prisoners – Emily Bay top of photo (www.bing.com/images) 2021

After five years of being stationed in Van Diemen's Land, he was given orders to go to the Swan River Colony in Western Australia. He left Hobart on the 27th January, 1847 on the troop ship *Java*. There were 100 soldiers in his regiment and another 350 from another regiment that was to go on to India. Edmund's regiment was to relieve a regiment of soldiers in the Swan River Colony who were also to go on to India. After several stops and starts due to both storms and calm weather along the way, he arrived in King George Sound (Albany) on the 13th February, 1847. Edmund didn't go ashore into Albany but his officer did and he described Albany as having … *"about forty houses in this Town, a Commissariate* [sic] *store and Barracks and a Church without a roof on it."*

On the 24th February, 1847, at the height of summer, they disembarked at Fremantle. There was no harbour at that stage so ships anchored off shore and people were rowed in. The Swan River colony was now only seventeen years old. Edmund was quite unimpressed with Fremantle and stated that there were four or five public houses, one church and chapel, and about 200 inhabitants who lived in houses made of white stone. The streets were ankle deep in sand and the glare effected the eyes badly. It was very hot and very unpleasant. Most of Edmund's regiment had to march to Perth and he described the route as being ankle deep in sand and the worst road on which to march that he had ever seen. He marched with the group for over a mile and even at this short distance the soldiers were tired, and they had another nine or ten miles to go!

Edmund and five other soldiers were told to go to the Courthouse (Round House), which was completed in 1831 and was the colony's first civil gaol. (AUSTIN, Tom, *Western Images* (St. George Books. 1996) p. 20. The group was to stay there until they were sent to Rottnest Island. At the Round House, they were put into an empty room to sleep. There were no facilities at all, no beds, no bedclothes, nothing. After two days sleeping on the floorboards, they went to Rottnest Island to guard the Indigenous Australian convicts there. Edmund got one shilling a day to supervise their work of growing food. It seems he treated the Indigenous men fairly and with respect. They were allowed to have Sundays off to go hunting and fishing and anything they caught they could eat. They were locked in their rooms at night where they would sleep on the ground, as was usual for them, and they were given a blanket.

It seems Edmund was respected and well-liked by his peers and by the Superintendent of Rottnest Island who was a very hard taskmaster. He was on Rottnest Island almost ten months and was asked to tutor the Superintendent's children while there. Prior to leaving the island, Edmund decided he had had enough of military life and requested to be discharged from the army; but this was to take some time.

On the 14th October, 1847, Edmund left Rottnest Island and was taken by boat to Perth where he was assigned to be a guard. Guards were required to stop the stealing that was occurring around the place and to protect the colonists and property.

In December 1847, Edmund and another soldier hired some horses and went for a ride to Guildford, which he described as a small town of only about twenty or thirty houses and some very good gardens.

On 21st November, 1848, Edmund's discharge application went before the Board of Officers and his papers were sent on to Hobart for approval. In December, while waiting to be discharged from the army, he received an order to proceed to York to relieve an officer there. He acquired a horse and rode via Mahogany Creek and the 'Half Way House' (the Lakes turnoff?) to York. After several months, at the beginning of April 1849, he was appointed as the first Post

Master for the district of York. He also became the tailor and storekeeper. He got the sum of £24 a year for the three jobs. However, this didn't last because he was ordered back to Perth to attend a farewell for the rest of his detachment who were being sent to India.

Soon afterwards, on the 10th May 1849, Edmund received his discharge from the army and, at the age of thirty-one, was doing quite well and had set himself up in business as a shoemaker.

He wrote the following letter to his brother in America.

"17th September, 1849

Dear Brother, I now sit down to write a few lines to you hoping to find you and the Family all in good health and circumstances as Thanks be to God it leaves me at present. I have to inform you that I got my discharge from the Army in May last and our Regt is gone to India. They left here a few days after my discharge. I have now set up in Business of Boot and Shoemaker and have one man and one Apprentice and am doing pretty well. I am still single but I have now a chance to marry a Widow woman about 40 years of age who has got several houses and Cattle and about 1800 acres of land, but I do not feel inclined to accept the offer though she often rides down from the country to visit me. She was down last week. I am still a Teetotaller and in a few days we are going to have a Teetotal Tea Party. Please let my Father and Mother, Brothers and Sisters know how I am getting on. Remember me to Samuel (name illegible) and all the (name illegible) and I should feel much obliged if you could find me some Teetotal Heralds tracts. I had years of service when I was discharged with a few days, but I had seven pounds to pay. I still pass for twenty four or so, I am at present stouter than ever I was. After a little while I shall try to get my Brother Ralph out to this country or I shall try to come home and out again for I would not stay in England if I was to come. Still I would like to (2 words illegible) more. They are about to open some Lead mines to the northward of this place about 300 miles and if it answers well this will be a flourishing colony.

But Dear Brother I must conclude for the present and remain your

Affectionate Brother

Edmund Ashworth Boot and Shoemaker"

(https://purl.slwa.wa.gov.au/slwa_b1827369_2.pdf?agree)

During his visit to Guildford three years earlier, he met 14-year-old Charlotte Pollard and later married her in the Wesleyan Church in Perth, on 26th April, 1850. She was seventeen and he was thirty-two years old. On their marriage certificate, Edmund put his age down to twenty-seven years old! Women were in very short supply and she could have chosen anyone but he must have been considered very good husband potential. They ended up having a large family of ten children.

He built a house in Guildford and was appointed Police Constable on 16th May 1854. Police officers at that time were volunteers and usually from the military so he didn't get paid but got a police uniform from England instead! He did one significant job as a police officer when he was ordered to Perth to attend the execution of two Indigenous men convicted of murder, then to take their bodies to York and display them in open coffins as a warning to others. He left the Police six months later on the 31st October, 1854.

He was also a Pound Keeper at Guildford. This was someone who impounded stray stock, horses, cattle etc. He would then advertise that they were in his possession and that they would be sold if no one came to claim them. If the owner came to collect the stock, they had to pay for the keep of the animals during the time they were in the pound.

Eventually, Edmund rented out his house in Guildford and bought some land near York. Later, he applied for and was granted ten acres in the town of York and in 1862 built a cottage on it. It was in Ulster Road, near Osnaburg Road – the house is no longer there. In that same year, there was a huge flood where the water came up from the river into the town streets. Over the next twenty-five years, he acquired hundreds of acres of farmland in the district. He bequeathed all of his land to his sons – in those times daughters were not generally beneficiaries.

It seems Edmund was a hardworking, conscientious man and a thoroughly good person (although, it seems, a little vain).

Upon his death in 1888 the following notice was published in the local York paper and it describes the type of man he had become.

> "*Edmund Ashworth death*
>
> *We have to record the death of an old and respected settler this week, in the person of Mr. Edmund Ashworth at the ripe old age of 71, which took place at his residence near York on Thursday morning last. The deceased who arrived in this colony in the days of its infancy, has had to contend with many difficulties, but notwithstanding they appeared at times almost insurmountable, with considerable pluck and energy he persevered until he had*

made a comfortable homestead, and, has always been looked upon as thoroughly straightforward and honest in all his transactions. His name has been associated with the temperance movement ever since its inauguration here, and he has always taken a most lively interest in the cause. The funeral took place yesterday afternoon and his remains were followed to the grave by a large concourse of people, including some of our leading citizens and the members of I.O.O. Rechabites to which lodge the deceased belonged The deceased leaves a wife and ten children but most of them are in a position to provide for themselves".

(*Eastern Districts Chronicle*, Sat 20 Oct 1888)

Note…a Rechabite, (pronounced Rek-a-bite) is a member of a society devoted to the total abstinence of intoxicating liquors; it was founded in England in 1835. (www.thefreedictionary.com/Rechabite)

Edmund Ashworth and wife Charlotte Pollard
(Photo courtesy of the York Residency Museum 2020)

The Pollards

Pollard Family Line

POLLARD FAMILY LINE

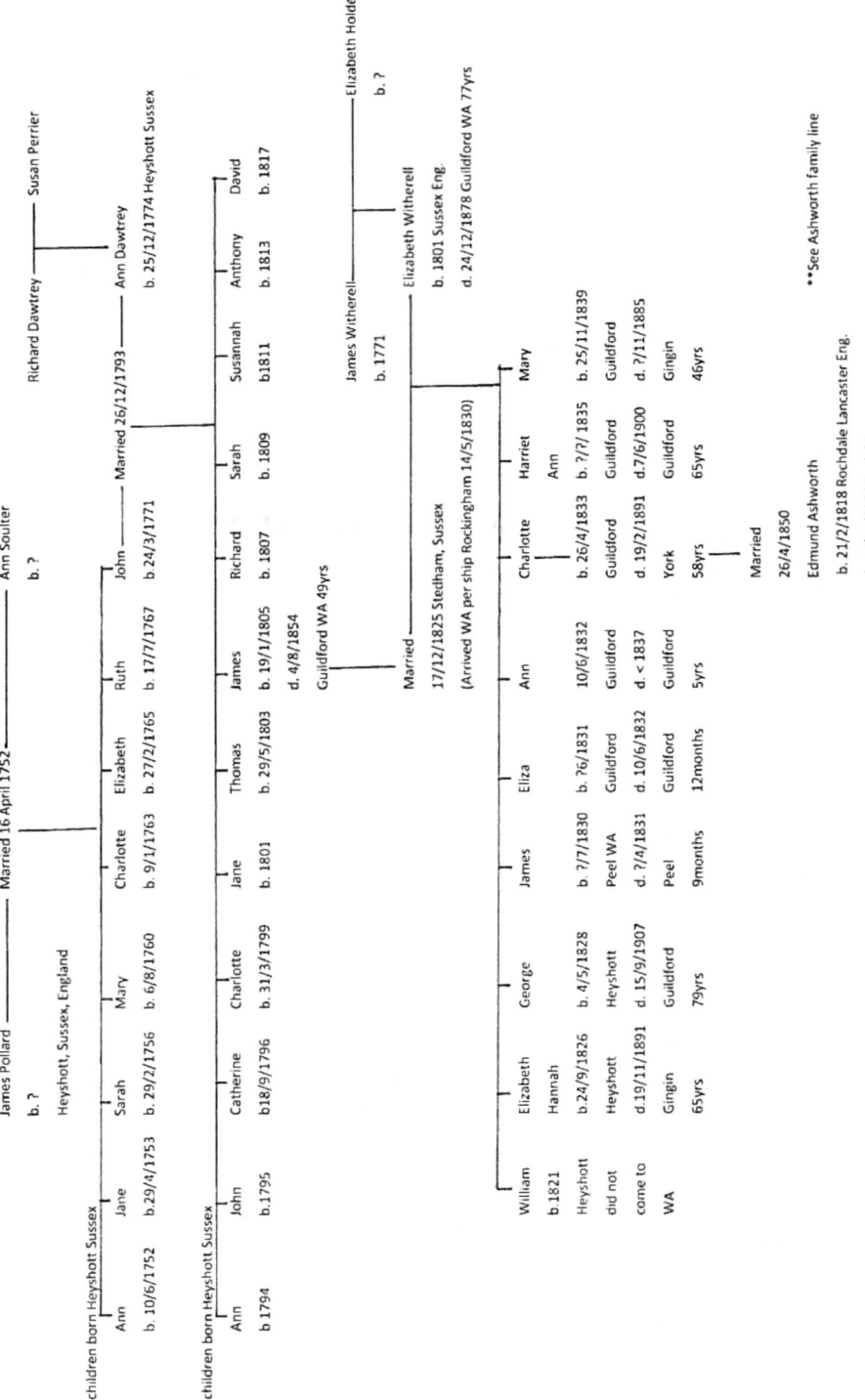

Edmund Ashworth's wife
Charlotte Pollard

Charlotte Pollard was born on the 26th April, 1833 in the very newly settled Swan River Colony which had its beginning only four years earlier. She died in York on 19th February, 1891, aged only 57, when their daughter, Sarah (McGlinn), was thirty-one years old. She was one of the first generation of non-indigenous Australian children to be born in Western Australia.

Her parents were free settlers and were farmers. Charlotte spent her childhood in Guildford, Western Australia. Unless Charlotte's parents were literate it is unlikely she was formally educated. There were very few schools (probably no schools) in the colony at that time and people's energy was taken up just surviving, and girls were not considered to require an education. She met Edmund Ashworth in Guildford when she was quite young and married him when she was only seventeen years old – and he was thirty-two. On their marriage certificate she signed her name in full which indicates by that time she was literate.

Charlotte's parents
James Pollard and Elizabeth Witherell

Charlotte's father, James Pollard, was born in the Chichester District of West Heyshott, Sussex, England on 9th January, 1805 and died in Guildford, Western Australia on 4th August 1854, aged 49, from *"Inflammation of the brain"* (https://www.wa.gov.au/organisation/department-of-justice/the-registry-of-births-deaths-and-marriages) four years after Charlotte's and Edmund's marriage. His death certificate stated that he was a Yeoman, meaning a person who was the owner of a small freehold block of land that he farmed.

Charlotte's mother, Elizabeth Witherell, was born in 1801 in Sussex, England and died in Gingin, Western Australia on 24th December, 1878, aged 77. After James' death, she married George Ruddock in 1857.

(https://www.wa.gov.au/organisation/department-of-justice/the-registry-of-births-deaths-and-marriages)

George lived in Wexcombe, Western Australia. Wexcombe was a nearby locality to Guildford and is now known as Stratton, a suburb in the Shire of Swan. Her death record in Births, Deaths and Marriages incorrectly shows her name as Elizabeth Rudrick.

James Pollard and Elizabeth Witherell were married on 7th December 1825. He was twenty and she was twenty-four years old. They had three children prior to coming to Western Australia and six after their arrival. Charlotte was their seventh child.

James and Elizabeth arrived in the Swan River colony on 14th May 1830 on board the sailing ship *Rockingham*. On board were twenty-five crew and 177 free settlers. The Pollards travelled in Steerage Class, a crowded and uncomfortable way to travel. The first fleet of settlers had only arrived in Western Australia in June 1829, eleven months earlier. After the long journey, the ship that belonged to Thomas Peel sailed into Cockburn Sound. Peel, unwisely, insisted the settlers and cargo be brought ashore immediately despite the worsening weather. The *Rockingham* was close to shore when a huge storm with crashing waves and freezing gale force winds blew up during the night. The crew couldn't control the ship, which foundered and was washed ashore. The ship's capstan broke due to the strain, the rudder was damaged and the strong winds drove the little sailing ship broadside onto the beach. Fortunately, no lives were lost and the passengers, including over fifty children, were able to be landed in the huge surf. The passengers were taken ashore but all their possessions to start a new life in the colony were lost. The location in which the ship initially foundered became known as Rockingham.

As the storm raged it would have been terrifying for the passengers. It must have been extraordinarily difficult for the Pollards at that moment. Elizabeth was heavily pregnant and had her two small children, aged three and two, to protect during this terrible and frightening time with the howling wind, raging surf, and being tossed and thrown about on the stricken ship. Once ashore, they had absolutley nothing for the children, who were soaking wet and freezing. They had no extra clothing for any of them, no bedding, no food and no shelter.

The family were now about to experience extreme hardship. "A period of semi-starvation followed. A wooden house had been thrown overboard from the ship during the storm and was secured and erected to accommodate some of the stranded migrants. The remainder had to find cover at night as best they could … but when winter came the weaker ones died from exposure and the lack of bare necessities of life." HAMMOND, J.E. Western Pioneers : the battle well fought. (Facsimile edition Hesperian Press, 1980) p. 170.

The ship "Rockingham" being blown ashore in Cockburn Sound.
SHARDLOW, R.H. The Ship Rockingham. (Shire of Rockingham (no date)) p. 3.

On the 2nd July, only two weeks after the wreck, and in mid winter, Elizabeth gave birth to their son James under these very primitive, trying and cold conditions. Sadly, baby James died nine months later.

James Pollard was a poverty-stricken farm labourer back in Sussex, as were most of the rural people in England at the time, and was contracted to work for Thomas Peel for a period of about one year as an indentured labourer after he arrived in Australia. Unfortunately, Peel was a victim of his own incredible greed and, as the colony was keen to get new settlers, it sent out a notice saying that anyone bringing people into the colony was entitled to 200 acres per indentured labourer over the age of nine years. Peel brought out enough people for him to be given over 250,000 acres! Of course, he couldn't possibly have supported these people without housing, food and tools for them to sustain themselves, let alone make money from the poor quality farm land he had. Governor Stirling found the situation to be dismal and allowed the settlers to leave their contract to Peel and go to Perth to work. Soon afterwards, in 1832, the notice was rescinded and no one could get the amount of land promised.

In order for the people to leave the 'Peel' settlement, the settlers had to build a boat and go by sea to Fremantle. There were no roads from "Rockingham", or anywhere else at that time, so going by sea was their only option.

James Pollard and his family were among those who left, and he went to work for Major William Nairn, who had property along the Canning River. James worked there for a short time to fulfil his contract before moving to Guildford to work and eventually was granted a small holding to farm.

James and Elizabeth had nine children altogether; three were born in England. Their eldest son, William, either died there or did not come to Australia. He was born in 1821, well before James' and Elizabeth's marriage. James was only sixteen when William was born and Elizabeth was twenty but James had probably been working since he was nine years old so would have been considered an experienced man by sixteen. After the death of baby James in the Peel settlement, the next two children born in the colony were girls. Tragically, both of these girls also died. The first, Eliza, died on or around the day Elizabeth gave birth to her next child, Ann in June 1832. Sadly, Ann also died at about five years of age. Charlotte Pollard was the fourth of their children to be born in Western Australia. She and the later three girls all survived well into adulthood.

Early colonial life was very difficult for the new settlers and there were shortages of just about everything until trade was in place for food and goods to be delivered, particularly from Tasmania where the population had had time to get their farming practices and businesses in order. Within a few years, crops and farm animals could sustain the growing colony but some items were in short supply because there was still no industry nor manufacturing. A letter to England from a woman named Jane Dodds, a shop keeper in the early Swan River Settlement in 1832, stated that there was a great need for personal items such as *"Men's canvass trousers and frocks ... blue and red striped shirts, shoes ... green canvass for windows (we do without glass), green coarse gauze for mosquitoes, caps, dark coloured stuff for women's dresses... coloured cotton hose for men ... small common parasols (those of green cotton are good enough ... there has not been a single good dark printed cotton sent into the Colony" Swan River Letters* – Part 1. Ian Berryman, ed. (Swan River Press, 2002) p. 236. However, there was great positivity among the people who were willing to work hard to make a success of their lives.

The Pollards were among these positive hardworking people and they became successful in their undertakings. Some descendants remained in Guildford until modern times.

James Pollard and Elizabeth Witherell's parents

James Pollard's father was John Pollard and his mother was Ann Dawtry, both born in Heyshott, Sussex, England. They had twelve children, six girls and six boys. James was their seventh child.

Elizabeth's parents were James Witherell and Elizabeth Holder, both born in Heyshott, Sussex.

The Gawneds

Gawned Family Line

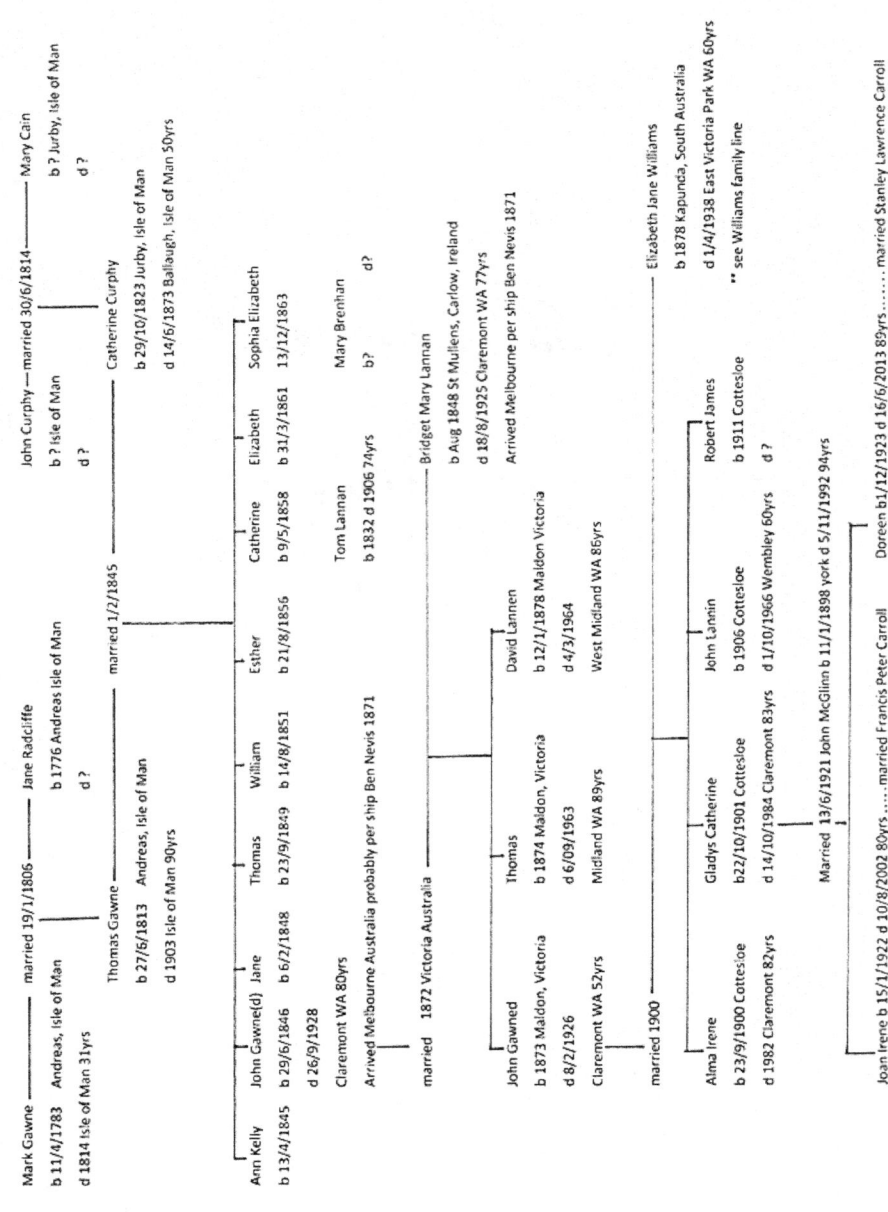

Doreen McGlinn's mother
Gladys Catherine Gawned

Gladys Catherine Gawned was born on 22nd October, 1901 in Cottesloe, Western Australia and died on 14th October, 1984, aged 83, in Claremont, Western Australia.

Apart from spending a short period of her childhood in Kalgoorlie around 1910, she lived in Cottesloe and Claremont, Western Australia. Gladys was educated at Cottesloe School and, on the completion of her schooling at the age of fifteen, she became an apprentice Seamstress Dressmaker, and no doubt helped her mother and grandmother in their boarding house businesses.

In Gladys's youth, women still had to make their own clothes and those of their children, or if you were well off you could have them made for you. Off the rack clothing for women was yet to become popular, but they were now available, in limited supply in shops. Dressmaking, tailoring, and being a milliner (hat maker) were large employing industries, along with boot and shoe making. Most clothes and shoes were sewn and made by hand. Visiting the draper's shop to buy fabric and haberdashery, such as buttons and trimmings, was a special and important event. The drapers' shops were full of all sorts of fabrics to make clothes, curtains, and bed clothes and, as can be seen on page 200, in those days men dominated behind the counter. Drapery and haberdashery were big business.

Dressmakers and tailors would inspect the bolts of fabric that were presented to them by an experienced draper. It was very serious and time consuming, and people could not be wasteful. Their choices in fabrics were important.

However, times were changing for the professional dressmakers and tailors of the day. The newly invented sewing machine for home use was making it easier and more time-efficient for women to make their own clothing at home.

In addition, paper patterns for simple clothing were sold to the home market to help with making stylish clothes at home by untrained women. Drapers became even busier as home dressmaking boomed. The time it took to make clothes was drastically reduced from the time-consuming hand-sewn items; now the wardrobe of just a few items of clothing expanded and there was no longer the one good outfit; now there could be multiple outfits for all occasions.

The Draper's shop 1918.
(In Old Kalgoorlie; the photographs of J. J. Dwyer. Pasco, R. WA Museum, 2010. p.143)

Newly invented hand driven sewing machine for the home.
Photo (www. bing.com/images) 2021

When World War I began, Gladys Catherine was only thirteen years old and she would have been exposed to the high anxiety of the population with the men leaving in great numbers to fight overseas and a great many of them not returning, or returning wounded or with "shell shock", Post Traumatic Stress Disorder as it later became known. She would have also seen that this war caused a very unusual situation for women because now they had to go and do the men's work while the soldiers were away fighting. A thing that was unheard of before the war! What was deemed as impossible for women to do suddenly became the norm!

This new work changed what women were prepared to wear. No longer would they put up with clothing that impeded their work by wearing the long bulky and heavy Victorian dresses that were underpinned by a severe corset to keep the waist thin, and the many petticoats. Shorter, lightweight dresses were becoming popular and hair fashions changed from the severe plastered down styles to the softer and more flattering styles.

The new softer and more comfortable clothing for women brought about during WWI (www.bing.com/images) 2021

Trousers too were becoming more acceptable for women's wear – certainly a shock to the previous generation and absolutely frowned upon.

Gladys left school towards the end of the war and her new dressmaking skills allowed her to become an elegant and stylish young woman in this new era of clothing. No doubt her mother and grandmother would have disapproved of this 'immodest' clothing! But, as with each generation, the times were changing. In addition to the change in clothing, women's makeup also changed. *"Makeup became more established during the war. Maybelline started in 1915, and it coincided with makeup … becoming more acceptable, particularly as working-class women … could now afford it. Powder, kohl eyeliner and mascara were popular... Body hair was on its way out. Women's uniforms had shorter skirts than were customary in 1914 – they were now at six to 10 inches off the ground. The reveal of a bit of leg was part of the change in perception of body hair, from something erotic to something unsightly. Gilette introduced Milady Decolletee razors in 1915. Shaving legs became part of standard female grooming".* (www.theguardian.com/fashion)

Gladys Catherine Gawned prior to her marriage in 1921 (Family photo)

By the time the war ended in 1918 Gladys Catherine had entered a new age for women. She had already met her future husband, John McGlinn, and was now seventeen years old and a young working woman. She was a happy friendly girl who enjoyed the company of others. She mixed easily but had a stubborn streak and, as she got older, she expected certain prim behaviour from others and was quite prim herself in her outlook. Her mother's and grandmother's expectations had rubbed off on her.

The Williams

Williams Family Line

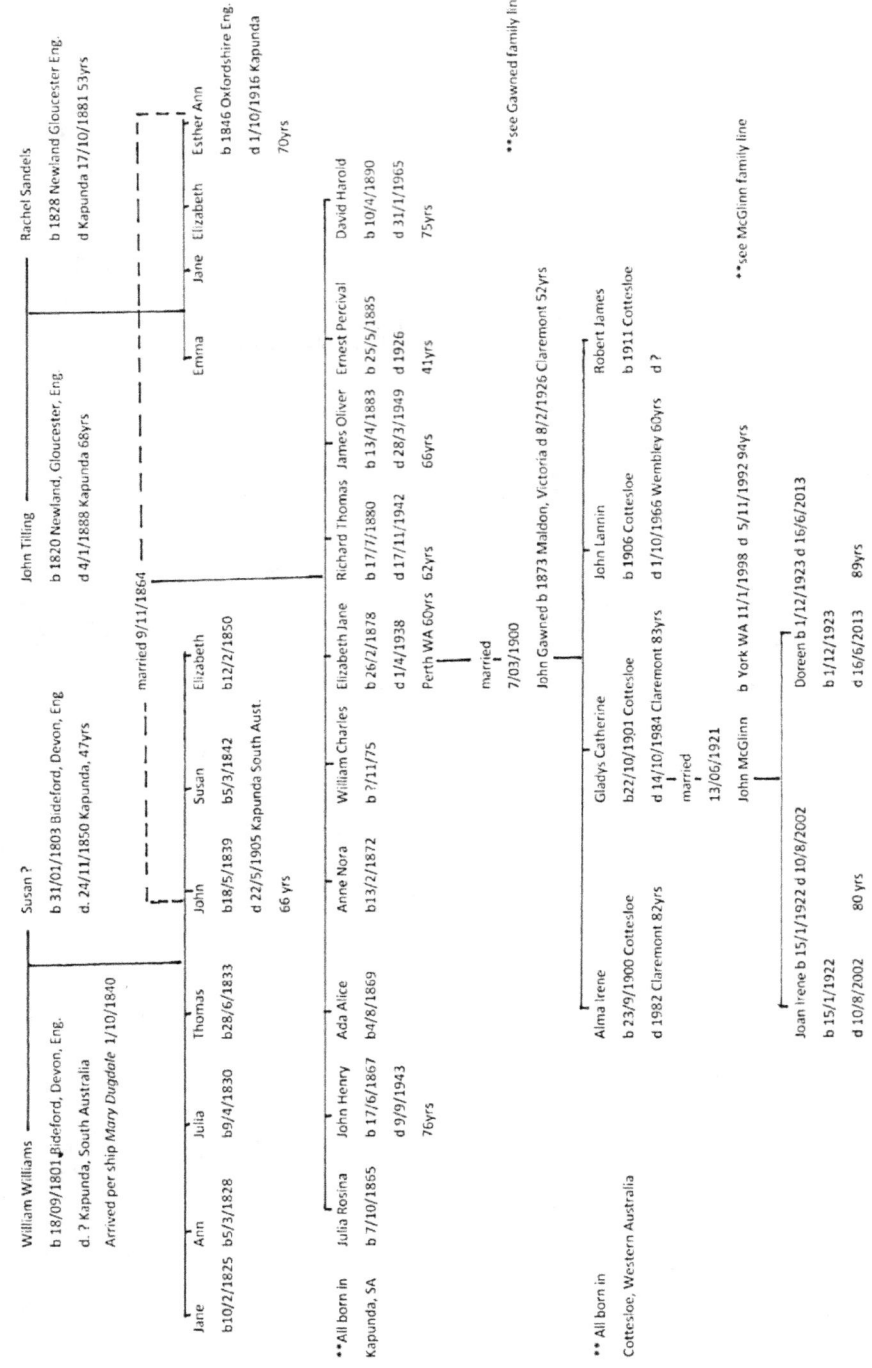

Gladys Catherine's mother
Elizabeth Jane Williams

Elizabeth Jane Williams (also known as Joan) was born in Kapunda, South Australia, on 26th February, 1878 and died tragically in a road accident in Victoria Park, Western Australia, on 1st April 1938, aged 60. Kapunda is a small town approximately 70km north of Adelaide, and was the site of the discovery of copper in 1842.

Elizabeth Jane Williams in her hand-sewn clothing (Family photo)

The reason for Elizabeth Jane moving to Western Australia is a mystery. She was engaged to be married so she may have accompanied her fiancé to Western Australia. On her marriage certificate, her occupation was stated as being a nurse so she may have had better employment opportunities in the booming Western Australia.

Note the fashionable corseted prim late Victorian clothing she is wearing. A beautiful, but uncomfortable outfit that she probably made herself.

Elizabeth Jane's father
John Williams

John Williams was born on 18th May, 1839 in Bideford, Devon, England and arrived with his parents in Australia at the age of about four and a half months. He died in Kapunda, South Australia on 22nd May, 1905, aged 66.

The family were free settlers and probably came to South Australia with the promise of new opportunities in farming. No convicts were sent to South Australia and migrants were encouraged to come and settle and farm there. Perhaps the family went to live in Kapunda, South Australia to farm in that region. Later, John was employed as a miner, presumably in the copper mines. He married Esther Ann Tilling on 9th November, 1864 and they had ten children – six boys and four girls. Elizabeth Jane was their sixth child. Both Esther Ann and John were illiterate; on their marriage certificate each of them signed their name with an 'X'.

John's parents
William Williams and Susan Williams

William Williams was born in Bideford, Devon, England on 18th September, 1801 and presumably died in Kapunda, South Australia, date unknown.

Susan Williams (unknown maiden name) was born in Bideford, Devon, on 31st January, 1803 and died in Kapunda on 24th November, 1850, aged only 47 years. She died when her youngest child was only eleven months old, leaving William to bring up the children alone. Fortunately, there were several daughters old enough to take care of the younger children.

The town of Bideford in Devon is a historic and very busy port town on the estuary of the River Torridge in north Devon, south-west England.

William and Susan, and their five children, arrived in Australia on 1st October, 1840 on the ship *Mary Dugdale*. They went on to have two more daughters in Australia.

Elizabeth Jane's mother
Esther Ann Tilling

Esther Ann Tilling was born in Chipping Norton, Oxfordshire, England in 1846 and came to Australia with her parents and three older sisters. She died in Kapunda on 1st October, 1916, aged 70. World War I was in progress and she too would have experienced the general trauma of war.

Esther Anne's parents
John Tilling and Rachel Sandels

John and Rachel originated in Newland, Gloucester, England and must have moved to Oxfordshire before leaving England for a better life in Australia. John was born in 1820 and died in Kapunda on 4th January, 1888, aged 68. Rachel was born in 1828 and died in Kapunda on 17th October, 1881, aged 53.

Gladys Catherine's father
John Gawned

John Gawned was born in Maldon, Victoria on 12th May, 1873 and died in Fremantle Hospital on 8th February, 1926, aged only 52, after a long illness. He had cancer of the colon with secondaries throughout his body.

John's early life is not known but in January, 1897 at the age of twenty-three, he came to Western Australia on the ship *Bulimba*. He immediately secured a job with the Western Australian Government Railways, firstly as porter at Cottesloe Station then signalman at various stations, including Cottesloe Beach, North Fremantle, Fremantle and Perth.

It is not known how John Gawned and Elizabeth Jane Williams met but it might have been during the time she worked in the home of the Mills family of the famous Mills and Wares biscuit and cake making company in Cottesloe. The company was founded by William Mills and Henry Ware in 1898 and these men would have been extremely busy establishing their new company. Elizabeth Jane may have been hired to care for William Mills and his family and she may have been nurse to their children. Elizabeth Jane became extraordinarily good at making the most beautiful home-made cakes and biscuits and she passed this skill on to her daughters. She and John Gawned lived in the same vicinity so it is likely they met at a social event or even on the railway station.

Whatever the reason, they met, courted, and married in Fremantle on 7th March, 1900. She was twenty-three and he was twenty-seven years old. They had four children, Alma Irene, Gladys Catherine, John Lannin, and Robert James. All were born in Cottesloe, Western Australia.

In January, 1909, he and Elizabeth Jane and their three children at that time, moved to Kalgoorlie into a house near the railway at 138 Forrest Street. He secured the job of 1st Class Signalman but not long after arriving in Kalgoorlie, things started to go bad for John; he began making mistakes in his job and was cautioned a couple of times. The dreadful heat in Kalgoorlie during summer may have been a problem for the family and his health was failing so he requested a transfer back to Perth.

John Gawned 1900 (family photo)

In March, 1910 the family moved back to Perth where John worked at Perth Railway Station in the demoted position of 2nd Class Signalman. He went back to Kalgoorlie for a short while to sell their furniture. He advertised to sell everything.

> *"Mr. J. Gawned to sell all his HOUSEHOLD FURNITURE -- 1 Sideboard (bev. glass) 1 Oak Ex. Table, 6 A.B. Chairs 1 Rocker, 1 Chiffonier, 2 Tables 1 Rocking Horse. 2. Double Bedsteads 1 Duchesse Chest, 1 Washstand and Ware, 1 Sup. Child s Cot, 1 Cane Chair. 1- 8-day Clock, Lino, Crockery, Tubs, Cooking Utensils, Safe, Curtains, and Sundries. NO RESERVE. WEDNESDAY, 1st. JUNE. At H. D. PELL & O.O. SMART"* Kalgoorlie Miner. (Mon 30 May 1910) p. 7.

On his return to Perth, he requested a transfer closer to home at Cottesloe Station, but as a consequence he got a significant drop in pay and worked as Head Porter for a short time. *Railway records,* (https://slwa.wa.gov.au/eresources) 2021)

Not long after the family returned from Kalgoorlie, they had their last child, Robert James, in 1911. Sadly, when Robert James was a toddler, John Gawned was playing with him by throwing him into the air and catching him. This was a good game until, for whatever reason, John missed catching him and the child fell to the floor sustaining a lifelong brain injury that was debilitating but not severe. No doubt poor John felt a lifetime of guilt from this accident. John may have suffered weakness due to his illness and this may have been the reason for the accident.

His health was failing and it wasn't long before he could no longer work. Elizabeth Jane now had to support the family and, with the help of John's mother Bridget Mary, she managed to help the family survive. It took John another sixteen years of illness for him to pass away. It was a long, drawn-out life of pain and sickness. As his health failed, John and Elizabeth Jane became more involved with his mother, Bridget Mary's, businesses. He knew Elizabeth Jane would be alright with her help after he died. There were still no benefits for widows and she would have to survive on her own merits.

John Gawned's father
John (snr) Gawned

John (snr) was born in Ramsay, in the Isle of Man, on 29th June, 1846, during the time of the terrible European Famine, and died in Claremont, Western Australia on 26th September, 1926, aged 80. His family lived in Andreas and their surname was GAWNE. Apparently, when John (snr) arrived in Australia (some say he jumped ship), he adopted the name GAWNED and went to live in Maldon, Victoria. On his marriage certificate, he states his occupation was a Carter – that is someone who drove a horse and cart and transported goods. It is probable that he carted goods between Melbourne and Maldon.

John (snr's) parents
Thomas Gawne and Catherine Curphy

Thomas Gawne, was born in Andreas, Isle of Man, on 27th June, 1813 and died there in 1903, aged 90.

When Thomas was old enough, he went to work as a labourer on the wealthy Dhowin farm, which is just north of Andreas. The farm employed several people as labourers, farm hands, and servants. Thomas was allocated six acres of that farm to work and was paid for his work. He met his wife, Catherine Curphy, on Dhowin farm where she too was employed, probably as a servant or dairy maid.

Catherine was born in nearby Jurby, which is west of Andreas, on 29th October, 1823 and died there in 1883, aged 59.

Thomas and Catherine married on 1st February, 1845 in Andreas. He was thirty-two and she was twenty-two years old. They had nine children, three boys and six girls. John (snr) was their second child and eldest son. They too were victims of the famine that raged in Europe. The farm failed and famine gripped the land. Thomas and Catherine had to leave the farm and went to live in Andreas where Thomas took up the trade of boot and shoe maker.

It seems John (snr) didn't want to stay in the Isle of Man – perhaps there was no future for him there and the famine would have been having a very negative effect on the family. Agriculture was failing and things were very tough on the land and elsewhere. It might not have been viable for him to stay because there was no work. He went to sea and worked on a ship.

Thomas Gawne's parents
Mark Gawne and Jane Radcliffe

Thomas's parents were also born in Andreas, Isle of Man. Thomas's father's name was Mark Gawne and he was born on 11th April 1783. He married Jane Radcliffe on 19th January, 1803. Jane was born in the Isle of Man in 1776. She was seven years older than Mark.

John Gawned's mother
Bridget Mary Lannan

Bridget Mary Lannan (also known as Mary) was born in St Mullen's, Carlow, Ireland on about 6th August, 1848, during the great famine, and died in Claremont, Western Australia on 18th August, 1925, aged 77. Her story may be similar to that of Jane (Walshe) Carroll. She became known by Lann<u>e</u>n in Australia. Her son David's middle name is <u>Lannan</u>, and her grandson, John's middle name is <u>Lannin</u>. On her marriage record, she is noted as Bridget Lannen and her occupation was Domestic Servant.

Bridget Mary Lannan was twenty-three when she travelled to Melbourne, Australia in 1871 on the sailing ship *Ben Nevis*. On board were many single women being brought to Australia to fill the need for servants in the flourishing colony. The shipping records stated that she was a servant. It is highly suspected that John (snr) Gawne was a crew member of that ship and they met on board. There were strict rules on these ships and fraternization was discouraged and often the girls were banned from talking to the crew, but many got to know some crew members intimately. When the ship docked and Bridget Mary was to leave to go to the official quarters set aside for the incoming girls, John (snr) may have decided to jump ship to be with her. It is probable they wanted to disappear so went to the busy inland goldfield's town of Maldon in Victoria. It may have been at this stage John (snr) added the <u>D</u> to the end of his name and became John Gawned and Bridget Mary's name changed from Lannan to Lannen. Their marriage record states they were married in Maldon on the 6th July, 1872. He was twenty-six and she was twenty-four years old and they were both literate.

On Bridget Mary's marriage certificate, she put her parents as Michael Lannen and Christine Murphy and that they were farmers.

John (snr) and Bridget Mary only had three children, a small family for those days, all boys, John, Thomas Collyn, and David Lannan, all of whom were born in Maldon, Victoria.

When their eldest son, John travelled to Fremantle in Western Australia in January, 1897, there was great unemployment in Victoria and times were tough so a new start may have been necessary. He may have told them of the rich gold finds in the eastern goldfields of Western Australia so, with nothing to lose, they too moved west. It seems they did not go straight to Perth as John had done. They, like thousands of others, went to Kalgoorlie and, like the Carroll brothers, they travelled by ship to Albany and went to the Kalgoorlie goldfields, possibly via the

Holland Track.

However, their stay in Kalgoorlie lasted for only a matter of months and they may have been disillusioned by the crowded, hot, dusty town and there may have been few decent jobs available to them. There are Western Australian Government Railway records that show John (snr), and his sons David Lannan and Thomas Collyn worked for the government railways in Kalgoorlie from about July to December 1899. The blistering heat would have set in by December and they were probably not used to it. They wouldn't have experienced this heat before and it may have been too much to bear, so they decided to leave and go to Perth. Another reason for leaving Kalgoorlie may have been to attend their son John and Elizabeth Jane's wedding in March 1900.

After they arrived in Perth in early 1900, Bridget Mary didn't waste time in establishing a boarding and lodging house in Forrest Street, Cottesloe. By this time, the Claremont Power Station had finished being built and, fortunately for the family, in 1901 they would have been connected to electricity. This would have made life so much easier by not having to light and use the fuel-based pressure lamps and 'hurricane' lamps. Illumination of the house would have meant they could just flick a switch and the room would be lit up. What a change!

Soon after establishing the boarding house, Bridget Mary advertised for a "respectable" girl to assist in doing the housework. Then, in August that year, she placed an advertisement in the newspaper to sell the boarding house. The advertisement is as follows.

> *"BOARDING HOUSE for Sale, near station, good position, eight permanent boarders. Apply Mrs. Gawned, Forrest Street, Cottesloe."* The West Australian (Tue 28 Aug 1900) p. 8.

Bridget Mary certainly had an eye for where her businesses were going to be successful and she ensured there was public transport close by for her tenants. The Forrest Street boarding house was close to the railway station and close to the popular Cottesloe beach where crowds would gather on hot days, even though it wasn't considered as being 'nice' to swim because the prim Victorian era was still in vogue and modesty wouldn't allow it.

Forrest Street Cottesloe in 1915. Electricity was now well established in the suburbs (www.cottesloehistory.wordpress.com)

After they sold the boarding house, in about 1903, they moved to John Street, Cottesloe, before moving again in 1906 to where Bridget Mary bought a new business and applied for a license to operate in the Cottesloe Hall (Wells Hall) which was an entertainment precinct for dances, theatre, and restaurants. The hall was on the busy corner of Leake Street and the Perth Fremantle Road, (renamed in 1930 to Stirling Highway), Peppermint Grove, where the Cottesloe Central Shopping Centre now stands. As can be seen from the following newspaper article, the Cottesloe Hall must have been a popular and lively place prior to Bridget Mary entering into a business there. An advertisement in the newspaper in 1897 about the new hall stated the following:

> *"COTTESLOE HALL. Arrangements have been made for the holding of a series of entertainments in the Cottesloe Hall. These*

will include caf concerts and dances, with refreshments provided. The originator of them, Mr Tottenham, seems to have considered his preparations sufficiently well to command success. The return railway fare, from the city will be 1s (one shilling), and from Fremantle 6d. (six pence)" The West Australian, (Sat 11 Dec 1897) p. 5.

Bridget Mary lodged an application to begin a business there and her advertisement was placed in the newspaper in 1906.

"APPLICATION for an EATING, BOARDING, and LODGING HOUSE LICENCE. To the Worshipful the Justices of the Peace acting in and for the District of Perth, in Western Australia. I, MARY GAWNED, Restaurant keeper now residing at Perth-Fremantle road, Cottesloe, in the District of Perth, do hereby give notice that it is my intention to APPLY at the next Licensing Meeting to be held for this district for an Eating, Boarding, and Lodging House LICENCE, in the shop or rooms which I now occupy, or intend to occupy, situated at Perth-Fremantle-road, Cottesloe, and being part of Cottesloe Hall, now held under a temporary licence. Given under my hand this 14th day of May, one thousand nine hundred and six. MARY GAWNED" The West Australian, (Sat 26 May 1906) p. 5.

Wells Hall / Cottesloe Hall behind the Cottesloe theatre
(www.peppermintgrove.wordpress.com)

Bridget Mary's tea rooms and restaurant were where the Milk Bar is situated and the boarding rooms were above the shop and theatre as shown in the above photo. Inside the hall was the Boronia Lodge, the one to which John (snr), and later his son John, and John McGlinn belonged, and the same one that helped Elizabeth Jane during her husband's illness and funeral. Apparently, John (snr) spent a lot of time hanging around in the Lodge and not doing a lot of anything else! (personal comment Joy Anderson/Gawned). John (snr) became the senior caretaker of the Cottesloe Hall when Bridget Mary had her business there, between 1907 and 1912.

Many of the women in the Gawned's extended family went to stay with Bridget Mary for the later stages of their pregnancy and she assisted with the births of their children. She must have been a very capable and remarkable woman. Elizabeth Jane would have had her children with the aid of Bridget Mary. In those days, home births were common.

The business in the Cottesloe Hall may have been getting a bit much for her to handle, and even though Elizabeth Jane helped out, it was sold. In about 1912, when Bridget Mary was aged sixty-four and John (snr) sixty-six, they moved to a new smaller business, the Claremont Café in Bay View Terrace, Claremont. She kept a few rooms in this building for boarders. They operated this business until about 1920 when they retired. John (snr) was seventy-four and Bridget Mary was seventy-two years old. Cafés in those days were more restaurant than café as they are known today and Bridget Mary hired women to work there. They then moved in with son John and Elizabeth Jane who were living in Divers Street, Claremont. Divers Street was where the "Claremont Quarter" is today. It no longer exists but there is a Divers Link which no doubt was where the street was. In about 1925, Elizabeth Jane bought the boarding house *Woodlands*, which was situated on the north side of St Quentin's Avenue, Claremont. Eventually, they all moved in there. The block on which the boarding house stood ran between St Quentin's Avenue and O'Beirne Street where the shopping precinct now stands. They lived in the house at 25 O'Beirne Street that backed onto the boarding house in St Quentin's Avenue. Interestingly, the big apartment complex on the western end of St Quentin Avenue is called *Woodlands*, possibly named after the boarding house. John (snr) became 'famous' in Claremont; he had the reputation of being the "Biggest man in Claremont" – he was very tall and well built.

Possibly the John Street house with the family and perhaps tenants – about 1903 Left to right, Joe Rule, Unknown, Unknown, David Lannan Gawned, David's wife Rachael, Thomas Collyn Gawned, John Gawned (snr), Bridget Mary Gawned, Unknown, John Gawned, Elizabeth Jane Gawned, (Photo – Joy Anderson /Gawned)

Possibly the Divers Street house, Claremont, post WWI, approximately 1919. Back row: John Gawned, Alma Irene, John McGlinn, Elizabeth Jane, Gladys Catherine, Joe Rule. Front row – John Lannin, John (snr), Robert James, Bridget Mary. (Photo – Joy Anderson/Gawned)

In the photo above, it can be seen how thin and gaunt John McGlinn looks after returning from WWI. He looks much older than his twenty-one years.

Bay View Terrace, Claremont (looking towards Stirling Highway) The Dining Rooms on the left side of the street was the Claremont Café belonging to Bridget Mary and John (snr). (Simon Neville. Perth and Fremantle Past and Present. (Simon Neville Publications (no date)) p. 101.

Claremont Railway Station where John McGlinn worked – opposite Bay View Terrace, Claremont. Horse drawn taxis await train passengers. (Simon Neville. Perth and Fremantle Past and Present. (Simon Neville Publications (no date)) p. 100.

In the two Gawned family photographs on page 217, there is a man named Joe Rule. There is a story that comes with his being in all the photos. Joe was a close friend of the family – perhaps he was adopted by Bridget Mary along the way and he became good friends with son John. He was born in Victoria and might have known the Gawned family then. He stayed with the Gawneds prior to, and after World War I. At forty-four years of age, he enlisted to go to war and was assigned to the 44th AIF Battalion that fought on the Western Front. In October 1917 his battalion *"fought around Broodseinde Ridge, where it suffered heavily – out of 992 men committed, only 158 finished the battle uninjured"*.

(https://en.wikipedia.org/wiki/44th_Battalion_(Australia)

Joe was badly gassed. Chlorine, phosgene and mustard gas poisoning were terrible things. When the men were exposed to it, they screamed for water as their throats and lungs burnt. Many went blind and their skin blistered and hung from their bodies. They spat up blood and struggled for oxygen and some men begged to be shot. Joe was sent to England then sent home to Australia as medically unfit to serve any longer. His lungs were in a bad way and he could no longer do the labouring work he did prior to the war. He was cared for by Bridget Mary. He must have lived with the family in their boarding houses.

Bridget Mary and John (snr) lived into their old age with son John and Elizabeth Jane. Bridget Mary died in 1925, aged seventy-seven – probably from exhaustion – and then son John died nine months later, aged only fifty-two. Joe Rule and John (snr) were then cared for by poor Elizabeth Jane. Joe Rule wanted to marry Elizabeth Jane but she refused and who can blame her; she must have been exhausted and she'd surely had had enough of looking after people and didn't want to take on another invalid. However, he continued to live with her, along with her 'invalid' son Robert James, in her boarding house, *Woodlands*. John (snr) died seven months after John in 1926, aged eighty. This must have been a very tough and sad time for Elizabeth Jane losing her husband and parents in-law in the space of only one year.

The death notices for Bridget Mary, John and John (snr) were in the newspapers and are shown below…

Bridget Mary's death notice

"GAWNED. -- The Friends of the late Mrs. Mary Gawned, of O Beirne Street, Claremont, dearly beloved wife of John Gawned, senior and loving mother of John, Thomas, and David, are respectfully invited to follow her remains to the place of interment, the Congregational Cemetery, Karrakatta. The Funeral is appointed to leave her late residence, O Beirne-street, Claremont, at 10.45 o clock THIS (Thursday) MORNING, per road. Friends wishing to attend

the Funeral may proceed by the 11 a.m. trains leaving Perth and Fremantle". *The West Australian* (Perth, WA : 1879 - 1954) (Thu 20 Aug 1925) p.1.

John Gawned's death notices

"GAWNED. -- On February 8, 1926, at Fremantle, John, dearly beloved husband of Mrs. E. J. Gawned, of O Bierne-street, Claremont, loving father of Alma, Gladys, John and Robert; aged 52 years. A patient sufferer at rest. Asleep with Jesus.

GAWNED. -- On February 8, at Fremantle Hospital, John, eldest son of John and the late Mary Gawned, dearly beloved husband of Elizabeth, father of Alma (Mrs. J. T. Cavanagh), Gladys (Mrs. J. McGlinn), John and Robert, brother of Thomas and David, grandfather of Joan, Doreen and Leonard; aged 52 years. A patient sufferer at rest." Family Notices *The West Australian* (Perth, WA : 1879 - 1954) (Tue 9 Feb 1926) p. 1.

John Gawned (snr's) death notice

"ARTHUR E. DAVIES and CO., Undertakers, Fremantle and Claremont. Tel. B225. GAWNED. -- The Friends of the late John Gawned, of Woodlands, St. Quentin-avenue, Claremont, loving father of Jack (deceased), Thomas and David, are respectfully invited to follow his remains to the place of interment, the Congregational Cemetery, Karrakatta. The Funeral is appointed to leave the Private Mortuary of Messrs. C. H. Smith and Co., 281 Newcastle-street, Perth, at 2.15 o clock THIS (Monday) AFTERNOON, per road. Friends wishing to attend the Funeral may proceed by the 3 p.m. train leaving Perth". *The West Australian* (Perth, WA : 1879 - 1954) (Mon 27 Sep 1926) p. 1.

Elizabeth Jane stayed and continued to live and work for another ten years in the O'Beirne Street residence and the St Quentin Avenue *Woodlands* boarding house until 1936 before selling up and buying a shop at 46 Cargill Street, Victoria Park, in 1937. She is listed on the Australia Electoral Roll as a "business proprietor" along with her son John Lannin Gawned "shop assistant". Elizabeth Jane's invalid son, Robert James Gawned, who could not work, went with her. With the imminent sale of the boarding house, Joe Rule moved in with Elizabeth Jane's eldest daughter, Alma Irene. He wasn't with Alma Irene for long because he got married very soon afterwards, in 1936, at about the age of sixty-four, to

Pamela Ellis. He then returned to his birthplace, the gold mining town of Bendigo, Victoria and died there in 1955, aged eighty-three. He must have been well cared for!!

Joe Rule. (Photo Joy Anderson/Gawned)

Elizabeth Jane helped out in the Victoria Park shop and generally took care of the household and her two grandchildren, Fay and Joy. Her son John Lannin and his wife Hazel ran the shop.

In April 1938, she and Robert James went to the local shops on the Albany Road (now Albany Highway) and as she went to cross the road she was hit by a truck and tragically killed. She was only sixty years old and had had no time to rest and enjoy any free time; she had worked so very hard throughout her life. The newspaper article below described her death.

> *"WOMAN KILLED. Fatal Confusion in Traffic. Becoming confused in traffic when she was crossing Albany-road, Victoria Park, early last night, an elderly woman made a hurried backward movement and was knocked down and killed almost instantly by a utility truck. She was GAWNED, Mrs. Joan Elizabeth (60), of Cargill-street, Victoria Park. Mrs. Gawned was going towards the south side of the road in company with her son, Robert James Gawned. The son said after the accident that when they moved on to the road they noticed*

a motor vehicle approaching them but they had ample time to give it room to pass behind them. His mother, however, appeared to become confused by the approach of a tramcar and she stepped back two or three paces, right into the path of the vehicle, which was then almost level with them. An ambulance was summoned, but she died before she reached the Perth Hospital. The truck, which was travelling in an easterly direction, was driven by Reginald F. Howard, of Berwick-street, Victoria Park. Inquiries into the accident were made by Constables Beaton, McLaughlan and Eastwood". The West Australian (Perth, WA: 1879 - 1954) (Sat 2 Apr 1938) p. 19.

She died of a fractured skull. The family were heartbroken at the loss of this wonderful woman.

Her invalid son, Robert James Gawned, who before this time could not work, found a job and moved out of the shop and eventually married Mary Gill. The shop was run by Elizabeth Jane's son, John Lannin Gawned's wife, Hazel, for the duration of World War II, until he returned to Australia after being a prisoner of war in Germany. They then sold the shop and moved to a similar shop at 36 Grantham Street, Wembley, Western Australia. John Lannin Gawned was in the same Signals Corps, 2/11th Battalion as Stanley Lawrence Carroll! A small world!

The Wembley Shop, purchased after the sale of Elizabeth Jane's Cargill Street shop. It is of similar style. Left to right John Lannin Gawned's family – daughters Joy and Fay and wife Hazel. (Photo Joy Gawned/Anderson)

Doreen's parents
John McGlinn and Gladys Catherine Gawned

Their Marriage and Later Life

John McGlinn met Gladys Catherine Gawned in 1916 while he was staying at her grandmother, Bridget Mary's boarding rooms above the Claremont Café, in Bayview Terrace, Claremont. He was eighteen years old and she was fifteen and they met in the corridor outside his room. At that stage, he was working at the Claremont Railway Station and had met up with the local train driver, David Lannen Gawned, who told him to go see his mother Bridget Mary and she would give him a room. She put him up in a room out the back that he had to share with a 'rough type', as he put it, who scared the hell out of him. Later, she moved him to another room upstairs. He was just leaving his room one day when Gladys Catherine was in the corridor. They started a conversation which lasted the whole of their lives – they were attracted to each other immediately. He stayed with Bridget Mary for about four months and got to know Gladys Catherine well before he returned to York.

John's relationship with Gladys Catherine must have been intermittent and they would only have seen each other on his trips to Perth. World War I was in progress and no doubt the war would have been at the forefront of most conversations. John probably told them of the death of his brother, Ernest William, his cousin Christopher James, and that William Patrick Kett had died of illness. There would have been such sadness in his family and he would have received a lot of sympathy from Gladys Catherine's family. They were romantically attached at that stage and they may have corresponded, especially after John left to go to war. Letter writing was the only form of communication available to them.

When he returned from the war in 1919, it was a couple of years before he and Gladys Catherine married and it makes sense that their romance and courtship began in earnest after the war.

Poor John had seen the horrors of war, the killing, and the very hard times and would have grown up and become a man in a hurry. In the photo of the Gawned family at Divers Street, John looks drawn and aged – the war had affected him greatly. He would have become very worldly during military life and in the cities and bordellos of Egypt. On his return to Australia, he would have had to adjust to the ordinary day to day life of a returned soldier – something many of the returned servicemen found very difficult to do. Gladys Catherine would surely have been smitten by this very handsome and worldly young man.

The Wesley Church, Subiaco, where John and Gladys Catherine married in June, 1921
(Personal photo, 2021)

John McGlinn and Gladys Catherine Gawned – possibly on their wedding day
(Family photo)

After returning from the war, John got his job back with the railways and passed his "Fireman" exam in July, 1920 and was transferred to Brunswick Junction, 102 miles (164km) south of Perth in April 1921. John and Gladys Catherine's relationship blossomed and they married in the Wesley Church, Bagot Road, Subiaco, on 13th June, 1921. He was twenty-three years old and Gladys Catherine was nineteen. Gladys Catherine was seven months pregnant when they married which makes it possible that John was not able to make it back for a 'sudden' wedding. You couldn't just take time off in those days and he probably had to get permission to go to Perth.

Unfortunately, the spread of the railways was now slowing and railway jobs were diminishing. Staff were no longer required in the high numbers used during the expansions and it wasn't long before staff layoffs began. John was retrenched by the WAGR but telegraph lines were still in the process of following the rail lines so he got a job with the PMG at Brunswick Junction and worked further afield. He and Gladys Catherine rented a small house in Brunswick Junction but, when he got the job with the PMG, they moved into a tent (town) that was set up by the PMG for the families.

Gladys Catherine may not have accompanied John to Brunswick Junction until after the birth of their first child, Joan Irene, on 15th January, 1922. Almost two years later their second child, Doreen, was born on 1st December 1923. Both of their children were born in the old King Edward Memorial Hospital for Women in Subiaco, and both were breech births – meaning they were born buttocks first instead of head first, a very painful form of natural childbirth. (Ouch!!) Gladys probably did not want any more children after that! However, small families were becoming the norm.

The use of the cervical cap for birth control was introduced in the early 1920s. This must have been a welcome relief from the multiple births of the previous and earlier generations. Gladys was a modern woman and probably took advantage of the new birth control method. Birth control was illegal up until about 1914 and people were prosecuted for publicly advocating it. However, it wasn't long before the groundswell of objection by women was quelled and the law was overturned, making contraception legal. Women wanted to control the number of children they had and wanted to enjoy sex without the fear of pregnancy.

They lived in the 'tent town' for several years. John talked of killing kangaroos for meat; he would hang them up and skin them, gut them, and leave them to 'set'. He said he would cut off sections as needed and cover the cut section with cloth until the meat grew a tough outer 'skin' that kept flies and maggots out and preserved the meat. They also ate feral rabbits, and possibly possums and parrots.

Fortunately, Gladys Catherine was not isolated from her family because there was a railway to Brunswick Junction from Perth. Gladys Catherine probably visited her parents and family on a regular basis.

John and Gladys Catherine's daughters - Joan Irene and Doreen (right)
(Photo Kaye McCallum/Carroll)

John was a bright young man, but very quiet, and it can be seen from his war letter that he was well educated for those times and consequently, would make a good clerk. He applied for a job as a clerk in the PMG and got a job in the Head Office in Perth. The family moved back to Perth and, more than likely, stayed with Elizabeth Jane until eventually they moved into their brand-new War Service home. 'Cheap' loans were made available to soldiers who served overseas and saw active combat. Their lovely new home was at 17 Waroonga Road, Claremont, Western Australia, not far from Gladys Catherine's mother's place.

John and Gladys Catherine's home at 17 Waroonga Road, Claremont. 1975. (Personal photo)

Looking from the street, the house design was as follows: the front left window was the lounge-room behind which was the kitchen dining area. The right window was the main bedroom behind which was another bedroom that had its doorway off the kitchen dining room. This was Joan Irene and Doreen's bedroom. Past that was an open verandah that went across the length of the house with a bathroom enclosed in the righthand corner. Later, John enclosed the back verandah to make a sleep-out and small room. The laundry was in an outside 'lean-to' that housed a copper and troughs. The toilet had a plank seat with a hole over a bucket that was collected each week by the 'night soil' collector. It was up the back yard next to the laneway that ran along the back of the houses. The night soil collector would travel along the lanes to collect the full buckets and replace them with empty ones. These toilets were called "dunnies or thunderboxes!"

Commercial toilet paper was not yet available and little squares of newspaper were cut up and hung on a piece of wire close to the toilet. Doreen remembered as a child going to the old plank seat toilet and finding someone had put a little face of stones on one of the poos in the toilet. These plank seat bucket toilets just filled up with poo and wee and you had to wait for it to be collected once a week. A very smelly affair. When you think of the horror of a floating poo now…well even visitors had to brave the plank seat. Because the toilet was outside and usually up the back yard, a 'potty or po', like a big china or enamel cup, was placed under the bed to be used at night. No one wanted to brave the dark. Later, the toilet was moved closer to behind the laundry and was converted to the new porcelain pan and flushing toilet that flushed into the new septic tank that was dug into the backyard. A very modern addition and no more 'night soil' to be collected. The 'night soil' collectors became redundant. The flushing mechanism of the toilet was from a concrete trough placed high above the toilet and fixed to the rear wall. A chain was connected to the trough and was pulled to release the water and flush the toilet. It seemed each toilet had its own peculiarities and there was a knack to the chain pulling to get it to flush. Absolute luxury.

John was a keen gardener and had a big vegetable garden and a chook pen up the backyard and he grew beautiful flowers around the house. He built a shade-house out the back behind the laundry and shed and grew lovely ferns. Home gardeners were common back then; many people built up the skills from an early age when a lot of people had home vegetable plots and chickens and knew the science of gardening. Many vegetables and eggs were unavailable or not easily sourced so, at times, people had to fend for themselves, particularly during the Great Depression and the wars.

John stated that he was the first person to take about twenty or thirty Zinnia plants (flowers) to Woolworths in the city; there were no shopping centres then and this was the only Woolworths store. He offered them for sale. They were snapped up immediately by the shoppers and he was asked to bring more plants into the shop to sell. He thinks that was the beginning of the shops selling plants.

When John was transferred to the clerical job with the PMG, he worked in the central headquarters in Perth. This lovely building still stands and is situated on the western side of Forrest Place, Perth. He worked there until he retired at the age of sixty-five.

John was a bit of a drinker and smoker after the war (as many men who went to war were) and sometimes this usually mild-mannered and gentle man got fed up. His daughter, Doreen, laughed as she remembered one instance where the wooden back doorstep had been highly polished, and was NOT to be stood on – by orders from Gladys Catherine. John walked on it and slipped, lost his temper and tore the back door off and heaved it up the back yard!! Another incident was when he had had a bit too much to drink and rode his bicycle up the hill to the little shop on Stirling Highway. He wore long trousers and got the leg of his pants all wound up in the chain and he became stuck to the bicycle and had to carry it home with his leg attached to the chain, cursing all the way!

The Post Office (PMG) Head Office, Forrest Place, Perth. (Personal photo 2020)

John McGlinn during his working career in the PMG head office Perth (1950s?)
(Photo Kaye McCallum/Carroll)

Then suddenly, John had a haemorrhage in the stomach and had to have an operation to repair a perforated ulcer. From then on there was no grog and no smokes. He drank a glass of barley water and took a tablespoon of olive oil each day for the rest of his life. It certainly didn't do him any harm – he had the most beautiful skin, even into old age.

It is unknown whether John ever drove a car after the war: it appears that he didn't. He travelled to and from work in the city by an electric tram that had two long rods protruding from the roof and connected to overhead electric wires; the wheels ran along metal tracks in the road. These trams were superseded by the electric trolley bus.

Sometimes he would ride his bicycle up the hill to the bus stop and leave it at the little shop on Stirling Highway at the foot of Loch Street. On his way home, he would buy the *Daily News* newspaper, which had several editions each day, and ride home. There were far more newspapers back then than there are today. Public transport was much better back then too and, if John and Gladys Catherine went to visit anyone, they would take either the bus and or the train. Public transport was more regular and came more often and seemed to have more spread to locations which, admittedly, were then quite limited.

John liked to go to the horse races on a Saturday with his eldest brother David. He wasn't a gambler, often it would be a 5-bob (50c) bet. Horse racing, the trots or races, were extremely popular and would attract large crowds. It wasn't long before that time that people used horses for transport and to do deliveries etc. so there was a closeness to the horse. Of course, John had an affinity with horses that may have been more acute because of his "war horse" and his exposure to horses during his younger life.

It was probably during John's illness and after his operation when he couldn't work for a while that Gladys Catherine had to go to work to bring in an income. She got a job as a cleaner at the University of Western Australia, Winthrop Hall and she worked there until her retirement at the age of sixty.

While cleaning at home one day, Gladys Catherine stood on a small table to clean the windows; she stepped back; it tipped up and she fell to the floor breaking her wrist. John always maintained it was that fall that started her very debilitating rheumatoid arthritis.

Winthrop Hall University of Western Australia. (www.bing.com/images) 2020

Gladys Catherine was always conscious of keeping an image of class and decorum about her. She was an absolute lady and had high expectations of others. She was still a victim of her upbringing and still had quite a "Victorian" attitude like her grandmother Bridget Mary and mother Elizabeth Jane. Her pride was strong and she expected her family to behave accordingly and was very stubborn about it. She kept her house spotless and was a wonderful cook. She made the best sponge cakes ever! She liked her girls to be well behaved, elegant and well dressed and, between her and her daughter, Joan Irene, who was also a dressmaker, they had the skills to maintain this. Visitors to the house were always made to feel very welcome and were treated to some wonderful home cooking. They were very popular and there were many visitors.

Gladys Catherine always wore an elegant and clean outfit and was fussy with her appearance right into old age. She always wore make-up (face powder) and lipstick.

John and Gladys Catherine lived in their Waroonga Road house until it was time for them to go into an aged care home, the Returned Soldiers' Home in Mt Lawley, where they got a small self-contained unit. In that unit, they had a "lolly" drawer that would tantalize the great-grandchildren with a huge assortment of the most wonderful sweets.

Later in Gladys Catherine's life, she became so incapacitated by her arthritis that John could no longer care for her so they moved into the Alfred Carson Silver Chain nursing home in Claremont, just around the corner from their Waroonga Road house, until Gladys Catherine died in 1984, aged eighty-three. John, who was still able to care for himself in a limited fashion, moved back to the Returned Soldiers' Home until he died in 1992, aged ninety-four. They were a devoted and gentle couple who loved their family dearly and who were loved by all of their family.

John and Gladys McGlinn about 1975, at their Waroonga Road house before they moved to the Returned Soldiers aged care units. (Personal photo)

John and Gladys Catherine's daughters
Joan Irene and Doreen McGlinn

Doreen McGlinn was born in Subiaco, Western Australia, on the 1st December, 1923 and died from heart failure in Hollywood Hospital on 16th June, 2013, aged 89. It was her choice to die – they offered her medication to prolong her life but she refused.

Joan Irene was born on 15th January, 1922 and died on 10th August, 2002 from breast cancer, aged 80. She had had a mastectomy many years earlier when she was in her 40s.

Doreen's and Joan Irene's childhoods were happy ones. They did not experience the same poverty and hardship as that of the Carrolls. Doreen remembered the tent town in Brunswick Junction where she spent her early childhood but nothing else about the time she was there. Soon after leaving Brunswick Junction, they moved into their lovely new home in Waroonga Road which was in a new housing development in Claremont. While there, the girls had many happy visits to their Grandma, Elizabeth Jane. Doreen always spoke fondly of her.

She and Joan Irene were educated at "Prac" East Claremont Primary School which was a demonstration school where highly skilled teachers worked with new teachers in the modern education techniques of the day. Many teachers considered it a privilege to be chosen to teach there. Doreen spoke fondly of her time at "Prac" but lamented that she wasn't good at spelling and was always in trouble for her poor work in that area. However, she was good at maths and excelled in mental arithmetic which helped her later in her career.

Both McGlinn girls went to Claremont High School, the same school the Carrolls attended. It is suspected that Joan Irene met Francis Peter Carroll there and their romance and marriage blossomed from there. They were only one year apart in age so were attending at the same time. Stanley Lawrence Carroll was much older, so his and Doreen's time there didn't coincide.

Doreen McGlinn top left, class at Claremont Prac School. (Family photo)

Claremont was just developing from the rural setting of farms, back yard dairies and vegetable gardens. The river foreshore was still quite wild, with large trees and shrubs, and there were many wildflowers. New red brick houses were being built and these houses now took over from the weatherboard houses of the earlier type that the Carrolls had just three streets away.

Services, like trams and other public transport that took over from the horse-drawn transport, were being extended into these new areas. This meant the family could go on outings, and it was easier and more comfortable to get into the city to the big shops and to the Perth Railway Station to go further afield. Now that public transport was available to them, John, Gladys Catherine and their girls could go on visits to their extended families and could go further afield to places like Midland Junction, Darlington and York. For the first time, Perth Zoo could be easily visited even though it was a lengthy trip via the Causeway, and South Perth. There was no Narrows Bridge or freeway, so the long way was the only way.

The first electric trams to Loch Street Claremont, near Waroonga Road. (BERSON, Michael. Prac – East Claremont Primary School, 1905 – 1985. (East Claremont Primary School P & C Association, 1985) p. 53.

Doreen McGlinn - centre front holding the ball (Family photo)

Doreen was very keen on playing sport and she was very good at it. She played basketball (netball) and was captain of her team. She excelled at playing tennis and her love of the game stayed with her well after she was married and had children. She excelled at her sports and was a popular and fun-loving girl.

She and Joan Irene were very close to their cousin Leonard Ernest Cavanagh (Lenny), Gladys Catherine's sister Alma Irene's only child. Alma Irene had a tennis court in her large backyard at 19 Knutsford Street, Swanbourne, and Doreen, Joan Irene and Lenny would play tennis there as often as they could. Perhaps this is where Doreen's love of tennis began.

Joan Irene, Leonard Ernest Cavanagh and Doreen (right) in the tennis court at 19 Knutsford Street, Swanbourne, about 1936. (Photo Kaye McCallum/Carroll)

Doreen told of Joan Irene, Lenny and her hiding behind the shed in the backyard at the Waroonga Road house and breaking bits off the cane chair to smoke (and choke)! Also having a go at Woodbine cigarettes, a very strong cigarette that was popular with the soldiers of WWI and WWII. They were cheap so Doreen and the others could get a small pack of five cigarettes, break them in half and share them. They had a lot of fun together and were a tight-knit group. Doreen and Lenny were only five months apart in age and were particularly close.

Doreen was a fun-loving girl and she had lots of friends. She spoke fondly of them, especially Peg (Margaret) Hamley, who lived across the road from the McGlinns. Doreen and Peg spent a lot of time together and often Gladys Catherine would scream "DOREEEEN" from the front door of the house to get Doreen to come home. (This was something Doreen copied from her mother because she continued with this yelling from the back door of her house when she had children of her own).

She would be a bit too fun loving and daring at times and sometimes would hang onto the pram racks on the back (outside) of the bus and travel part of the way to Cottesloe Beach where she regularly swam! It was a very popular beach and a place for many surf club events. Many people would travel there on the train and walk up from the railway station as the McGlinn family did during Joan Irene's and Doreen's childhood. The jetty was initially built in her grandparent's time for people to 'promenade' instead of swim. Unfortunately, after a huge storm, the jetty was damaged beyond repair, and in 1953 was blown up and destroyed. Swimming was frowned upon in earlier days, particularly for women, but new freedoms meant swimming was now popular for both men and women.

Cottesloe Beach in the 1930s, where Doreen would regularly swim (photo Grove Library 2021)

On a few occasions, Doreen went on school holidays to stay with her father's eldest sister, Aunty Ada Jane McGlinn (Jones), in York. She said when she was a child, she remembered being told of the flood in 1926 that came up into the town and how the water rushed over the bridge that spans the Avon River and how amazing and frightening it would have been. Northam and Perth too were flooded at that time.

York floods of 1926. The water is over the bridge. (Family photo)

Doreen loved her Aunty Ada Jane and maintained a wonderful relationship with her until Ada Jane became ill and died of cancer in 1947 at the age of sixty-eight. Doreen had a very close relationship with all of her father's sisters but she had an especially close relationship with her mother's sister Alma Irene.

The McGlinn girls and their eldest brother; L-R. Selina Mabel, Gertrude Eva, Sarah Ruby, Maud Bertha, Florence Hilda and seated, their eldest brother, David McGlinn. (Ada Jane had passed away) (Family photo)

Doreen was a gregarious girl and full of life. Her cousin, Joy Anderson/Gawned, who was several years younger than Doreen, said Doreen would often say to her – 'Come on, would you like to go' here, or there – and Joy would be thrilled to go along with her. She said Doreen was always very friendly, happy, and lots of fun and a thoroughly good person.

Joy Gawned – Doreen's cousin (family photo)

She also said Doreen was excellent with children and that she loved them. When Doreen got older, her skilled and confident manner with babies and children was obvious; she certainly had a natural talent, (especially at keeping them in line!) Her confident manner gave the children a sense of security. She could quieten a crying baby in no time by wrapping it securely in a blanket or cloth and holding it close to her body. She was amazing. A true 'child whisperer!'

Joan Irene did not often go on adventurous outings with Doreen; she was quieter and more 'refined' and did not like the boisterous nature of activities and sport that Doreen preferred. Joan Irene's nature better fitted the behaviour that Gladys Catherine had in mind for a young lady. She was very feminine in her manner and quite reserved.

***Joan Irene a more 'delicate' child** (Photo Joy Anderson/Gawned)*

Joan Irene, an elegant woman *(Photo Kaye McCallum/Carroll)*

In the photo of Joan Irene, it can be seen that fashions had certainly become more revealing and no doubt her grandmother Elizabeth Jane and her mother would have frowned upon so much flesh being revealed in public. Her outfit was a shorts and top set that she, no doubt, made herself.

Doreen, on the other hand, was the tomboy of the family and she took after her father who was a little 'rough around the edges'. Gladys Catherine would be constantly trying to get Doreen to fit the mould of how she thought a young lady should act, but Doreen resisted and there was often conflict. Doreen said she always felt that Joan Irene was the favoured child. When Joan Irene didn't want to do something, she would feign sickness to get out of it and Gladys Catherine would fuss over her. Doreen was a teenager with a mind of her own and this frustrated Gladys Catherine enormously.

Gladys Catherine must have forgotten the big changes in her life during World War I and the resistance she would have got from her mother and grandmother. Doreen took advantage of the even more enlightened times and was fully aware of the freedoms for women and girls that followed World War I and were now becoming the norm and, naturally, she wanted to be part of this new norm.

From the 1920s onwards, there came a new freedom for young people, especially women and they behaved and acted a lot differently to their parents. Jazz music was introduced and dancing changed radically. Later, Doreen grew to love this new type of dancing and the new music that was frowned upon by the older generation. It was positively sinful! She, like Stanley Lawrence, loved music and it was always an important part of her life. She had quite a good singing voice.

When Doreen left school at the age of fifteen, the Great Depression was in full swing and work was almost impossible to get for a young woman just out of school. Gladys Catherine might have encouraged Doreen to do dressmaking, but Doreen's heavy handedness wasn't cut out to do these fine skills and she wasn't up to the task. When Joan Irene left school, she followed in her mother's footsteps and became a professional dressmaker, seamstress and tailor and was extremely talented and highly skilled at this creative task. Her cousin, Joy Anderson/Gawned, said Joan Irene's skills were such that she could lay out the fabric on the floor and just cut out the pattern without the use of the commercial paper patterns that could be purchased. She said Joan Irene's skills were incredible and her work was beautifully and meticulously done. She, therefore, could contribute to the household by doing dressmaking. Fortunately, Doreen was extremely lucky to get a part time job in the little shop where John McGlinn bought his daily newspapers, in Stirling Highway at the base of Loch Street.

The Great Depression brought many hardships and people just had to go without. It was a time of – repair, re-use, make do, and DON'T throw anything away, it might be useful somehow. This was the motto for most people and such was the effect of the Great Depression on those who experienced it that this behaviour continued for most of their lives, including Doreen's and the Carroll family. They couldn't stand wasting anything.

Entertainment during the Depression was cheap and going to the picture shows (movies) and the local dances were popular attractions. Being 'sporty', dancing became an absolute passion for Doreen. Dancing is very athletic and the endorphins flow just as it does for athletes. If the partner was a good dancer, it was a bonus. The new dances of the day were the Foxtrot, Rhumba, Quickstep, Waltz, Jive, and Jitterbug, among others. Doreen probably practiced and practiced with her friend, Peg Hamley, until she was confident enough to go to the local dances. These were held two or three times a week, at the end of her street, in the Loch Street Hall where many local teenagers and young adults went, and possibly the Carrolls. It is not known whether Joan Irene accompanied her. Doreen was growing up in a new era and was becoming a beautiful looking and popular woman.

Doreen McGlinn – growing into a beautiful woman in a new era (Family photo)

PART 2

World War II and beyond

Stanley Lawrence Carroll enlists and goes to war

Stanley Lawrence was still in Southern Cross when Australia entered World War II on 3rd September 1939, following the government's acceptance of the United Kingdom's declaration of war on Nazi Germany. There was a call for men to enlist in the militia to defend Australia at home; there was no call to go overseas at that time and there was no call for men to join the regular army. However, it wasn't long before England needed its allies to be ready for war, and a full-scale recruitment drive was done.

Both in WWI and in WWII, except for some of the fighting in New Guinea, all soldiers were volunteers, an unusual thing because most other allied countries had professional soldiers. In November, the war took on a new phase for Australia and it now needed more men to enlist. A call to arms went out for volunteers to go and fight. The selection requirements for the volunteers were age – between twenty and thirty-five years – minimum height: five feet six inches – plus other criteria, but there were some exceptions to these rules.

Stanley Lawrence packed up his meagre belongings and probably gave his prospecting equipment to his old friend and prospecting mate Mr Faulkner. The war was a form of escape from the hard and harsh life of the still-going Great Depression and even though World War I was still fresh in some people's memories, this was an opportunity to escape. The army offered pay, food, and security and many men who had lost everything, or were badly affected by the depression, went to the enlistment centres in droves. Perhaps ideology and patriotism were not the only motivating forces that made men 'join up'.

Stanley Lawrence was no exception. When he heard about the war, he caught the train to the closest enlistment office, which was at Merredin, just over 100 kilometres west of Southern Cross. It was the 13th November 1939. He was now twenty-four years and ten months old. As part of the requirements to be a soldier he was told to take off his shoes and stand against the wall to have his height measured and was bitterly disappointed when he was rejected – he was too short by just a fraction. Luckily for him, the newly commissioned Commanding Officer, Lieutenant Colonel Tom Louch had selected Lieutenant Ralph Honner to command the Western Australian 2/11th battalion. Lieutenant Honner was responsible for the recruitment of the men and he was very keen on selecting sportsmen and farmers from the Great Southern and, in particular, men from the goldfields. He was fully aware that sportsmen were physically fit and could participate well in team situations. He was also well aware that the men from the bush and goldfields knew how to work hard doing physical labour at the end of a shovel! To his relief, Stanley Lawrence fitted the criteria, was selected and passed as 'Fit for War'. He was among the first to enlist in the Australian Imperial Force (AIF) in Western Australia. He was given the Service Number - WX953 in the 2/11th Battalion. The soldier's number was allocated according to district.

The 11th Battalion was the Western Australian Battalion in World War I and was now called the Second 11th Battalion. (2/11th) The 2nd denoted World War "II". Stanley Lawrence was now in this battalion in the Sixth Division/C Company, Infantry, Rifles.

On his enlistment papers was his physical description, which stated that he had fair hair, hazel eyes, and no distinguishing marks. His medical condition was that of 'Class 1', meaning he had no disabilities such as bad eyesight, deafness or any other affliction, and his occupation was stated as 'Labourer'. Considering his hard life and varied background, he was still a very immature-looking young man, as can be seen by his photo below.

Stanley Lawrence Carroll WX953 Australian Imperial Forces 2/11th Battalion. (Family photo)

This photo is the official record of his appearance and was taken to give to the family at home. Most serving soldiers had their photo, some a portrait, others full length, done in case the soldier was killed and as such the family would have a nice picture to remember them. Many of these types of photos still adorn the walls of houses today in remembrance of those who died or served in the war.

On the top outside of Stanley Lawrence's left-hand sleeve can just be seen his 2/11th colour patch. This patch was allocated to the 11th Battalion prior to World War I, the battalion in which Ernest William McGlinn served and died. This colour patch was also used during WWII but had a grey border to denote service in WWII.

2/11th colour patch with border – Mid brown over sky blue

Stanley Lawrence - *The portrait version of his war photo (Family photo)*

Stanley Lawrence was always self-conscious of his height and he hated it. He stood five feet six inches, and was usually called Midge by his family, meaning midget. Because of this, he had what is commonly known as "Small Man's Syndrome". He had to prove himself over and over again as being a "big" man. This meant he was always ready for action and wouldn't back down in any situation and did adventurous and dangerous things that normally wouldn't be tried. He was the quintessential Aussie larrikin. He was reckless and would give anything a go. In sport, he'd go in for the tackle with great tenacity and as a consequence was often the best player. He was absolutely no coward! He had a reputation of being a 'Wild Child' and had a few 'talkings to' by his older brothers and his mother to improve his reckless behaviour. He did just that and became a very hard worker with no view to entitlement. He had a nice friendly personality, generous nature, an abundance of patience, and he spoke eloquently and was very popular. After he joined the army, his mates called him "Titch", which also means small.

By the 21st November 1939 he had reported to the Northam Army Base which had been hurriedly converted from the basic militia camp. Buildings were erected to house the men. *"The camp … was used to accommodate the 2/11 Infantry Battalion … the camp became the main training camp for Western Australia … infantry training battalions and specialist depots for artillery, engineers, medical, service corps, ordnance, signals, and all other corps. Almost every soldier recruited in Western Australia … trained at Northam."* (www.ozatwar.com/locations/northamcamp.htm)

Stanley Lawrence was allocated to one of the barracks which were *"48-men barracks … laid out in the camp area to form a Company, with each Company area having its own headquarters, Quartermaster's store, mess hall, cook house and ablutions blocks. The officers and NCOs had their own separate barracks and messing facilities. The YMCA, Australian Red Cross and Salvation Army had their own huts. The 38th Australian Camp Hospital was located in the middle of the Northam Military Camp. Entertainment at the camp included bridge games, table tennis, movies on Tuesday and Friday nights, plus the occasional concert and almost weekly boxing tournaments."*

(www.ozatwar.com/locations/northamcamp.htm)

Initially, there were no army uniforms so the men wore what were known as 'Giggle Suits', basically, similar to a pair of pyjamas! It wasn't too long before they were allocated their uniforms and full pack, including a rifle.

To harden the recruits, they were <u>all</u> trained in rifles and basic military practices to become combat soldiers ready for front-line duties. There was also the practice of discipline and procedure and, constant marches and parades which meant that, once uniforms were allocated, buttons and shoes were to be polished to the highest standard. Stanley Lawrence was used to shiny shoes: his father, George Thomas, always liked to have his shoes nice and shiny and to dress well as can be seen in the earlier photo taken at Nannine. Stanley Lawrence told of polishing his army boots to such a shine that he could see his face in them. He revealed the knack: dip the shoe brush in the polish then spit on it before using the brush to spread the polish over the boots, then with another softer brush polish with a brisk rub to bring out the shine, then rub the back of a teaspoon over the boot to really bring out the shine. Was this George Thomas's trick to get his boots to shine? The term "spit and polish" came about during World War I when a quick polish was required ready for inspection, and initially came from polishing shoes and buttons with spit.

Dormitory beds were to be made in military style with corners folded in a certain way to reflect the crisp corner folds, and barracks inspected for the slightest bit of dust. Uniforms were ironed to make sharp creases in the front of the trouser legs, and shirts and collars had to be clean with no wrinkles. Good personal hygiene and shaving was required, along with haircuts of short back and sides, especially for parade, which was often. All this was part of the discipline process.

Marching and parades were held often. There were also long marches in full gear, bayonet practice, and constant rifle drills. This bunch of motley men were brought into shape quickly and soon became a good fighting force. Soldiers then either requested or were allocated specialty duties, such as, artillery, transport, communications, machine guns etc. Stanley Lawrence was accepted into the Signals Division where he learnt Morse-Code using electronic signalling devices, telegraphy, flashlights, and flags, and the use of a heliograph. The Signals Corps recognised that it required men *"with a high degree of integrity of character. This integrity in each individual is an essential factor in the security of information which must be observed in the transmission and reception of the secret messages which are passed over the Army Signals communication channels. In them at all times rests the security and success of the operations in progress… It might be said that the Signals Corps is the nerve system of the Army; its communication channels run from the largest headquarters to the smallest unit… (and) information carried back and forth with the utmost speed and clarity"* Signals, Forward by General Sir Thomas Blamey, Commander in Chief Australian Military Forces. Halstead Press, 1944

Signals meant Stanley Lawrence was considered as having the integrity and mental ability to carry out this important position. He was to be with the officers who planned and invoked battle plans, and gave orders within a battle, sent messages to the back and forward lines etc. so very good communication between each other and the wider communications world was vital. A very important role.

It meant Stanley Lawrence must be able to accurately send the message and there must be NO ERRORS in the message. He said he recalled a practice Morse Code exercise, a 'chain of message', a bit like Chinese Whispers, where one person would tell the next person in line a message and so on until the line of men had been told. The message was "Send reinforcements we're going to advance". At the end of the line, the message ended up being interpreted as; "Send three and four-pence, we're going to a dance". He often chuckled at this when relating the story, but it displayed the degree of accuracy required and how, over a chain, the message can change. Even many years after the war, he was still very proficient at Morse-Code.

Stanley Lawrence's actual Morse-Code machine he used during WWII

Northam Army Base recruits in their "Giggle Suits". Stanley Lawrence – bottom row 3rd from right – 1939 (Family photo)

After initial training at Northam, on the 12th December 1939, the new recruits were sent home for a few days before being shipped to NSW for further training. This was the first big trip on a ship that many of the soldiers, including Stanley Lawrence, had experienced. They were fortunate that the military had requisitioned luxury passenger ships on which the troops were sent. The journey was very pleasant.

Their first camp was at Rutherford, which apparently was a filthy camp, but it wasn't long before his division was then moved to a camp near Greta, NSW. He wrote a letter to the family telling them he had met a girl who took him home for some home-cooked meals and family company. He sneaked out of camp on several occasions to see her, got back late, was caught, and was fined 5/- each time and, at the time of his letter, he was up to 15/-, a considerable sum. *"A very typical young man in search of a good time, booze, and girls"*. (CARROLL, Max. *Memoir*)

Many men became disenchanted with the routine and went 'AWL' (Absent Without Leave). They were bored and the training was ordinary; they wondered why they had been sent to NSW. Even their commanding officer agreed that there had been no use in the move to NSW and they would have been better to stay at home and do their training there.

Stanley Lawrence wrote a letter home from Ingleburn, New South Wales, where they underwent further training. It was written on his 25th birthday, 6th January 1940, where he stated that his Paybook had been lost for five weeks and he hadn't had any money. A soldier's Pay Book was sacrosanct. It had to be carefully guarded and looked after; after all, when it was missing you didn't get paid and it took a long time before you were issued with another one, then receive the back pay! Fortunately, he had recently been issued with a new one and now had £10/10/- to 'live it up' during the New Year celebrations.

The division moved again to an area twenty miles from Sydney where the local RSL arranged for the troops to be billeted out for New Year, 1940. It turned out that Stanley Lawrence was billeted to the mayor's house, and he said, best of all the mayor had a seventeen-year-old daughter who took him to a New Year's Eve dance, then during the next few days to Bondi, and Manly. He went sightseeing with his mates to all the tourist places, like Taronga Park Zoo, The Aquarium, and the Sydney Harbour Bridge. He was very impressed by them all. There was nothing like these grand things in Perth.

During this time, Stanley Lawrence contracted (German measles) Rubella, and was isolated in hospital for a short time.

He later met a woman who was visiting from Greta where some of the troops were still stationed and he said in a letter home she had told him *"That the whole bloody town had gone mad, married women, young girls, even kids were becoming women overnight*". A new mentality was manifesting itself in the young people. World War I was still very fresh in people's memories and many were keenly aware that life may be very short and every opportunity was taken to live life to the full – right now. Incidentally, there is a small plaque on the Albany foreshore in Western Australia where the Australian troops left for WWI. On the plaque, it states that, even though this was in an era of very prim behaviour, a woman said she saw girls and women lying on the beach and in parks kissing the soldiers and embracing them before they left for war. This seems a natural phenomenon in times of desperation and distress. Stanley Lawrence was probably no exception. He would have liked to spread his genes among any willing female participant. It is a biological fact that occurs across most species in the event of stress, even in trees, which will flower profusely and shed a lot of seed to ensure the species' survival.

In late March 1940, the men left NSW and travelled by train back to Western Australia and went on six days of pre-embarkation leave. Stanley Lawrence immediately travelled to Greenbushes to be Best Man at his older brother John Raymond's marriage to Audrey Knapton on the 13th April. He now had his full military uniform and looked very smart indeed.

On his return to the Claremont camp, Stanley Lawrence, along with the rest of the troops, became restless and bored so to keep them out of trouble they were sent from Claremont on a route march through the bush to Rockingham and back. It was the longest march they had ever done and the conditions were hot and uncomfortable. Within a day or two, they were informed they were to go to war. There was a march through the streets of Perth in front of large crowds of cheering people. Women cried and threw flowers; they ran and kissed the troops as they marched by and there was a swelling of pride among the men. It was certain that not all of these young men would return.

It was during the pre-embarkation leave that the photograph of the Carroll family, on the next page, was taken.

Max Carroll stated that Stanley Lawrence had all of his issued gear with him – that is, his "*kit bag, uniform, tunic, trousers, slouch hat, full webbing equipment, belt and shoulder straps, basic pouches, haversack, backpack as well as rifle*". Young Max Carroll was intrigued by the war and tried on all of this gear. (Max grew up to become a career military man and subsequently ended up as a Colonel in the Australian Army. Colonel Owen Maxwell Carroll, OAM).

*The Carroll Family shortly before Stanley Lawrence left to go to war
(Photo – Max Carroll)*

This was perhaps the final farewell to Stanley Lawrence and his friends before they were shipped out. No one knew where they were going, and very soon they would be gone to war.

Stanley Lawrence was the first in the family to enlist, and he would certainly have been very proud of the fact. Finally, he must have felt he was doing something for which the family could be proud. He would have felt he was now worthwhile and of importance to the family and his country.

His friend from Bridgetown, Harry Draper, and his friend, Alan Knee, from Mt Barker spent the last night with the Carroll family before they were told to report to the army camp at Claremont Showgrounds ready for embarkation. No one knew just where these men might be sent.

The night before they were to be shipped out, the local Perth soldiers removed the pickets from the back fence of the Claremont Showgrounds and sneaked out to their waiting families for a teary farewell. Their mothers, sisters, wives, and girlfriends cried to see these men leave for they knew that there was a very real possibility that they would never see them again. Their menfolk too would have been emotional at the occasion. Stanley Lawrence said he was much relieved that his parents put on a brave face and joked and laughed with him; it saved them all from an emotional and traumatic farewell.

Stanley Lawrence goes to war

On the 20th April 1940, the troops marched to Fremantle and boarded the ship *Navasa,* which was headed to the Middle East, although they were unaware of the destination at that stage. This ship was very uncomfortable and not built to be a troop carrier. It was hot and there was not enough refrigeration for food, and facilities were abysmal. The food was of poor quality and there was not enough to go around. They slept below deck on hammocks that were so close together that getting out of them without disturbing someone was impossible. He continued to write letters home but now they were censored by the army. He said the trip was interesting and described some of the towns they visited but, owing to censorship, no names of the places could be written. It is now known the ship called into Colombo, Ceylon (Sri Lanka) where Stanley Lawrence, among quite a few others, overstayed his allotted time and was fined for going AWL, again. Colombo was a very new experience for the men – it was their first experience of a different culture. The local rickshaw drivers were encouraged to sit in their rickshaws as passengers and the Australians would be the runner and race up and down the streets. The poor rickshaw drivers had probably never been in the passenger seat and were most disconcerted. Personal Comment. Arthur Leggett, Signalman 2/11th Btn, 2022.

During the journey, Stanley Lawrence had his first real experience as a Signalman: he sent signals between ships and used flags for communication.

For part of the trip the ship was in 'black-out', meaning no going on deck to smoke nor have any light showing to the outside world. At that time, there was no going outside at night. Port holes were covered so no viewing of the outside could be done. He said it was a relief when black-out ended and they could go on deck, get fresh air, lie around, and smoke. They had concerts and plays in which the soldiers performed and, in all, he found the trip quite good. At one stage they were required to wear their life-belts and the thrill of danger went through the ship.

On the 18th May 1940, they arrived at Kantara in the Middle East. They were given a meal then trucked to Palestine. Stanley Lawrence said it was reminiscent of the goldfields with camels and donkeys about the place, but the surrounds were very different. There were small patches of cultivation with swarms of goats, sheep, camels and donkeys going in all directions. He said the people appeared to have remained content with the customs of the days BC (Before Christ). The troops travelled for hours through deserts and small settlements until reaching The Bitter Lakes where they had a swim and got cleaned up. They had been on the crowded ship, which had no bathroom facilities, for one month. They were then sent by train to Palestine where they finally arrived at their camp in Gaza. The camp was known as Kilo 89. He said he was used to camp life so it wasn't a problem for him; he set up and settled in. Others found it difficult to adjust but he found camp life pleasant enough but a bit boring. The YMCA (Young Men's Christian Association) provided games, and the canteens had beer. He mentioned that this area was where some of the fighting took place during WWI and that the cemetery was something he would like to visit. Perhaps he was where his future father-in-law, John McGlinn, had fought during WWI.

In a letter to his brother, Francis Peter, Stanley Lawrence stated that during brief periods of leave many of the young, and some quite innocent, men lined up at brothels where they had to wait in long queues, then perform in front of their mates. There was no privacy! Stanley Lawrence said he failed miserably so he and his mate, Alan Knee, also a signaller, decided to buy a night with two prostitutes. He said it was much better and they had a good night, however, halfway through the night they swapped girls, to break the monotony! He said it was well worth the money! It is suspected that, for many of the men, it would be their first experience with sex and they were going to make the most of it. After all, if you were going to be killed soon, you'd better have a bloody good time now.

During another period of leave, he and Alan Knee went to the Café Metropole in Cairo, which was reserved for the rank of sergeant and above. Neither Stanley Lawrence nor Alan Knee had sergeant stripes so they got some from somewhere and put them on their sleeves. They were having a good time and reckoned the women were of a higher class and seemed to like these two culprits. The military police soon discovered them and put them on a charge. They were thrown out and fined four shillings each.

However, it was not all fun. After one sightseeing tour, they went straight out on a bivouac that covered all sorts of terrain for over 100 miles, in full pack, with minimal food and water. Their rations were awful. During the march, an Arab came along on a camel and had a cargo of watermelons he wanted to sell to the troops. Stanley Lawrence grabbed some of the greasy rations from the men and ran over to the Arab and haggled to swap the rations for watermelon. The Arab agreed and the men in Stanley Lawrence's group had a nice refreshing change of watermelon. From then on, training was constant and hard and only short periods of leave were given. There was never a time of feeling at ease: any moment they could have been sent into battle and their lives could be snuffed out in an instant. For these innocent men, the thrill of battle meant they were raring to go and fight to see how they would go against the enemy. There was the occasional air raid to keep them on their toes and to give them a sense of war.

The dynamic duo – Signalmen WX953 Stanley Lawrence, left and WX 688 Alan Knee (Family photo)

"A touch of desert madness"

Stanley Lawrence "Training in the field"

Stanley Lawrence on the camel   (Photos Stanley Lawrence Carroll)

In the photo below is a woman handing Stanley Lawrence oranges at a railway station in Gaza. He said you couldn't trust what they were giving you and you had to be wary. The soldiers were warned by their Commanding Officers that the local people used one hand to eat and the other to wipe their backside – so make sure the fruit was well washed! Dysentry was always a problem and was a very debilitating condition.

Stanley Lawrence "Gaza 1940 Cigarettes for oranges en route to camp, Kilo 89"

They left the Palestine camp, Kilo89, and were sent to Burg el Arab, Egypt, near the coast for further training and then on to the desert country in Libya for desert training. The troops became a hardened and tough fighting force.

To fill in some of his spare time in camp, he played rugby and cricket. In a game of rugby, he went in for a tackle and as he did one of the players landed on his leg, wrenching it sideways. He was sent off to hospital to clean sheets, good food, and a masseuse. Bliss! He said it was worth the bump!

Just before Christmas, 1940, a two-mile cross-country run was organised in which there were over two hundred participants. Stanley Lawrence was an excellent runner and joined the group to go in the race and represented Headquarters Company. They marched two miles to the start line and had to race in their heavy trousers and army boots, very hard going. The starter used Italian hand grenades to start the race, so it can be imagined the bolted start they got. There were several hundred men in the race. Stanley Lawrence stated in a letter to his mother Maria Ellen, *"Using my head as I thought & remembering a few tricks I had learnt when running in the five milers at home, I went straight to the front & made the pace pretty hot. When only a half a mile to go two chaps joined me & after a hard struggle I found my condition failing me & just managed to scramble in third. Nevertheless I got five bottles of beer out of it so Xmas night was pretty gay after all".* He was an excellent athlete.

Stanley Lawrence in his Cross County running outfit 1940 (Family photo)

It was close to Christmas day and the officers expected the men to leave for battle within a day or two, so they thought their men should have a nice Christmas lunch of lamb and vegetables, plum pudding, and a free bottle of beer each. This was a real treat after the monotonous food they had to endure. The battle plans were delayed so the men, much to their delight, were treated to another Christmas dinner on Christmas day.

During periods of leave in these ancient areas, Stanley Lawrence visited all the places of interest, for example, the Pyramids, Jerusalem, Haifa, Nazareth and others. He was amazed by the sheer age of these places and the primitive way the people lived. An absolute eye-opener for a boy from Western Australia.

Then a rumour went through camp, and with it the thrill of anticipation. War for them could be very soon, and it was. When they were ordered to move out, Stanley Lawrence was still in hospital with the knee injury! One of his fellow signallers went and told him it was time to go so he discharged himself from the hospital and off they went. Stanley Lawrence's role as Signaller was now to begin in earnest. In stationary battles, all communication lines between Commanding Units were run with wires, which had to be laid out by the Signalman, often over several miles – a very dangerous operation because sometimes wires had to be run over open ground and, if they were broken during battle, the signaller would have to go and fix the problem and would be very exposed to artillery and gunfire. Communication between Command Posts was vital for battle plans to be implemented or changed as required. In a moving battle, as many are, Signalmen would run on foot to get messages between command posts.

The days of true trench warfare were mostly over. The men would usually go to the battle front at night and dig a 'weapon pit', which was a hole big enough to hold two men lying side by side. This was the case for Stanley Lawrence. He would normally be with a commanding officer and maintain communications for him. Among all of his usual kit and webbing, he would take his rifle, telephone set, wire cables, repair kit, heliograph and tripod, a Lucas Lamp and a satchel with message pads and pencils! The life of a signalman was tough. LEGGETT, Arthur. *Don't cry for me: an autobiography*. Linellen Press, 2019. p 143.

Signalman with all his equipment in his (half dug) 'weapon pit' during the battle at Bardia. Photo - Signals. Halstead Press, 1944. p41.

Into Battle – the Middle East

Just over eight months after arriving in the Middle East and experiencing little of war, apart from the occasional bombings and air raids, on the 5th January, 1941, the 2/11th 6th Division was ordered into battle. It was the day before Stanley Lawrence's 26th birthday. They had been trucked to Italian-held Libya and close to the town of Bardia (Bardiyah), just north of the Egyptian border. During the trip to the battle front, the troops had to camp overnight. The convoy would stop during the evening and the men would be fed from the kitchen trucks. There were no other facilities so the men would just sleep on the ground for the night.

During the evening prior to the battle, the men would go forward as quietly as possible and dig in. The Signalmen had to run wires from Headquarters (HQ) back to the transport divisions then from HQ to the front lines, the various Company positions, often over quite long distances. At the junction of the wires, a telephone exchange was installed and manned to direct the flow of information. All of the signalling equipment was WWI issue and was obsolete, but expected to be used in this modern war.

They were about to engage in several battles during the next month and many were hard-fought and very dangerous.

Below is a letter from Stanley Lawrence written after these battles to his brother, John Raymond, describing his first experience of war. No names of places are given so the family had no idea where he was. The battles the 2/11th engaged in were for Bardia, Tobruk, Derna, and Benghazi.

WX953
Signaller CARROLL S.L.
H.Q. Coy Sigs 2/11
ABROAD
10th Feb 1941

Dear Jack

Received your very welcome letter some weeks ago & have made several attempts to answer same. Each time the order came to move on & now I am hundreds of miles from the front lines with the legs under a table. The papers have no doubt given a detailed account of the doings in Libya, so will try & describe what my experiences were.

We have been very fortunate having gradually got used to the fireworks before going into action. In Palestine we saw nothing at all except for a tour of Tel-Aviv where the air raids took place. In Egypt we witnessed several bombings and had a couple in our own area. As we moved up we passed over several battle fields & saw the ruins of several towns plus acres of captured material.

(Bardia) Two days before our turn came we stood back & watched the arty (artillery) send over their barrage. During the night it was a great sight, as far as the eye could see flash after flash appeared on the horizon. It sounded and looked like a terrific thunderstorm, first the flash & then some seconds later the boom, but no hailstones came our way.

We were still some miles from their first line of defence. Under cover of darkness we moved up to take our positions & during a halt near the arty (artillery) I met Vic Kennedy, he's a transport driver with the R.A.A. (Royal Australian Artillery). Just after dawn we crossed the antitank trench, the barbed wire had been ripped down for hundreds of yds (yards) by the boys who made the dawn attack.

Our job was to follow on & relieve them as soon as they broke through. They cheered us on as we moved through the area they had taken, groups of prisoners were everywhere. Our own guns lost no time in moving up, after an hour's spell we prepared to make our debut. In broad daylight we went over the ridge & then all hell broke loose at least I thought it had, but it was only our big guns giving the dings (Italians) the works.

It's a queer sensation, very much like going on to play a big football final, you want a leak every few minutes & realize that you should have had a bog, an excellent cure for constipation. We were informed that rum demijohns (earthenware bottles that held the rum rations) got broken an old story I believe, but being new chums we fell for it.

The enemy abandoned their forward positions & fell back about three miles, so it developed into a bit of a race over very rocky country. Up went their signal for defensive fire & up went the dirt around us & believe me their hundred pounders go off with a bang when they land. It lost its grand final touch here, instead of flying for the marks we flew for the dirt.

Some of the shells landed half a mile from us, but when they start to chuckle overhead one thinks they are going to drop right in the arse pocket. It doesn't take long to get used to judging their flight, when you can hear them dying down it's time to do the ostrich trick & bury the head. The nearest I got, ripped a crater in the ground about a hundred yds (yards) behind me & when I swallow dived my telephone set clouted me behind the ear. Very gingerly I felt to find how much of my head was left, because I heard several lumps whine over the tin hat.

As soon as we got within range the Eytie (Italians, a name coined during WWI) tossed it in & the procession started. Hundreds of them poured out with the hands up waving the white material they all seem to have in readiness. It looked a strange sight two or three hundred being escorted by a couple of guards. The old bayonet does the trick, let the sun flash on them & the game's over. The remainder of the day was spent chasing the stragglers out of their dugouts.

A day's spell & we were on their wheel again. As we rode along we had a glimpse of the equipment they had abandoned, what a collection. Vehicles of every size and description, thousands of them were strewn about for miles on both sides of the road. Aerodromes with planes, some intact, others destroyed, appeared at intervals along the track. Alan was attached to another coy (company) during the bout & the day after being my birthday he drove along in a little Fiat sedan & gave it to me a present from Musso (Mussolini). It was almost brand new, had only done twelve hundred kilos (kilometres) & what a heartbreak to have to leave it behind. I had a 3½ camshaft Benelli (Italian motorbike) for a couple of days a 1940 model & could it move. They are fitted with two hydrolic [sic] shock absorbers on the back wheel, just like floating on air to ride. Finished up getting a puncture & left it by the wayside.

We kept worrying them until the time was ripe to have another crack & during that time they pumped a couple of tons of shells into our area & treated us to several air raids. It was all waisted, [sic] they never made a hit, a lot of noise but we were well dug in. A couple of times I had to sneak out & repair my line, once I got the job half done & had to dive into the hole that caused the break. When I got back I found my burrow had been visited & my great coat minus one sleeve, left it on the side of the hole when I went out. One had landed a few yards away, blew my mate's bayonet to pieces & set the rounds off in his pouches. He was covered in dust but still laughing at the way I had scuttled for cover when she came down. I don't think I'd have the heart to shoot a rabbit after watching the boys scoot for their holes & when the dust dies down you can see heads popping up everywhere. Once the officer was using the phone & I heard one coming. I dived for my tin hat & tried to make room for him in my funk hole. In he tumbled boots first, stamped on my head a few times & brought half the desert in with him.

This went on for about ten days, down the hole all day & come out at night when the ration truck came up & then go forward and give them a few rounds to go to bed with. We were eventually relieved & went back to the ocean to have our first wash in three weeks. B.O. (body odour) & toe jam was a little bit high. The water looked a little cloudy after we had finished wallowing in it but we had at least dumped a bit of the Western Desert in the Mediterranean.

(Tobruk) Sixteen days after the first campaign we made another dawn attack. Once through the barbed wire, the same old story again, apart from shell fire the coy (company) I was with only drew fire three times up till midday. The lads welcomed this bit of resistance & proceeded to give them a bit of their own medicine. Not even a blade of grass to take cover behind, so our O.C. (Officer Commanding) ordered fix bayonets & go for them. Out they came as usual, but not before we had given them a hail of bullets to go with.

By nightfall we were almost in the town itself, except for a few bombs dropped by our bombers all was quiet. We had covered about eighteen miles since dawn, so you can imagine how much they held the advance up. We even had time off for lunch, what a war, more like a route march.

Before ten o'clock on the second day we were making ourselves at home in the town, partaking of Italian delicasies, [sic] very tasty after tin dog.

(Derna) No time was waisted, [sic] after a swim a change of undies & a good hot meal we clambered aboard the trucks & away to the next joint. A few bridges had been blown up, but the road gang was on the job, only a few minutes delay at each holdup. This time we bowled straight into them & here's where I made my exit. Got a belly full of shell fumes, a dud lobbed right in front of me & sprayed me with some yellow muck.

I thought I had swallowed a hot spud, the tonsils were on fire & the top of my head felt as if it had caved in. When I went back to guide the line party up the boss sent me back to sig (signals) office & from there the Doc (doctor) sent me back for a spell. I went back alright first in an ambulance then in a hospital ship and found myself on a red cross train bound for Cairo.

Seven days after leaving the unit I was in a N.Z. (New Zealand) hospital. Had recovered days before but it was no use arguing I had to do as I was told & here I am back in Palestine.

I may get back before it peters out, if not my term in the front lines will have been very short.

One thing about it I had a chance to see Cairo & all its historical places. Dan Smith came back with me, he had a poisoned knee, so we had quite an enjoyable two days touring. Dan not being a lady's man we restricted our leisure time to sightseeing. Went & explored the Pyramids, the Sphinx all the ancient temples & mosques.

If you are thinking of joining up, you can tell Audrey that there are any number of units to join besides the front liners. We certainly have all the fun & get our share of foot slogging, but it takes eight men behind the lines to keep one man up there. The infantry, artillery, some of the engineers, tank & anti tank Corps have to face the music. Not every man that joins the army is in danger, some of them might never hear a shot fired, but his job has to be done by someone.

With your experience as a linesman I would suggest Corps of sigs (signals) or Divi sigs (Divisional Signals). There's not much sense joining the foot sloggers when one is experienced in other units work. They have a special squad to repair the civilian telephone lines & do they need it, miles of wire is torn down & twisted everywhere. An occasional air raid may happen along, but as a rule all is quiet after the infantry has gone through.

The postal corps is another crowd who deal with the mail part of the business. Practically no danger at all & the living conditions are almost on militia lines. Every comfort, food & usually situated well back where leave is pretty prevalent. People seem to get the idea that every man that joins up is in the firing line, but it's not the case. Where you have a thousand in action you have (?) thousand backing them up. In my opinion no married man should be in the infantry.

Well Jack I've just about exhausted my supply of news, will be writing home again shortly, until then Cheerio. Give my love to all at home. Best of luck old chap.

Brother Stan"   (Signed by the censor)

Best mate, Alan Knee WX688. Despatch Rider, on the captured Benelli Motor Bike mentioned in Stanley Lawrence's letter above Photo – OLSEN, Wes. Battalion into battle. Wesley John Olsen, 2011, p. 93.

In another letter to other members of the family, he explains the incidents in John Raymond's letter in different detail, and he added to some of the detail. One was the time the dud bomb hit and spewed yellow stuff over him. He said he was knocked unconscious and when he came to he saw a penis near him, said he got the shock of his life and checked to make sure he was still intact! Sadly, he also said that Harry Draper, his friend from Bridgetown, who had stayed with the Carrolls the night before going to the Claremont Showgrounds to leave for war, had been killed at Derna. Death and injury were becoming a harsh fact of life for these young frontline men.

Stanley Lawrence was not able to give any locations and his letters were censored by the army. Giving out information on their whereabouts was a dangerous security breach. The battles he participated in were at Bardia on the 5th January, Tobruk on 21st and 22nd January (where the famous Rats of Tobruk fought later against the German Field Marshall Erwin Rommel). On the 25th January he was at the battle for Derna where the dud bomb fell – he was very lucky to survive. If the bomb hadn't been a dud he would certainly have been killed. He now had had two very close calls in the short time he had been in action and he certainly had other close calls while running, and or repairing telephone wires at night. The last battle, in which Stanley Lawrence did not participate, was the push towards Benghazi when the Italians surrendered on 7th February 1941.

Whenever there was a moving battle or advancement of troops Stanley Lawrence was a runner and would take messages from his commanding officers and run to where ever the message was to be sent … sometimes right into the thick of battle at the front lines.

Stanley Lawrence's friend Harry Draper is killed

It was during the battle to seize Fort Rudero at Derna that Harry Draper was wounded. Twenty-eight 2/11th men were wounded or killed during this battle which was a dangerous forward push across an open aerodrome tarmac.

When Stanley Lawrence described Harry's death to the family, he said that, when a man died in battle, he wouldn't have known it, it was that quick. Again, as with WWI soldiers, he was putting a positive spin in his letters to his family because he didn't want them to worry. He described Harry's death in his letter, making it seem painless and quick, but Harry died of a head wound so, unless he was unconscious, he probably suffered a lingering and painful death – he survived for approximately fifty days. In the letter to his brother Arthur Henry and his wife, Thelma, he states: "*Young Harry made his exit very suddenly*", however, he may not have known Harry had survived when he wrote that letter, and that Harry was severely wounded rather than killed.

At the front of battle, news about their mates probably took some time to filter through. By then it was too late to undo the message in the letter. After the war, Stanley Lawrence never spoke of his friend; it must have been too painful and he probably wanted to leave the sadness behind him and to try to stay positive. It is known that most soldiers only spoke of the frivolous aspects of their war or just skimmed the surface However, on ANZAC Day each year, he would remember….

Harry Victor Draper WX574 2/11th Battalion
Photo – OLSEN, Wes. Battalion into Battle. Wesley John Olsen, 2011, p. 97.

Harry Victor Draper was safely evacuated from Fort Rudero but died on the 17th March 1941 of wounds received during the battle for Derna. He was only twenty-one years old. He is buried at Chatby Military Cemetery in Alexandria, Egypt, the same cemetery Ernest William McGlinn and William Patrick Kett were buried during WWI.

Harry's name is situated on Panel 35 in the Commemorative area at the Australian War Memorial, Canberra.

North Africa, 6 January 1941: Australian troops advance across open ground into Bardia.
Stanley Lawrence would be here – it was his 26th birthday.
Photo - Australian War Memorial accession number 069221

After the war, each ANZAC day Stanley Lawrence would make a wreath from fresh ficus leaves and flowers and during the Dawn Service at the War Memorial in Kings Park would march down the path and lay the wreath, stand back and salute. He would then stand with his head bent for a moment, turn and then march back. He looked very serious and solemn; he was remembering… Very few people attended the Dawn Service in those days.

Stanley Lawrence Carroll - ANZAC DAY – A proud man remembering … (Family photo)

Pain from Stanley Lawrence's dislocated knee injury he received during the rugby match returned. He had to nurse it through some of the battles by having it strapped. He didn't want to complain and have to go back for treatment. Because of his dedication to his mates, he stayed and stuck it out with them.

The Battle for Greece

Following these battles in North Africa, the men were wondering where they'd be sent next. Stanley Lawrence thought Venice might be nice! He was sick of the Middle East and thought the romance of the East was thoroughly over-rated! It wasn't long before they were told to be ready to be shipped out. According to Stanley Lawrence's commanding officer Brigadier T.L. Louch, Churchill had wanted to send the Australians from the 6th Division, which was Stanley Lawrence's division, to Greece following the battle of Tobruk and not to worry about the push to Benghazi, which was an important strategic battle.

Louch stated *"Winston Churchill, whose fertile mind was never at rest and who always had some plan of his own up his sleeve - often to the embarrassment of his professional advisers – was keen to send an army to Greece."* A compromise had to be sought to placate him! The push to Benghazi continued! LOUCH, T. S. Early Days of the 2/11th Australian Infantry Battalion. (In The 2/11th (City of Perth) Australian Infantry Battalion 1939-45). John Burridge Military Antiques, 2000. p 29.

Eventually, after the battles in the Middle East, the Australians were deployed to assist in the defence of Greece against the Italian army that was advancing from the north. Early in April 1941, the 2/11th had been moved back to Alexandria, Egypt and was there for only one day before being urgently required and hurriedly shipped across the Mediterranean to Greece.

Prior to their arrival in the port of Piraeus, Greece, where they were to disembark, bombing of the port by the German *Luftwaffe* had taken place, closing the port. The men, including Stanley Lawrence, were dead tired and in need of a rest. Now the ship had to be re-routed further along the coast to where they disembarked from the ship *Pennland* at Phaleron Bay on the 12th April. The men were told to leave their personal possessions on the ship. A soldier carried with them bits and pieces of personal things that did not go in their kit bag. These possessions travelled with the soldier throughout the war and contained photographs and some of the more luxury items not normally carried into battle. These items were left at a depot or camp during battles and were collected later when the men went on rest. The withdrawal from Greece had already been planned but the Australians were still required to go into Greece and into extreme danger. There was chaos during the disembarkation: two small fishing boats ferried some of the troops ashore until the tide changed and the ship had to move out to sea. Some troops spent the night on the ship and those who went ashore had to march two miles to a position where they could be taken to Daphne where they slept in tents in a pine plantation. It seems that the British commanding officers in Greece had not planned well enough the arrival and movement of the troops so confusion reigned until the 2/11th commander, Tom Louch, got things sorted. The next day, the troops had to march to the railway line where they were entrained to the town of Larissa, a journey of over 300 kilometres to the north then trucked west to Trikkala, Thessaly in northern Greece to assist in the British army retreat. As soon as they had dug their weapon pits, they were told to retreat and to leave behind any possessions they could not carry. Some of the men had taken their personal possessions and were angry that they had to be left behind. Orders were orders!

The Greeks had held off the Italian push from the north through the Balkans but were not strong enough against the tremendous force of the now-advancing German army. The British army had already mobilised to the front lines but it soon became apparent, after severe battle losses, the British could not hold the line and their position was untenable. They were being bombed out of existence with many casualties; the Australians were now to take the full brunt of war to help with the retreat. They were ordered to be the rear guard for the retreating British forces. In other words, the British were important and the Australians were expendable! Fierce battles took place. The Australians fought gallantly in absolutely perilous conditions in the mountains.

During the battles, Stanley Lawrence had to ensure messages between officers was maintained. He was in great danger and sometimes had to run the messages between them. The very steep slopes and low vegetation would have made him visible and a prime target. There were some instances that telephone lines could be run out between Companies The signalmen managed to keep communications open but there were times that wires were cut by bombs and information was not able to get through, causing serious miscalculations in some areas. However, these breakdowns in communication didn't last long; repairs were carried out quickly and runners filled the need. Several signalmen were injured and one killed. Stanley Lawrence's signalling duties continued but at times he joined the men at the front line as a rifleman.

It is fortunate he was an extremely fit man who could endure running long distances carrying a heavy load. Many of the wire lines were run up goat tracks that were steep and slippery – exhausting in the extreme, but those brave signalmen pushed through.

During battle situations, there are no comforts at all. The men slept on the ground in the freezing cold with their one blanket and great coat if they were lucky. Food supplied to them was intermittent and of very low quality, often leaving the men hungry and thirsty. They had to make do with what they carried but they fought on courageously. Conditions were abysmal.

The defeated Greek soldiers were retreating from their battles with the Italians and Germans further north and staggered past the Australian-held lines and continued on the road down the mountain passes. One Australian noted their gallantry. He said *"I would have been proud to have been killed in an attempt to stand by these Greek soldiers and save their country from the Hun. Some of them had been four or five days without food, and during that time they had covered anything up to one hundred and fifty miles after they had been cut off by the German push. They were footsore, hungry and weary, some even without boots and hardly able to walk, and yet when they heard they were needed they turned around and went back the way they had come, to stand side by side with us and try and hold the onrushing German mass. If that isn't guts I've never seen it."* OLSEN, Wes. *Battalion into battle.* Wesley John Olsen, 2011, P113-114.

The Australians managed to keep the enemy tanks, artillery, and infantry at bay but then the German air offence began. They almost carpet bombed the area the Australians held, but it was the continual diving of the Stukas screaming overhead and their machine gun strafing and bombing of the area that made the Australian retreating defence impossible. Evacuation was ordered and the withdrawal began. Stanley Lawrence said that the battles in the Middle East were like glorified bivouacs compared to the battles in the Greek mountains.

At Brallos, the men were told to make a stand and fierce fighting took place with many Australians killed. The men were fully aware that they had no backup or air support and they were on their own; they felt disillusioned and abandoned. It was during the battle at Brallos that Stanley Lawrence had another close encounter with a bomb that exploded close to him and knocked him off his feet, bursting his eardrum and causing concussion. He pushed on; there was no help. The withdrawal continued. The Australians were constantly bombed and strafed and the German infantry was on their heels. The Australians fought another rear-guard battle at Skamnos when further withdrawal was ordered.

During one of these battles, Stanley Lawrence's commanding officer, Tom Louch's car was bombed, wrenching his shoulder. His driver was shot through the head and killed by strafing from a Stuka. Louch's mental health failed and he was sent on down the mountain and away to hospital. It was at this stage Major Ray Sandover took over command of the battalion and became Stanley Lawrence's commanding officer for whom he would do signals.

Major Raymond Ladais Sandover commander of the 6th Division 2/11th
Photo – (www.prabook.com)

Stanley Lawrence said he had never been as cold as when they were retreating through the snow-covered mountains, and on down the bitter wind-swept passes. They had no bedding, only their great coats and had to sleep on the ground. Obstacles in their path included destroyed bridges across rivers that caused slow troop movement. German aircraft, Stukas, continued to harry the troops. They hurriedly continued their evacuation in open-sided canvas-covered trucks that were harassed by the German Luftwaffe. The troops were crammed into the back of trucks with one man posted as lookout for the enemy aircraft. When he saw them coming, he yelled out and the men would scatter in all directions hundreds of metres from the tracks and hide in the low bushes. The aircraft would bomb the line of trucks then turn and strafe the area either side of the road where the men were hiding. On one occasion, some men scattered either side of a small valley and on one side a bomb was dropped that killed eight or nine men. Their commander was on the road directing them when he was bombed and blown to bits – the only bit left of him was a small section of his spine that could be held in one hand! JOHNSON, Kenneth (Katy) Lieutenant. *Australians at War Film Archive*. 2003. (Australians at War Film Archive (unsw.edu.au)

The withdrawal was extremely difficult but they managed to leave the German ground forces behind by blowing up bridges and roads, blocking their way. Stanley

Lawrence was in one of the canvas-covered trucks during the retreat when an explosion near his truck caused the driver to swerve and hit a ditch and roll over, causing the troops to be thrown out, injuring a few. Stanley Lawrence hurt his lower back, neck, and shoulder but had to continue on without complaint – there was no option. The men were picked up by the following trucks and continued on down the mountains. This harassment continued all the way south to the coast.

Incidentally, this retreat went through the mountainous Thermopylae pass where in 480 BCE, the famous Battle of Thermopylae took place. *"Over 7,000 Spartans waited on a rise to defend against over 100,000 Persians but they couldn't hold the line and the Spartans were all killed."* (en.wikipedia.org/wiki/Battle_of_Thermopylae) This battle is often referred to in war books when describing disastrous losses. Fortunately, history did not repeat itself.

On the 24th April 1941, the 2/11th, which by now consisted of totally exhausted hungry and thirsty men, arrived at Megara to the west of Athens on the Isthmus of Corinth. They had no food nor water having been told to leave their webbing and ration packs in the mountains. Now at Megara, the soldiers were told to destroy the vehicles and other items that might be used by the enemy. They did a good job on the vehicles: they smashed windscreens, smashed the sumps, and emptied the oil from the engines then ran them until they seized then cracked the heads with a hammer. Then they shot the tyres and the radiators! Nothing was to be left for the Germans. Unfortunately, nothing was left for the troops either!

It was 25th April 1941, ANZAC Day. The injured Tom Louch had left his hospital bed and found his troops and was intent on commemorating ANZAC Day. He managed to clean himself up and honour the day. He said he had now experienced three memorable ANZAC Days – the first his landing at Gallipoli in 1915, the second, the battle for Villers-Brettoneux in 1918, and this one in Greece of which he said was the most trying of them all! The soldiers would now reflect on the mates who had been wounded or killed during their short war, and there were many.

The battle for Crete – a nightmare

The planned evacuation from Greece was to be on the nights of the 25th and 26th April. The navy was to be ready to evacuate over 4,000 troops, 1,500 wounded, and eighty nurses, but disaster struck. One of the ships, *Pennland*, had been sunk by German aircraft and the destroyer *Griffin* had picked up the survivors of that ship and was taking them to Crete. Orders then had to be changed and new pickup arrangements had to be made. The men, dog-tired and hungry, fell asleep in the olive groves where they were protected from continual menacing by German aircraft until they were roused to march to the pickup area and board the ship *Thurland Castle*. Not all could be taken, but the 2/11th – Stanley Lawrence among them – was marched to the pickup area. The embarkation of the men and the nurses began at 10.30 pm and finished at 3 am. They were told to leave everything behind and only take what could be slung on their backs. Their rifles were a priority and had to be taken but all other heavier armaments had to be left. Stanley Lawrence slung his rifle and telephone set across his shoulders, and in the dark climbed the long rope ladders to the deck of the ship. Many found the rope ladders daunting, especially some of the officers who complained that it was a very difficult climb to such a great height. The men were crammed into the ship.

Stanley Lawrence's commanding officer, Ray Sandover, noted that the ship was *"loaded with well over 3,000 instead of an intended 1,500 wounded. It was standing room only."* OLSEN, Wes. *Battalion into battle*. Wesley John Olsen, 2011, p. 139.

In the early hours of the morning on the 26th April, the *Thurland Castle* sailed from Greece escorted by five destroyers.

Against their officers' orders, some men managed to get a few Bren light machine guns and heavier armaments aboard. As daylight began, it brought the danger of enemy attack from the air. It was fortunate the men had strapped the guns to the ship's railings during the night because the ship was attacked many times by German aircraft en-route to Crete. Having been told during the battles in and around Brallos not to shoot at the German aircraft so as not to give their positions away, the soldiers now let go and shot at the aircraft with everything they had. Some even used pistols! The deafening noise from the gunshots drowned out the scream of the Stukas in their vertical dives. These aircraft were deadly accurate when dropping their bombs and strafing with their machine guns. Stukas were fitted with a siren that would scream with a frightening sound as the aircraft dived to attack; the faster the aircraft went, the louder and shriller the sound. It was horrifying and a great psychological hit to those below.

The ship was attacked five times during the voyage and several German planes were shot down. On one occasion, a bomb exploded under water just outside the hull of the ship, denting it severely, but didn't totally breach it. These bombs were designed to be dropped next to the ship to fracture the hull. To the great relief of the soldiers who were crammed in the hold, including Stanley Lawrence, only a minor leak occurred. If the hull had given way none of these men would have survived and they knew it. The navy personnel reassured the men and almost as a reward they told the men to help themselves to the food, drinks, and cigarettes stored there in the hull. There were many delicacies the men hadn't tasted for a long time so they really made a feast of it. The last of the airborne attacks was defended by three of the Royal Airforce's Bristol Blenheim fighter bombers that chased the enemy aircraft away and shot one down.

Unfortunately, during the chaos of trying to evacuate over 50,000 men from Greece, time ran out. The German army was now breathing down the necks of the men waiting to be evacuated. For those left behind, surrender was their only option. There were nearly 14,000 men left behind, and sadly they were to become prisoners of war, among them were 2,030 Australians.

Winston Churchill had decided that Crete was to be held at all costs. By his calculation, Crete was important in saving the Middle East and its vital oil supplies. He had already sent troops to defend the Middle East and Malta, and estimated that the only troops available to defend Crete were the troops evacuated from Greece. He would have been very aware that these troops lacked in all equipment for war. Because everything had to be left behind in Greece, there were severe shortages in everything, including tanks, artillery, mortars, transport, tools, and ammunition. Even boots and food were in very short supply. If an attack occurred, it would be an almost suicidal battle.

Churchill didn't care about the implications of war without weapons and ammunition! Disgustingly, he made no plans for evacuation in the possibility of withdrawal. He obviously thought these men were expendable – again! Analysis by war historians concluded that it was a disgrace that so many young men were sent into an unwinnable battle! According to some, Dunkirk was a picnic compared to Crete! (*WW2: Battle of Crete*. Pilot Guides. DVD. 2020). It seems Churchill's over-inflated skills at war strategies was a disaster in several theatres of war, including the Gallipoli campaign that he planned and implemented – another unwinnable disaster. It seems this man certainly knew how to 'talk the talk' but, unfortunately, not 'walk the walk'!!

On Crete, supplies were short. Some of the supply ships carrying food for the troops were sunk and only about one third got through. There was therefore some reliance on the Cretan people for food supplies. The commander on Crete, General Freyberg, soon learned that *"the only artillery he had on Crete was a handful of guns that had been shipped from Egypt. For the same reason, he had no trucks other than the few already on the island, few tools of any kind and no direct naval support"*. He believed Churchill was living in a dream world. LAFFIN, John. *Greece, Crete and Syria*. Time-Life Books, 1989. p. 58.

In Crete, during the late afternoon on the 26th April 1941, the damaged *Thurland Castle* arrived at Suda Bay with her cargo of exhausted and demoralised men and women. All were disembarked and, at last, a sense of security and safety (and quiet) ensued. That night the exhausted soldiers huddled together and shared the few blankets they had and slept on the ground.

Once again conflicting orders from the British hierarchy made life difficult for the soldiers. The 2/11th was ordered to march out towards the eastern town of Retimo (Rethymno), then were told to march back to Suda Bay. Stanley Lawrence's commanding officer, Major Ray Sandover, halted the troops and didn't move them again until those above came to a consensus. Many men complained and some caustic remarks were made about the excellent organisational skills of the navy compared to the poor decisions made by the British army hierarchy.

Those wounded in Greece and many of the nurses, plus some of the troops who could not be gainfully employed on Crete because there was not even enough small weaponry for them to use, did not stay on Crete. They were sent on to the relative safety of Alexandria in the Middle East. They were the lucky ones.

The Battle for Crete was the only time, other than at Gallipoli in WWI, that the Australians and New Zealanders fought together as a single unit. A true ANZAC force.

At that time, Hitler hadn't planned to attack Crete. He was more interested in invading the Soviet Union. However, he was harassed by his drug-addicted *Reich Marshal* Hermann Goering who was in charge of the Luftwaffe (the German airforce), and eventually Hitler gave permission for an all-out air and paratroop assault on Crete. This was the only time a solely air and paratroop attack was undertaken during WWII. Hermann Goering's Luftwaffe was an elite and crack force and many were dedicated to the ideology of Nazism. Kurt Student was a German General in the Luftwaffe during WWII and was in overall command of developing a paratrooper force to be known as the *Fallschirmjäger*, and would be in charge during the battle for Crete.

Once orders were received and Sandover agreed, Stanley Lawrence's group along with the Australian 2/1st Battalion, were instructed to march to Retimo, approximately fifty kilometres east of Suda Bay, to defend the airstrip there. A Greek force was to be there too.

Even though the Allied forces had no air support and therefore no real need for airstrips, it was ironic that the defence of them on Crete at Maleme, Retimo, and Heraklion, and the harbour of Suda Bay were considered vital. British intelligence received had told of German air attacks in the near future. Perhaps if the airstrips had been destroyed the Germans may have not had the ability to land their aircraft and deliver arms and transport requirements.

The troops marched into Retimo, and Sandover addressed them and gave them the orders for setting up battle lines. *"…Sandover took up defensive positions in the hills around the airstrip of Rethymno, … along with the 2/1st Battalion, supported by elements of 2/3rd Field Regiment, 2/1st Machine Gun Battalion and members of the Cretan Police. Lieutenant Colonel Ian Campbell, commander of the 2/1st Battalion, was appointed overall commander of the Rethymno Force."* (en.wikipedia.org/wiki/Raymond_Sandover#Battle_of_Crete)

After their arrival at Retimo and battle lines chosen, Stanley Lawrence reconnoitred the area and set up signal stations. He dug himself a lookout on higher ground to watch over the battle area so he could communicate to his Commanding Officer some of the battle situations. He and other signalmen ran what wires they had between command posts. The rest of the troops dug weapon pits and slit trenches among the olive groves and around the airstrip. Daily patrols were undertaken and the few armaments they had were strategically placed. There was very little signalling equipment so the main telephone line to headquarters at Maleme and General Freyberg's command post was via the Crete public phone system.

Because of Stanley Lawrence's fitness and endurance skills, he was appointed to be a "Runner". Messages would be relayed to battalion positions around the airstrip by physically running between them with messages from his commanders. The field telephones were in use but were minimal and used where they were most needed. His primary role was to deliver critical information from one command unit to another. *"A runner was a soldier responsible for passing on messages between fronts during war. This was arguably the most dangerous job of all, since these soldiers obviously had to leave the safety of a trench, bunker or any other kind of shelter in order to move from one front to the other".* (www.military-history.fandom.com/wiki/Runner). Runners seldom got through enemy fire!

Operation Mercury
Germany's paratroop assault begins

Germany's Operation Mercury was about to begin.

The morning of the 20th May 1941, at Retimo was just like every other blisteringly hot, boring day of routine, cleaning rifles etc. until the throb of aircraft engines could be heard coming from the north. All eyes turned and watched as hundreds of enemy aircraft flew towards them. Adrenalin made the men prickle and they came to a very alert state. Sandover quickly ordered battle stations. They all watched and must have wondered if this day would be their last, but to everyone's relief the aircraft turned westward and flew away from Retimo. A great feeling of relief must have been felt among the men.

However, later that day, at 4pm, another wave of German aircraft fighters and fighter bombers appeared again from the north and this time they didn't fly away; they began to bomb and machine gun the area around the airstrip. The men in the 2/11th dived into the trenches or hid behind whatever cover they had. It was this day that the battle for Crete began. About twenty Messerschmitt Bf 109 fighters and twenty Bf 110 fighter bombers flew over and began dropping their bombs around the perimeter of the airstrip, mainly on the 2/1st Battalion and the Greek troops. The 2/11th wasn't targeted so Sandover assumed the enemy wasn't aware of their positions. He ordered that no one fire upon the aircraft so as not to disclose their positions. One Bf 109 was shot down by the 2/1st Battalion.

At 4.30 pm, another wave of aircraft, in perfect formation, flew in from the sea. These aircraft were Junkers – Ju 52 Transport planes –that flew in flights of three. Twenty-four sets came in the first wave and there were several successive waves. As they approached, the aircraft began dropping their loads of paratroopers. Hundreds of them descended into a storm of bullets and many were killed. Some of the frail-bodied Junkers were hit by rifle fire and exploded into flames. The paratroopers' chutes caught fire and they plummeted to earth. Some had their chutes caught on the following aircraft and were dragged off to certain death.

Paratroopers descend from Ju 52 aircraft onto Retimo, there were hundreds more...
Photo - Bundesarchiv, Bild 110-670-7410-10. Photographer: Kleiner

Hundreds of paratroopers were killed or captured. They landed with only a Luger pistol, a flick-knife, and some rations and water but were ready to fight within thirty seconds. Their fighting equipment was dropped separately in big containers that they had to find while under a barrage of bullets. The Retimo airstrip had an apron fence that the paratroopers encountered and couldn't go over and they were shot. It was a bloodbath but many managed to gather into groups and hide to become a menacing fighting force. They were very well trained and had an obsessive pride in their ability to win. They wore very heavy uniforms, quite unsuitable for the oppressive heat, so many of them cut the legs and sleeves off their uniforms. Captured by the Australians were the intelligence papers of tactical use to the paratroopers. Some included an explanation of the colours of the parachutes and their meaning, which were mainly white or camouflaged green and brown, and some were coloured chutes that denoted the rank of officers. The camouflaged ones were to be used as camouflage for their machine gun and mortar positions and the white ones were for making signals by laying symbols and letters on the ground for their aircrew. Bombs could then be effectively dropped for the most damage and death. Once the Australians knew what the signal parachutes were used for, they made signals that directed the enemy onto their own men.

During the first three hours of the battle, the Australians had used almost half of their ammunition, but this was alleviated somewhat by the capture of the

German's parachuted equipment that had come down by the box full ready for their paratroopers. The fighting here, and at Maleme, had been particularly bloody. The Germans that had managed to get away from the Australians gathered in groups and formed into substantial and dangerous fighting units.

A total of 10,000 paratroopers and twelve thousand glider-borne infantry were sent to Crete with 1,000 aircraft. Four thousand were killed or wounded on the first day. MacDOUGAL, A.K. *Australians at war.* Five Mile Press, 2002. p. 201.

The fighting to the west, at Maleme, was bitter and there was much bloodshed on both sides, but the Germans ended up as the victors. At the end of the Allied fighting ability, the New Zealand Maori unit fought a heroic and bloody front with minimal ammunition. No one knew at the time but it was later noted that Germans were also at the end of their abilities to continue. They had no ammunition and, had the Maoris been given the opportunity to attack with the very little they had in way of ammunition, the battle for Crete may not have been lost. It was the New Zealand commander who was stationed on high ground overlooking the battle area who commanded the surrender of the Allied troops. Apparently, he had a mental breakdown, was delusional, and wrongly surrendered his troops. The last-ditch attempt by the Maoris was the performance of a ferocious-looking Haka that spooked the Germans who ran off. These proud warrior Maoris were prepared to fight to the death and faced the Germans front on.

That order to surrender meant capitulation of the island. Many of the Australians, New Zealanders and British were either captured or headed for the mountains in the hope of escape. Without any defence, the Germans were able to land their aircraft at Maleme and bring more weapons, heavy transport, and many more troops. Crete was lost.

Allied ships in Suda Bay had been heavily bombed and many destroyed. The navy had tried to support the troops and fight off the German air attacks but, to do this, they had to sail north of the island and right into German air power. Ships were sunk with heavy losses of life.

Retimo Force continued to fight on for a few days after the surrender at Maleme. The Retimo commanding officers had no idea that the surrender had taken place – there had been no communication – the wires had been cut. Those at Retimo kept up a fierce battle against the Germans. The following is an excerpt from the book *Battalion into Battle*. It displays the courage and tenacity, against the odds, by the Australians. Stanley Lawrence was in the thick of it. He had to relay messages to and from the commanders of the battles and would have been in immense danger. On this day, his company, "C" Company, now consisted of just sixty men and, along with another two companies, were stuck in a nine-inch-deep ditch near the German front lines without any chance of escape. The excerpt below gives an idea of how battle plans must be implemented in the thick of battle in order to save lives ... One of the commanders, Honner, needed to give those in the ditch the opportunity to get out before many deaths occurred.

This battle took place after Crete had fallen but they weren't aware of it. It was early morning, Tuesday 27th May 1941. The battle had now been raging for seven days.

> "Honner knew from the volume of fire emanating from the German trenches, and the upper windows of the houses, that he would lose men if he ordered a frontal assault. He also knew that time was critical, and believed Robert's platoon (in the ditch) would be overwhelmed if he did not move quickly. The task though, was daunting. The forward German trench was seventy-five yards away, and the only cover was a low stone wall surrounding a well about fifty yards away. If his men were to have any chance of crossing no-man's-land in the rapidly improving light, it was vital that he get a machine-gun behind the wall to cover the assault. Honner ordered Lieutenant Stoneham to get a Bren gun to the wall while the remainder of the company provided covering fire. The task fell to Corporal Tom Willoughby's section.

Honner recalled:

> As the rest of the company opened rapid fire on the trenches and houses to quieten the enemy guns Willoughby's gallant team leaped from the ditch and started racing along a low hedge leading past the disabled tank to the well. Willoughby was nearly there before he fell. Behind him the Bren-gunner went down. The next rifleman caught up the gun in passing and went on until he was killed, and so the Bren was relayed through the next section until it almost reached the well in the hands of the last runner; and he too was killed as he went down kneeling over it, guarding it even in death.

> Eight brave men ... fell trying to get the Bren gun to the well ... A stretcher-bearer then raced out to assist the first man to fall, dived down beside him, but discovered him dead. Suspecting the others were also dead, he decided to lay low and feign death Sandover, having received Honner's report of the situation, now

decided to abandon the attack. He ordered that the men still sheltering in the ditches remain there until dark Later in the morning Sandover proceeded to Hill "C" with Campbell to reassess the situation. Once there, Campbell watched as the Luftwaffe dive-bombed and machine gunned Sandover's forward troops." OLSEN, Wes. Battalion into battle. Wesley John Olsen, 2011. p. 185-187.

While these battles were raging, Stanley Lawrence would have had to run messages between commanders. He could have easily been a victim along with the many others who fell that day. This day was no different to the next three days: battles raged and more men were killed or wounded. It was a terrifying and precarious time. This group of men had to contend, not only with the German troops on the ground, but had to endure the constant air attacks with both machine guns and bombings. The Australians had no protection from the air – the British Airforce was no help.

The Germans were able to pincer some of the Australian troops who had to surrender. Others fought on and it wasn't until the Germans could be seen advancing in the distance and began to arrive on motorbikes and other heavy transport that the order was given to withdraw. There was no possibility the Australians could continue and, finally, word got through to surrender. Stanley Lawrence was out trying to contact the 2/1st battalion but had no luck. They had been captured. All the phone lines were down and contact with anyone was now impossible.

Sandover, who didn't like the idea of surrender, offered his troops the option – either surrender to the Germans and become a prisoner of war, or, it's every man for himself. This order gave the opportunity for any soldier to try to escape. Without this order of every man for himself, men could not escape; they would be considered going absent without leave and could have been court-martialled. Stanley Lawrence, being a fighter who didn't mind taking risks, decided to make a run for it and escape. He asked another of the signalmen if he would like to go with him. This man was to be his future uncle in-law – John Lannin Gawned. John Lannin declined and decided to surrender – he had two small daughters at home and didn't want to risk being killed. He went to the same prisoner of war camp as Stanley Lawrence's close friend, Alan Knee, photo on next page.

Alan Knee, a POW in Stalag X111C Germany. (Family photo)

Stanley Lawrence wrote home to his family expressing his sadness at Alan being taken prisoner and how much he missed him.

Fifty-eight of Stanley Lawrence's group were killed, 126 wounded, and 535 were taken prisoner of war.

The next section is Stanley Lawrence's official account of what happened during the occupation of Crete. The battalion's diarist had been injured during the bombing of the *Thurland Castle* and had been evacuated from Crete to Alexandria. Therefore, there was no diarist in the battalion so Stanley Lawrence provided the official information to the hierarchy after his escape from Crete. He hand-wrote the following official account of the Battle for Crete … Acronyms have been removed and written in full and some explanations of terms have been provided.

This is Stanley Lawrence's true and correct account as written by him. His document is now housed at the Australian War Memorial in Canberra, Australia.

This was written on "Australian Comfort Fund" (ACF) paper and "Australian Young Men's Christian Association (YMCA) Write Home First" paper that was supplied to soldiers to write letters home. CARROLL, Stanley Lawrence, *Report of WX953 Pte Carroll, S.L. Citation* - Australian War Memorial - 3 DRL 6045

(After leaving Greece) Arriving Crete on the evening 26th April went ashore in invasion barges, Australian Infantry Forces assembled and were marched to reception camp several miles west. Here a good mug of hot tea, biscuits etc were served, oranges, chocolates and cigarettes to follow. This cheered the boys immensely, they sat around in small groups discussing their various experiences, some quite humorous, others perhaps a little exaggerated but never the less very interesting.

An atmosphere of security was very much in evidence the moment we set foot on the island. Sleep had been sadly neglected and nerves a trifle frayed during the seventeen whirlwind days spent in Greece. Long before midnight silence reigned, huddled together to share what blankets were available we literally died until reveille next morning. After a fairly substantial breakfast we were again assembled in our respective units and moved off in the direction of Suda Bay. The general impression being that we were to embark for Egypt.

Heading inland gave us a considerable food for thought and as usual the inevitable rumours began to circulate. The distance to the camp varied from two to twenty miles, causing a number of complaints, always to be expected on a long march, but moreso when arms, ammo and rations have to be man handled.

A few (to use the army term) bludgers fell out in hopes of bumming a lift but the majority plugged on. The Battalion reputation had to be maintained, especially with such units as the Field Ambulance, Army Service Corps etc strung out in the rear.

At 15.00 hours camp site was reached, except for an occasional enemy aircraft passing over the area, all was very peaceful. To lie on grass in the cool shade of the olive trees, was something we had dreamed of for months.

The following day another move was made, Companies taking up positions, lookout and battle stations. A very pleasant week was spent here, hot meals, cigarette issues & more blankets were available, quite like old times. An air raid on Suda Bay from time to time, reminded us that the war must have been still in progress.

It was here, a general muster of representatives from all Australian units in the area was made. The General commanding the entire forces on the island had a few words to say. As usual the case on these occasions, he referred to we Australians as being a tough looking bunch, whom he felt sure could deal very effectively with parachutists. Our reputation with the bayonet should discourage any would be invaders. I for one, up till that time, had slaughtered many a bag of straw in camp with the bayonet & felt the two hairs on my chest bristle in anticipation. We had just experienced our first taste of real warfare, (in Greece) the Libyan Campaign being in comparison a glorified bivouac.

A further movement brought us to a position overlooking the ocean, it seemed that we had already walked twice around the island. The first pay since leaving Egypt was made here, the result being several charges of excessive consumption of vino or crassi. (alcoholic drinks).

For some unknown reason the final movement order had been delayed. Unit was instructed to occupy position Retimo aerodrome that night. A gallant attempt was made to comply with order and the troops expressed their disapproval in no mild form. The night was very bright, but the atmosphere quite the reverse. Battalion Head Quarters staff and batmen (a batman is assigned as a 'servant' to the Commanding Officer) experienced great difficulties, endeavouring to keep the seats of their trousers from dragging on the cobblestone roads. (They were very tired).

A number of stragglers managed to reach Retimo, remaining there until the piquet (a Piquet is a small group of soldiers who were used for some temporary assignments) rounded them up the following day. Commanding Officer's orderly room was well attended, at least twenty defaulters daily. During the ensuing few weeks, the generosity of the Greeks threatened to interfere with Battalion routine consequently all cafes were placed out of bounds.

The area known as Retimo sector took the form of an island, being surrounded by a first class road. A thin strip of flat land extending from Retimo township to a headland some five or six miles east along the waterfront, was regarded as the only possible area where parachutists could make a successful landing.

The defensive positions were dug in on the forward slope, which made a gradual rise in terraced formation and was completely covered by olive groves. An apron fence concealed among the vines and trees extended along the entire front, a death trap for a considerable number of Germans.

2/1 Battalion occupied the right and eastern end, the Greeks the centre overlooking the aerodrome, 2/11 Battalion left and western end, the rear being practically unprotected except for one or two patrols.

About 1000 hours on the 20th May large enemy aircraft were sighted inland flying in an easterly direction. These machines appeared to be towing gliders. Another formation could be seen out to sea, also towing gliders and flying in the same direction.

Message from Brigade "Parachutists landed Canea, Heraklion, Georgeopolis." Battle stations were manned. Further message Brigade "No Parachutists Heraklion, approx 500 landed Georgeopolis, dispersed in surrounding hills."

1600 hours

Large number enemy fighter planes attacked Retimo sector. Flying at low altitude severely strafed the whole area, Bren guns opened fire, bringing one plane down 200 yards from Battalion Headquarters. From signals Observation Post report sky black with large aircraft approaching east, flying very low. Within a few seconds sky was full of planes and parachutes. The enemy appeared to operate in formations of five troop carriers in waves of twenty. The first descending on and in front of 2/1 Battalion lines, the second on the aerodrome, a third on our immediate front whilst a fourth in the vicinity of Perivolia. This procedure was repeated at intervals of about five minutes. Each (German) Transport Carrier dropping an average of fifteen parachutists, 2 inch field pieces, motor cycles, mortars and large containers were dropped at intervals. Parachutists were of different colours denoting rank and section, Medical Officers, Engineers etc. information from captured papers and prisoners. During the remaining hours of daylight operations depended mainly on communications. Platoons being transferred where ever weakness occurred. B. Company acting as reserve working between rear, left flank and front.

Enemy patrol entered Advanced Dressing Station (medical) Adele (place) informed staff and patients they were Prisoners of War and would be taken to Retimo that night. Stretcher bearers working between unit and Advanced Dressing Station were intercepted, some detained for questioning failed to return.

Patrol consisting of signals, batmen & a section of mortars, were detailed to investigate. Engaged enemy patrol vicinity Marulas, returned an hour later with several prisoners. Mortars scoring direct hits disposed of patrol, few managed to escape.

To prevent further infiltration in rear, Greek battalions moved from Adele to fill existing gap between 2/11 Battalion left flank and Marulas. Midday on the 21st May position was well in hand, enemy operating in isolated groups, withdrawing to positions on outskirts Perivolia.

An attempt during daylight to prevent enemy consolidating in Perivolia was cancelled owing number of casualties inflicted by severe ground strafing by low flying enemy aircraft. B & C Companies repeated attack, dawn next morning. Greeks were to participate with one of their dashing attacks, which never eventuated.

By 0800 hours our troops had covered the two miles separating our forward positions and Perivolia. Through signals telescope in Observation Post enemy could be seen retreating, running from house to house. Artillery had silenced three field pieces and several mortars, leaving machine guns and rifles being used against our advancing Companies.

Greeks were of little if any assistance. Transport making an encircling movement between Marulas and Perivolia, were fired on from left. An investigation proved that both Greek civilians and soldiers were responsible. The whole show would have undoubtedly been closed before nightfall. The Greeks had managed to cut off the retreat in direction of Retimo. A squadron of fighter bombers appeared about 1000 hours. The enemy signal, one green very light (A "very" light is a flare fired from a pistol) was fired in direction of B Company meaning bring fire to bear on area. A little later repeated in direction of C Company.

Within an hour the whole area was in flames, crops and trees being set alight by tracer and explosive bullets. A number of bombs were dropped on Sesmes and along the road. Troops were pinned down for remainder of day.

B & C Companies retired at dusk, A & D Companies moved into sheltered positions half mile forward of Sesmes. Further operations during daylight were impossible as enemy aircraft working in relays continued to bomb & machine gun from dawn till dusk. Artillery, Machine Guns, and mortars being likewise effected.

The Commanding Officer had for days endeavoured to obtain the assistance of two Infantry Tanks from the 2/1 Battalion. With their aid, plus two carriers attached to 2/11 Battalion, it was hoped to stage a dawn attack in the way of an armoured sortie. Rations & ammo were almost exhausted & Retimo was our only means of securing same.

2/1 Battalion were experiencing similar difficulties, fresh supplies were dropped to enemy daily. (German) Troop Carriers were making crash landings in the fields and although the artillery were blowing them up as soon as they landed, the enemy managed to get more field pieces & mortars.

(27th May)

Seven days after the fighting commenced received message "Loaded lighter will land stores beach vicinity aerodrome, between 0200 and 0300" (A lighter is a type of flat-bottomed barge used to transfer goods and passengers to and from moored ships.) All available transport including carriers stood by to collect cargo, returning at 0430 hours empty. At first light lighter was sighted approx 1½ miles east aground. Fortunately most of the cargo, ammunition and rations had been brought ashore by 2/1 Battalion personnel, before enemy aircraft bombed and sank the lighter. R.A.F. (Royal Air Force) dropped medical supplies during the early hours the same morning. Bandages were fluttering in the trees like streamers for hundreds of yards around, the remainder of the stuff was scattered in all directions. A message was sent out in "clear" requesting that the Germans drop medical supplies for their wounded.

(28th May)

Early next morning a troop carrier flew low over our lines, one man sitting on the fuselage holding what appeared to be a white flag with a green cross in the centre. Two containers were dropped in C. Company area containing medical supplies of all descriptions, also a full kit of surgical instruments.

It was decided to make a night attack on German line, extending from beach to southern end of Perivolia, four Companies taking part. Tommy guns 75%, German hand grenades and bayonets being used.

Moving under cover of darkness to a position well forward, the attack was launched at 0300 hours.

Each Company working in sections were to advance to outer buildings in allotted area and attack known Machine Gun and mortar positions at an appointed time, retiring before first light, when the prearranged signal went up. Greeks were to attack at dawn from the rear enemy positions. Proceedings were suddenly interrupted when signal came from D. Company. It was later learned that the Officer Commanding had been badly wounded. A.C.D Companies retired, B Company had gone right through and were forced to remain in the village, being caught in line Machine Gun fire. (and were cut off from the others).

During these operations, a thin line of defence had to be maintained along the Battalion front, in the event of further landing of parachutists. By night, Head Quarters Company, transport & a section of Machine Guns patrolled and manned listening posts from Greek left flank to village of Sesmes. Advantages gained in surprise attacks could not be followed up after first light.

Two snipers rifles were used to advantage. Germans were compelled to expose themselves when using ground strips and collecting supplies dropped. Enemy ground strip and 'very' light signals obtained from captured papers were used by both 2/1 and 2/11 Battalions. A number of containers being dropped in lines.

These containers are a large wooden box braced with angle iron, an aluminium buffer at each end and fitted with two small pneumatic tyred wheels a handle fitted underneath sliding out.

Activity next day was almost nil, not knowing the whereabouts of B. Company artillery were restricted to a very small area, Machine Guns and snipers were the only safe means of retaliation.

At dusk A. Company moved forward to cover should B. Company attempt to withdraw. Mortars using 4" German smoke bombs concentrated an area along water front, whilst artillery shelled visible enemy positions. B. Company failed to put in an appearance next morning, but managed to reach Greek lines, arriving Battalion area 1400 hours from the direction of Marulas.

Considerable information had been gained. Exact enemy positions, ammunition dumps, Head Quarters beneath Regimental Aid Post estimated number enemy casualties and fighting strength. Battalion Medical Officer went forward carrying Red Cross flag and entered enemy lines. He was intercepted & blind folded. Attended to both Australian and German wounded. A request was made that they remove ammunition and Head Quarters also allow truck load badly wounded through to Field Ambulance.

The Greeks became very restless, news had reached them that 300 German motor cyclists had arrived in Retimo. They were told that British reinforcements had arrived on the island but it was useless to try and hold them, they vanished overnight, leaving the entire centre and left flank unprotected. Leaflets dropped by enemy planes might have been responsible. 2/11 Battalion were immediately withdrawn to Greek position overlooking aerodrome. C. Company forming road block forward of Sesmes at fork road. During this movement information regarding capitulation of island was picked up by wireless attached to 2/1 Battalion.

Officers conference was summoned result being, destroy weapons and surrender or every man for himself. C. Company had engaged enemy and were last seen fighting at close quarters.

Remaining old position to keep communications open to C. Company and section Machine Guns, I couldn't understand Machine Guns and rifle fire coming from front. All lines were destroyed, failed to raise Battalion, Artillery and forward troops.

(30th May)

Arriving new position found it almost deserted. Bullets were clipping leaves and bark off the trees all round me. Hearing whistles blowing on the aerodrome, I went forward on my hand and knees. A number of (German) troop carriers were approaching from out to sea, the road was lined with small armoured cars & motor cycles. Germans were everywhere

Crete was lost.

A hand written page from Stanley Lawrence's official report of the battle for Crete is below.

> The enemy appeared to operate in formations of five troop carriers in waves of twenty. The first descending on and in front of 2/1 Bn. lines the second on the aerodrome, a third on our immediate front whilst a fourth in the vicinity of Perivolia. This procedure was repeated at intervals of about five minutes. Each T.C. dropping on an average of fifteen parachutists. 2" field pieces, motor cycles, mortars and large containers were also dropped at intervals. Parachutes were of different colours. denoting rank and section, N.C.Os, EN.Os etc. information from captured papers & prisoners. During the remaining hours of daylight operations depended mainly on communications. Platoons being transferred where ever weakness occurred. B. Coy acting as reserve working between rear, left flank and front

Written by Stanley Lawrence after his escape from Crete in June 1941

Stanley Lawrence escapes from Crete – sailed alone across the Mediterranean

Below is Stanley Lawrence's personal account of his actions during the last moments of the Battle for Crete and his escape. Rather than include the official version that continued on the above document his more personal account written in a letter to his brothers soon after his escape has been included here. Some acronyms have been included in full wording along with some explanations. Spelling and grammar have been left as is.

WX953 Signalman S.L. Carroll
2/11th Battalion. ABROAD
25/7/1941

Dear Jack and Art

My letters home just about cover all events of the past, so will give you the story of my escape from Crete. British War Correspondents took a few pictures and a story when I arrived in Egypt, but I don't know whether it has been published.

We cleaned the G's (Germans) *up on our front and were sitting pretty, but they gained a footing on other aerodromes and came by road in hundreds of armoured cars and motor cycle outfits to show us where we got off.*

The battalion had just taken up a new position overnight and I was left behind to keep communications open until Headquarters was established. Mortars were crashing all around me and explosive bullets were clipping the bark and leaves off the trees. I couldn't make out what was going on, all lines were disconnected and there didn't seem to be a soul about.

Disconnecting the instruments I put the lines straight through and took off for the new position. When I arrived there it was deserted, so crawled forward to see what all the noise was. The position we were holding was on the forward slope of a hill overlooking the aerodrome and was covered with olive groves. Whistles were blowing and chaps were shouting, bullets whizzing in all directions, talk about a din. Several big troop carriers (German aircraft) *were circling low over the drome and all I could see was G's, thousands of them.*

Stripping my webbing I took water bottle, haversack and bolted for the mountains reaching the south coast at midnight, a distance of about forty miles. A Blenheim (British plane) flew over in the early hours of the morning so I opened up with my signals torch and called him. He circled a few times and then dropped about a dozen bags of ration chocolate and some medical supplies.

There were hundreds of us all along the coast so I sent the pilot a message telling approximately how many were there. He acknowledged the message sent good luck and headed out to sea. That was the last we saw or heard of anything except enemy planes, they didn't forget us (and) kept up a continuous reconnaissance. We hung around for eight days signalling to sea every night without result. Our numbers were dwindling, the German patrols had us cut off, we were out of food but water was still plentiful. It was a bit risky hanging around with the crowd, so I headed back into the mountains and travelling by night managed to get across the road they were patrolling. I kept going for about twenty miles or so and then returned to the coast and luckily met up with two other chaps, one was a tommy (English) officer and had about forty Greek quid (money) on him, so we set about getting a boat. There wasn't much left to choose from, all the ocean going craft had gone off or had been machine gunned from the air. We found a little 16ft (foot) tub that looked in pretty good nic. (condition) but the owner wouldn't sell, he wanted to get to an island about thirty miles off, but wasn't game to tackle it.

Something in our attitude must have made him suspicious because the swine removed all the fittings and riggings. I ripped a piece of canvas off the wall of a flour mill. The old miller went dead crook but wouldn't accept any payment.

The rest of the crew, which now amounted to four, another tommy had blown in & knew nothing about sailing, left me to fix everything up while they attended to food and water. During the day a Greek nurse came on the scene and begged the tommy officer to take her to Alexandria. Ye Gods! Five in a jerry rigged tub to travel all that distance. We had a few arguments over the matter, neither of the other two wanted to stand down so I was elected skipper, but what I said didn't seem to go. On the afternoon of the eve of our departure, the other three chaps went in search of another water container and fresh bread, up until midnight had failed to return.

The nurse, only a young sort, was still hanging around so I sent her back to the village to wait until I called for her. Three patrols were combing the area and I thought she might give the whole show away. One section of them passed within feet of me several times. I had to slide into the creek and crawl for hundreds of yards and by god the water was cold.

As soon as things quietened down, I shifted the gear to a little cove about half a mile further up the coast and came back to pinch the boat. It was drawn right up on the beach and without rollers I had to drag it end for end. I've never lost so much sweat in all my life. Expecting to draw fire at any moment and struggling for about two hours to get it into the water.

With the aid of a floorboard I paddled back to pick up the works. The mast, boom, peak and sail were all in one. The peak was made out of a fishing spear, the centre prong bashed out to make the fork act as jaws. You've never seen anything like it. Bamboos, a piece of old drift wood for a mast and about fifteen square feet of ancient canvas reinforced with string. Luckily the rudder was under the seat and the tiller easily fixed.

By the time I got her rigged up she was half full of water, but next morning I found the drain cock wide open. When I pushed off and had put a hundred yards between me and shore I felt as if I had already reached safety and was as good as saved, but nearly three hundred miles lay before me.

My intentions were to make a big rock that stood off about three miles and give the whole outfit a good overhaul. The breeze had to be blowing in the wrong direction and trying to beat up into it, I drifted miles off my course. When dawn came I was becalmed in full view of the beach patrols and a sitting shot for the dive machine gunners. Without oars, I just had to sit there and wait for the recce (reconnaissance) plane. As soon as I heard him coming I swung the nose in the direction of land in hopes that he would mistake me for a fisherman. The trick didn't work. He came down and put one burst (machine gun) about twenty yards in front of me, circled around and ripped another burst alongside me, so I promptly took to the water. He must have thought that he had scored because he gained altitude and continued east.

My plans were badly upset, so decided to cruise along the coast and make for the place where I had left the crowd. There were three officers I had been with most of the time still hiding back in the hills so thought if I could creep in somewhere I might have chance of getting them off.

A breeze sprung up about 10 o'clock and keeping at what I considered a safe distance headed west. Each time I approached what appeared to be a quiet secluded spot, I drew fire and believe me some of those pieces of lead whined damned close. The ricochets were the worst, I nearly put my head through the floor boards several times. The boat seemed to be anchored to the spot, if I'd had a pair of spurs I think I would have used them, talk about ride her.

It seemed hopeless to try any further, so put her about and headed for Egypt. "Sydney or the bush" I preferred feeding the fish to being a prisoner of war.

The first night out it blew like hell. I reduced the sail to about six square feet and then the cords holding the jaws broke, down came the lot. The sail went overboard and dragging it back ripped all down one side. All I could do was sit tight and wait for the moon to rise. The wind eased off about midnight, but the water was very choppy, I felt as crook as hell and no sleep the night before didn't improve matters.

I stuck it out til day break and by this time the sea had subsided except for the swell. I was too tired to bail the bilge out so curled up on the little bit of forward decking. It was nearly midday before I woke up. I was wet through, the boat was drifting broadside on and every second wave dashed spray all over me.

With a pocket knife and some string I stitched the sail up and when trying to guide the mast into the block got bowled overboard nearly smashing the whole outfit. Luckily the boom was made of bamboos and bent instead of breaking. From then onwards I had mild weather, too mild in fact was becalmed on the fourth and fifth days, about six hours wind in forty eight. Had to cut down on water and rations. I had a two gallon tin and six tins of ration chocolate, enough to last me twelve days. During the night I used to signal in all directions with my torch, but not a damned thing ever answered. Except for a few pieces of drifting wreckage and some sea birds, I never sighted a thing throughout the whole trip.

Early on the sixth day a strong wind came up and by 8am had developed into a gale. It was a nor'-wester so had to alter my southerly course and run before it, the sea being too heavy to risk reaching. The boat was pointed at both ends and rode the surf wonderfully, I must have been doing twenty knots at times.

Without a compass and not a thing to steer on made it difficult to keep a straight course. The pocket knife with the blade stuck in the decking at right angles to the length of the boat, was a pretty good guide. When it cast the finest shadow I knew I was heading due south and without a plate it meant that I would drift sufficiently east to avoid landing in Libya.

For fifty two hours I ran before the wind. The waves were so big that I dared not leave the tiller or I would most certainly have been swamped. (During sleep, Stanley Lawrence tied the tiller to his neck so he could detect a change of direction.)

At about 9am on the eighth morning I sighted a sort of white haze in the sky to the south and soon after a tiny strip of land loomed up. Throwing all caution to the wind, I pulled in the sheet and headed straight for it. It was quite a battle holding her against the waves, they were thumping me broadside on. Each time she went down in the trough the sail was robbed of wind and the mast would kick back putting a hell of a strain on the planking, loosening the putty. She began to leak pretty badly and by midday I was nearly euchred, (exhausted) trying to bail and steer at the same time. The coast didn't appear to be far off so I didn't mind much if she did crack up.

She gradually got lower and lower in the water and finally rolled clean over. I got bashed about a bit before I could get clear and the mast had gone right through the bottom. I tied my tunic and haversack to the sheet rope clamps and set off for the shore on the water tin which still contained about a third of a gallon.

Swimming, surfing and floating I managed to gradually close the distance. It must have been much further than I anticipated, it took me seven hours to get in. Long before I reached shore I could hear a rumbling sort of a roar and from the crest of the waves could see the spray being dashed yards in the air. Not very comforting, but still it was land and that seemed to be all that mattered. Well I had a hell of a struggle when nearing the rocks. Trying to retain hold on the tin and avoid being carried on the breakers, I thought the game was up. (he would be killed)

The only chance I thought was to use the tin to take the impact and try and scramble clear before the next wave caught me. They must have been twenty feet high. Keeping on the bottom as much as possible I worked my way along for about a quarter of a mile and came across a small patch of sand. They were lovely dumpers, I must have turned fifty somersaults before coming to rest high and dry in a heap of seaweed. My legs wouldn't hold me up, I felt as if I had been on the beer for a week. My trousers was all I had left so wrung them out and stretched out for a spell, (rest) but it got too cold and decided to go in search of civilization.

The coast road wasn't far but the stones were too rough on the feet, I had to stick to the sandhills and head east. After walking for about an hour I came across an airforce listening post. Two little aerials and bell tent with a wireless van hidden in the hollow. There were two dark, foreign looking chaps messing around in the anti-aircraft pit. They had the blue peaked caps on and looked just like dings. (Italians) I thought then that I had run into enemy territory after all.

The van had British lettering and numbers on it so decided to try my luck, it had been pretty good up till then. I stood up and walked towards them. They got a hell of a shock and swung the gun on me. I must have looked a great sight, a badly torn pair of trousers and with a red handkerchief tied around my eyes to keep the glare out. (He also had a very sunburned and scabbed face and cracked bleeding lips.) They thought I was a wog. (a middle eastern man)

My left eye was completely blind and the right was badly affected from the glare of the sun. They called out to the wireless operator who had blonde hair and of course I thought he was a German. When I approached him he just stood and stared at me so all I could think of was to ask if he was a German. He seemed quite insulted and answered "Be buggered we are British". When I told him that I had just arrived from Crete he was astounded and rushed off to send a message to control. The two foreigners turned out to be Maltese chaps.

They carried me into the tent and in a few minutes had a lovely big mug of tea brewed, the first I'd had for nearly a month.

I couldn't eat much, so the operator produced a couple of bottles of Richmond Tiger (beer) and a tin of Craven A's. (cigarettes) Well I nearly lost my sense of reason. (At this stage he nearly broke down in tears at the relief of being safe, a very emotional time. Later, when he spoke of this moment his voice would catch – he was still affected many years later.)

I had a couple of smokes and knocked one bottle of beer off and passed clean out, properly blotto. (drunk) Didn't wake up till after ten next morning. My poor old watch had cashed in, (stopped) the water had got in somehow so am going to put it on Caris Bros for a new one. I took a stroll back along the beach to see if the boat had come in. It was there alright smashed to pieces on the rocks, but the tunic was missing and with it went my pay book.

About midday a car came out and got me and that's when the fun started. Interviews, cameras and war correspondents. Am now back in harness but don't know when we will see action again.

Well lads that's the story and I can tell you I don't fancy another dose just yet a while.

Give my love to all, will write again when more news is available.

Brother Stan

PS Alan is a POW. (Prisoner of War), I miss him terribly.

Illustration - Stanley Lawrence's escape from Crete 1941 – By Emily 2023

A note of explanation about the escape across Crete from Retimo. The men followed the road south and headed for the mountains. Many were exhausted and the climb up mountain slopes was very steep and perilous. They had had very little food and were extremely hungry, thirsty, and exhausted and the terrain was rocky and rough to cover. The Cretan people were very good to the soldiers and led them away from the road along goat tracks to avoid being seen. They gave the men what food and water they could and advice on where the German patrols were. If not for these brave people a lot more soldiers would have been captured or killed. Alarmingly, when the Germans found out the Cretan people had helped the escaped soldiers, they executed them, but in spite of this, the brave Cretan people continued to help.

The typical rugged terrain of southern Crete (Photo, Lindsay Carroll. 2008)

The mountain passes were rugged and had very little cover in which to hide and the nights were bitterly cold. On the 1st June, they made it to Agia Galini on the south coast. This is where Stanley Lawrence signaled out to sea and was threatened by his fellow soldiers who thought he would give their position away. They waited there for eight days. Stanley Lawrence and Alan Hackshaw didn't stay on the coast. Each day they went into the mountains and only came to the coast at night to continue signaling out to sea, and thus avoided capture. Unfortunately, many of those who stayed on the coast were captured by the German patrols and taken as prisoners of war. While on the coast, the monks from a nearby Monastery brought rice for the hungry soldiers. They also brought news of German patrols and advised the men when to move back into the mountains. When Stanley Lawrence decided to go it alone, he made his way east for about twenty miles across rugged country, then headed south approximately eight miles to the coast. He may then have been in the vicinity of Kaloi Limenes, where he managed to find the boat. The country was mountainous and covered in low rugged limestone rocks. There was only sparse coastal vegetation. At some stage, Stanley Lawrence hid under a bush as the German Patrols walked past; he was very lucky not to have been seen and thought his heartbeat would give him away. He set sail on June 11th 1941. Eight days later, he landed near Sollum, on the Libya-Egypt border in North Africa.

A 'double ender' boat similar to the one in which Stanley Lawrence escaped. Note the rugged country of southern Crete in the background. Crete, March 2008. (Personal photo)

After Stanley Lawrence had left the main group, Commanders Sandover and Honner arrived at Agia Galini. Several days later, they had gone with a group of other soldiers to a mountain stream to wash. A German patrol went through Agia Galini and discovered some of the escapees, who were rounded up and taken prisoner at gunpoint. By now the men were at the end of their tether. They were starving and exhausted and gave up without a fight, and without a choice – surrender or die. Sandover and Honner and the others headed for the mountains again and hid.

After Stanley Lawrence's escape, he gave the information about the escapees still in the vicinity of Agia Galini, and plans were put in place to rescue them. Lieutenant Commander F.G. Poole had lived in Crete and had volunteered to return to find the escapees. After he arrived in Crete, he told the Cretan people he was there to rescue the allied escapees, the Cretans then went and found several groups of soldiers and gave them the message to be ready to be rescued. Poole sent a message to Sandover to organize the soldiers to meet on the night of the 17th August on the coast at the Preveli Monastery. The men went through the mountains to get there and the monks hid them in caves in the surrounding areas until the 17th. On the nights of 18th, 19th and 20th August 1941, the submarines, *Torbay* and *Thrasher*, rescued all the men, including Stanley Lawrence's commanding officers, Sandover and Honner. To avoid detection that troops had been on the beach, the monks ran sheep along the beach to cover the tracks of the soldiers.

If Stanley Lawrence had not had the risk-taking, dare-devil approach to life that he had, he would have been too afraid to risk such a monumental trip alone in an unseaworthy small boat. The odds of him making it to North Africa were hugely against him. He could so easily have just disappeared into the depths of this vast sea, been reported as missing, his family never knowing what had happened to him.

Stanley Lawrence was the first of the escapees to arrive in North Africa and to alert the authorities of the events in Crete. This dangerous and very courageous attempt won him the Military Medal for Bravery, something he, and the rest of his family, felt very proud of. When he spoke of his escape, he would get quite emotional at the parts when he first saw land after crossing the 350 miles of ocean, and especially when he found the men in the Listening Post in North Africa were allies. His relief, after so much danger, must have been so immense that he never got over it.

After the war, he was asked to give a talk to the Returned Soldiers' League (RSL) about his escape. When writing his speech, he tried to explain how he felt while crossing the Mediterranean but couldn't. He had several attempts and even though he had good descriptive writing skills he couldn't convey the feeling. There is no description that would make an audience understand just what it was like if they hadn't experienced it.

Stanley Lawrence's parents received a telegram informing them that their son was missing. Apparently, Maria Ellen, his mother, said she wasn't worried; she knew Stanley Lawrence had been in many scrapes and was quite able to look after himself so she was confident he would come through.

On the return of the 2/11th escapees to Syria, there were only forty-two soldiers remaining. Of those were fifteen who did not go to Crete. Sadly, the rest had either been killed or were prisoners of war.

> R1053 PRIVATE CARROLL MISSING I REGRET TO INFORM YOU THAT WX953 PRIVATE STANLEY LAWRENCE CARROLL HAS BEEN REPORTED MISSING THE MINISTER FOR THE ARMY AND THE MILITARY BOARD EXTEND SINCERE SYMPATHY
>
> MINISTER FOR THE ARMY

The dreaded telegram that every family member would never want to receive. But there was still hope, it did not say he had been killed. (Private collection)

> R.2013 Further reports state that WX953 Pte Stanley Lawrence Carroll previously reported missing is now located in Middle East.
>
> Minister for the Army

This telegram was received 15 days later, there would have been such relief in the family. Stanley Lawrence was safe. (Private collection)

Stanley Lawrence suffered from the effects of exposure for some time. His eyes, sunburn, and the effects of starvation and thirst had taken their toll. After he had convalesced for a while, he was sent to work in an office and kept inside to avoid bright lights. He was now effectively an office person. From then on, he had to wear glasses.

Stanley Lawrence's younger brother, Francis Peter Carroll, arrives in the Middle East

A couple of months after Stanley Lawrence's escape, his brother, Francis Peter, aged twenty-one, arrived in the Middle East. He had enlisted on 28th January 1941, and, prior to his embarkation, was married on 15th March 1941 to nineteen-year-old Joan Irene McGlinn, Doreen's sister.

He arrived in the Middle East in July, 1941.

Francis Peter Carroll (WX 10885) (photo Kaye McCallum/Carroll)

Francis Peter Carroll and Joan Irene McGlinn in the dress she made herself on their wedding day - 15th March 1941 (photo Kaye McCallum/Carroll)

Before Francis Peter enlisted Stanley Lawrence had encouraged his brother to join the Postal Corp; he had seen enough of front line fighting to know he didn't want his younger brother anywhere near it. Francis Peter enlisted and joined the much-loved Postal Corps, and was attached to the 1st Australian Postal Corps. Mail was very important to the soldiers fighting away from home; it was their only means of communication to family and loved ones and a high morale booster.

The photos below arrived in the mail for Stanley Lawrence. They are his sisters, Kathleen Christine and Mary Ellen (Molly) with her daughter Patricia. He treasured these photos and carried them with him throughout the war.

Stanley Lawrence's sisters - Kathleen Christine

and Patricia, and Mary Ellen (Molly) (family photos)

Francis Peter had heard about Stanley Lawrence's escape and made a concerted effort to visit him. The following is a letter written to his parents and younger brother, William Kevin.

> "WX10885
> Pte F.P. Carroll
> 1st Aust Corp Postal
> A.I.F. Abroad
> 19.8.1941
>
> My Dear Mum, Dad, and Willy,
>
> Every day I have good intentions of keeping up my replies to the correspondence but by knock off time I feel more like shuteye than pushing a pen. Well since my last letter a lot of things have happened as for a fortnight I was in a rest camp, or should I say in and out of it, as twice I went down to see Stan, a trip of about four hundred miles.
>
> The first time I landed at about 7.30, and the truck which I came down in, let me out at the turn off. He was just slowing down when I saw a convoy of trucks turning off towards Stan's camp so I flew out of the Postal truck and just about dived under a staff car. I happened to glance at the officer who was in it, and damn me if it wasn't the Major in charge of the Postal Services. I slammed the hat over my eyes, and luckily for me he didn't sight me, as being some two or three hundred miles from the unit would take some explaining.
>
> I eventually got to Stan's Units Orderly room and enquired as to his whereabouts. The RSM (Regimental Sergeant Major) recognised me and asked if I was looking for my Brother, he told me they had sent him back to Crete with the boat, but I knew by the grin old Midge wasn't too far away. I looked in the corner behind the door and here was Midge meekly typing a letter.
>
> I completely surprised him, and he stood up and in his quiet way said "Gawd bugger me! How are you?"
>
> After a lot of happy yarning we adjourned to the canteen and picked up a supply of tongue looosener and by this time it was

getting dark as we sat down in a bit of a water course till about one AM.

Our talk ranged on about two thousand subjects and the one which interested him the most was the wedding, as he was highly enthusiastic over the whole affair. Gawd knows what time it was when we finally crawled into a shared bed, but I know that I no sooner hit the blankets and I wanted to be sick. I got up and stumbled up a hill and on the way I had a puke which when I felt it coming on I had enough brains to yank the fangs out. As I bent over for a heave I had a feeling I dropped the pegs out of the shirt pocket, and in scratching in the dirt for them I grabbed a handful of prickles. I got to the top of the hill and the old dysentery got me again so I made a proper do of it.

On the way down the hill I got up a lurch and ended up in a prickly bush at the bottom, but after a lot of scratching etc I finally got to bed (one blanket under and one over). The war has knocked the wild stuff out of Midge as you would hardly credit the change in him. He has settled down and his only thought is Soldiering. I am not bulldusting but with his experience and determination I would rank him with any front line soldier in the world as now it would take a big bit to make him panic or do his block.

I had to smile the other day while looking through a Western Mail, (newspaper) it showed a WA Batt. (Western Australian Battalion) on a route march from Northam to Perth. It said "On Reaching Bassendean oval they grimly Battled on and finally reached their objective at such and such a time." Midge covered Thirty miles over rough mountainous country in from 9.30AM till 12 midnight, and he had no made roads, and besides had to dodge and hide from the Jerries.

My next trip included orders from the Doc not to get too full so we had a couple of jars and a real good night and also he received a couple of letters from home so while he was reading one I had a screw at the other. I hope to be able to meet him at a town half way in about a month, and although I am in one country and he another it is company for both of us to know we are together this side of the equator. Tell Mrs McGlinn that he told me of the Christmas party they had in the desert and how Jack (John Lannin Gawned) (well under the weather) got up and made a speech which included a few complimentary remarks to "Lickem" (their Lieut) (Lieutenant) His effort was greatly applauded by both officers and men, but next day Jack wanted to know "why the B (bloody) Hell Stan didn't shut him up" He (Stan) also said that on Crete Jack's ear was crook (the old complaint) and like a fool he would go back to help the lads out and ended up in the boob with all his cobbers.

Well Willy I think I have clipped your wings as I will claim you on arrival and you can be a choco on this side. I think one night in Tobruk would be sufficient to convince you which is the best unit, as we see just as much of the world as anyone, and we are always not far behind the leaders. Plenty of work you know but you get used to it and take no notice of it, and we can always get places where an ordinary private can't go. One only has to mention Airmail aboard and the lads can't get the barricades open quick enough.

There are no heros [sic] in this unit but the boys would always prefer mail to meals and if you give them ten letters a day they would still be looking for more. "Smiths Weekly" (newspaper) annoys me with their little bits about the troops not getting their mail. I would like to have the editor working over here for a while as he would soon change his tune after lumping bags full of lumpy parcels for half the day. Some of the chaps annoy me with their complaints of non receipt of letters and parcels, but it seems funny that 90% of the troops receive their mail regularly while chaps for the same unit always seem to have mail astray. Half the time it is a case of the would be writers forgetting to write, or the blokes are those who if they were squatting on the top of the world would still find something to winge about.

One woman was horribly indignant that her old man wasn't receiving her letters so she wrote to the DoD (Department of Defence) Postal Services and wanted to know why. The Major went and interviewed the soldier in Person and it was found that he had received every one.

I have received all of my letters and four parcels so I can't grumble. I received three parcels in the last three days and the cakes soon disappeared at morning tea times. This morning when I produced the cake, Joan was the best girl in the world, but by the time it came to sort the airmail the lads were a bit crooked on her for putting dried fruit in the package, as it was a case of me having the frames to myself and sorting the lot or being kicked right out of the joint. The knitted things were bonza and I tried the lot on together and looked a bit like an eskimo, but at present they are not needed, but about christmas when a bloke is working in snow they will come in handy then. Well Dear folks the light is worrying the drunks who have just rolled into bed so I will draw to a close and don't worry over me as over here it is like a transfer to the bush in Aussie only the towns are much bigger and a bit cosmopolitan but I am quite happy and contented and have no regrets at taking the oath. Well so long till next time.

From your loving Son and Brother   Frank xxx"

Stanley Lawrence recognised for his bravery is awarded the Military Medal

On the 23rd September 1941, the 2/11th, complete with reinforcements, paraded before the military hierarchy. During this parade, Stanley Lawrence was called forward and was told he would be awarded the Military Medal for Bravery. A very proud moment.

His escape was now recognised as a mighty and gutsy achievement. Newspapers and magazines in Australia were filled with stories about his escape and contribution to rescuing troops and officers from Crete. It was recognised as a superhuman endeavour. The movie company Gaumont British Newsreel made a short re-enactment to be shown in movie theatres across Australia and they sent an invitation to his parents to watch the screening at a local theatre. He was a very real hero in Australia.

He could now be very proud of himself and all those who knew him would now be aware of this courageous young man and his bravery.

Sergeant Stanley Lawrence CARROLL.

His Majesty The King has been graciously pleased to award the Military Medal to Sergeant Stanley Lawrence CARROLL, Australian Military Forces, for courage and devotion to duty in CRETE.

Official recognition for the award of the Military Medal for Bravery (Family collection)

Stanley Lawrence's war medals – the one on the extreme left is the Military Medal for Bravery. (replica – family collection)

His feat of heroism should not be underestimated. After the war, many books were written by military experts and war historians and the Battle for Crete was often written about. From all the aspects written about the war in Greece and Crete, many wrote about Stanley Lawrence's escape and his amazing feat of human endeavour and physical endurance in crossing the Mediterranean. Even the series of war books by *Time Life Books* included his escape.

A newspaper article about his escape was seen by Alan Knee's mother who hadn't heard from Alan since the fall of Crete. She contacted the newspaper who contacted Stanley Lawrence. He was able to tell Mrs Knee her son was safe but a prisoner of war. Even though this was shocking news, she would have been very relieved that her son was alive.

Stanley Lawrence after his escape. September 1941 (Family photo)

Newspaper photo of re-enactment of Stanley Lawrence being washed up on the beach after his escape, 1941 (Family collection)

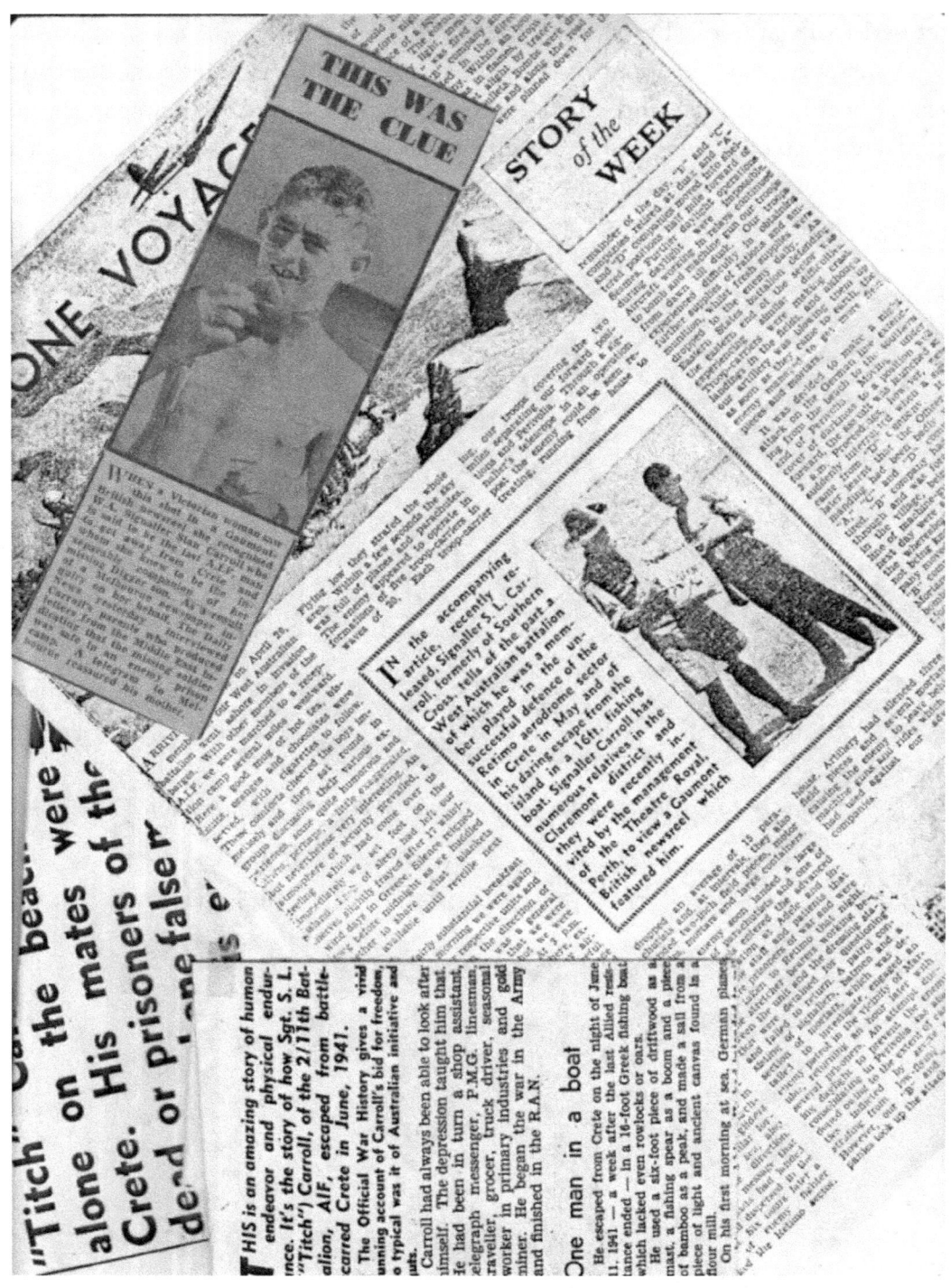

Some of the many newspaper and magazine articles about Stanley Lawrence's escape from Crete (Personal collection)

The youngest brother, William Kevin Carroll, enlists for war

William Kevin Carroll WX13227, 1941 – aged 17 (Photo – Lesley Watson/Carroll)

On the 21st May 1941, their youngest brother, William Kevin enlisted – illegally! He put his age up and, because he had joined the militia back in Perth, he was accepted. On his enlistment papers he had put his date of birth as 2nd December, 1920; but in actual fact he was born on 20th January, 1924! His age was taken as being twenty years and five months, the accepted legal age to enlist without parental permission, but he was only seventeen years old! His daughter, Lesley Watson, stated that he had to go to various enlistment centres to be accepted because they didn't believe him: he looked much younger than his alleged age. He was of similar build and height as Stanley Lawrence so was an immature-looking young man. His parents didn't find out he had enlisted until he was in the Northam Army Barracks training for war.

He left Australia for the Middle East in September, 1941.

When Stanley Lawrence found out that William Kevin had enlisted, he pulled strings to make sure he went into the postal corps and not the infantry. Francis Peter made arrangements for William Kevin to join him in his Postal Corps. Both Stanley Lawrence and Francis Peter would have told the authorities of William Kevin's deception if he had gone into the infantry. Neither wanted their youngest brother in danger.

Francis Peter left and William Kevin in the Middle East with their Postal Corps truck
(Photo Kaye McCallum/Carroll)

Stanley Lawrence would soon become just another signalman/soldier. Another move loomed and he was sent off to Syria with the now reinforced battalion on the 12th October, 1941 as a garrison force digging trenches and setting up for defensive works. As winter drew near, the weather became very cold with bitter winds that whipped up dust, making their lives miserable. Stanley Lawrence's hatred of dust must have given him grief. To brighten his life, he was promoted to Corporal in late November and the bonus of more pay.

At Christmas, snow fell; they had a white Christmas which was nice for the men who had never seen snow. Some, however had endured the snow-covered mountains in Greece, and some in Crete, so the novelty of snow did not bother them. Fortunately, the men had moved out of their tents into corrugated iron huts – bitterly cold but better than a tent. On the 23rd January 1942, the 2/11th was relieved, and five days later they were sent to Palestine. Here further training was given until the 10th February when they were entrained to Port Tewfik in Egypt. It was now clear they were to be sent by ship – to somewhere. They knew that Japan had bombed Pearl Harbour on 7th December 1941, and the Australians were now at war alongside the United States of America. The troops guessed they would be going to somewhere in the Pacific, perhaps to Singapore, or Burma, or even to Australia to protect their home turf.

Sandover, who had been away, was now back with his men and was again disgruntled at the confusion and bad planning by the British. He wanted his men to be combat-ready in the event of an attack, but the armaments were scattered, ammunition was not with the armaments and even the cooking and mess equipment were in different places. Sandover got the band to play their unit song *Sussex by the Sea* (the officer in charge of organizing things was from Sussex, England) and he managed to get things in order without too much hassle.

Francis Peter and William Kevin stayed on in the Middle East.

Stanley Lawrence returns to Australia

The ship that was to transport the 2/11th men was the *Durban Castle*. Rumours were rife about their destination. No one knew, not even their commanding officers. Eventually, on the 16th March 1942, they arrived in Adelaide, which was considered the safest port in which to bring the men. Further training and route marches took place to bring the men back to fighting fitness after a sedentary life on the ship. Three weeks later, they were sent by train to Perth. The train station platforms were full of cheering and waving people who searched for the faces of their returning loved ones. By the end of April, the entire battalion had arrived and all were sent to the military camp in Point Walter.

Not long afterwards, there was a sense of frustration that the men may not be sent further. They were now garrisoned to protect Fremantle and felt a sense of disappointment.

Stanley Lawrence and the rest of the men were given seven days leave. He went home to his family and no doubt was invited to his new sister-in-law Joan Irene's place for a meal. Here he met her now eighteen-year-old younger sister Doreen McGlinn, a blossoming beauty. By now, Stanley Lawrence was a very experienced man in worldly affairs; he could take care of himself in nearly any situation, and was a very war hardened soldier who had seen and experienced things no one should ever see or do. He was craving a female's touch and feminine company. He was a young man full of vigour – and testosterone. Doreen, on the other hand, was a protected and fairly naïve girl, but strong willed, and lived with her parents who saw her needs were met – and she liked to have fun. Now the McGlinns had a national hero in their family and for them it would have been extraordinary. Stanley Lawrence and Doreen McGlinn were smitten with each other almost from the first instance. He with her vivacious beauty and she with the hero serviceman in uniform. During the next few days, before Stanley Lawrence's leave expired, they were 'a couple'. Their time together was precious and they would have seen each other as often as they could, which wasn't often.

Doreen McGlinn and the outbreak of World War II

When World War II broke out in 1939, Doreen was only sixteen years old. Men enlisted to go to war and women went into the workforce to replace them. The Women's Land Army formed to ensure the farms continued to produce food for both the home market and to send food to the troops. Women worked in factories, offices, telecommunications, munitions, and other male-oriented employment. Except for during WWI, women mainly worked in female-oriented jobs – they were again to experience the change. The women had even more freedoms that they never thought possible. Doreen would have picked up on this and would have pushed the boundaries of her parents' rules. She was strong willed and liked entertainment – perhaps she had what is now known as Attention Deficit Disorder.

For women, there now came a confidence in their demeanour and attitude and they pitched in with passion to help the war effort. Women were chosen to carry out some jobs by the skills they had. Because of her wonderful sewing skills, Joan Irene was seconded to do the making and sewing of uniforms for the Australian Army, Navy, and Airforce. At Doreen's young age, she had no particular skills and was sent to the carrot canning factory that was reasonably close to her home. The carrots were processed, cooked and canned to send to the troops overseas. She did her bit and she got paid for it. In some ways, she became independent so could go out and pay her own way. She then moved from that job to The Central Provisions Store, a grocery store that stocked all sorts of groceries, clothes and small household goods but not green groceries. She moved to various branches throughout the war and, when she left that job, she was given some glowing references stating that she was a good and honest worker and they were sorry to see her go.

Wartime became a difficult time for the people at home. On 31st October 1940, her father, John McGlinn, at the age of forty-two, enlisted to fight but was discharged soon afterwards on the 29th November 1942. He may not have passed the medical and, being a World War I veteran, they may have thought he had done his duty. After what he had been through in the previous 'War to End all Wars', it is commendable that he enlisted and was prepared to go and fight and die in another war. He had seen it all before, not like some of the young men who signed up in naïve ignorance of what was to come in WWII.

Doreen worked, and continued her usual family life of visiting her extended family, cousins etc. but knowing that things were very different now. The war effort was everything and all things centred round it.

"Rationing regulations for food and clothing were gazetted on 14 May 1942. Rationing was introduced to manage shortages and control civilian consumption. It aimed to … limit impending shortages of essential goods. … Rationing was enforced by the use of coupons and was limited to clothing, tea, sugar, butter, and meat. From time to time, eggs and milk were also rationed under a system of priority for vulnerable groups during periods of shortage… Breaches of rationing regulations were punishable under the general provisions of National Security Regulations by fines of up to £100 or up to six-months imprisonment."
(www.awm.gov.au/articles/encyclopedia/homefront/rationing)

Petrol was also rationed so not many people could drive their cars. (If they had one.) Like many people, the McGlinns didn't own a car so it didn't bother them much; they relied on public transport.

Now with the men gone to war, Doreen would go to dances and dance with her girlfriends. The pictures (movies) were cheap and good entertainment for people and often they would go once or twice a week. Before the main feature, there was always the movie news with footage of the war.

The shops were limited in their stock so any items that were required often had to be ordered ahead. Gladys Catherine and Joan Irene had difficulty doing their dressmaking and tailoring. Getting dress fabric was almost impossible because 'frivolous' fabrics were now not being made in favour of military fabrics for uniforms. When Joan Irene married Francis Peter Carroll, she couldn't get nice wedding and bridesmaid dress fabric, there was a chronic shortage. She and Gladys Catherine, being very creative, made the beautiful dresses from curtain fabric which was still relatively plentiful. The bride's dress was white and bridesmaids wore pink.

Joan Irene would wait for letters from Francis Peter, and the family would be very interested in the goings on at war in the Middle East where John McGlinn had served in WWI. They would have been very aware of the adventures of his two brothers, especially Stanley Lawrence. They too would have seen the movie news at the pictures and seen Stanley Lawrence on the big screen and known he was a hero, and that he was Francis Peter's brother.

Doreen had turned eighteen when bombings by the Japanese reached Australia. They had bombed Darwin on 19th February 1942, then targeted the Western Australian towns of Broome, Wyndham, and Derby that were bombed on the 3rd March 1942: war was now on Australia's doorstep.

The McGlinn and Carroll families, along with most people in Western Australia, prepared for war by digging air raid shelters in their backyards and covering their windows with materials that didn't let light out. They had blackouts often and air-raid sirens sent out alarms to let people know an air-raid was imminent and to head for the shelters. John McGlinn dug a large air raid shelter in his backyard and stocked it with food, water, and torches at the ready. A nervousness descended over the population.

Stanley Lawrence and Doreen 1942
Marriage

During his short leave, Stanley Lawrence and Doreen went to the movies and she was shocked when the British Movietone Newsreel came on with war footage of bombings. At the first sound of bombing the servicemen who had been to war quick as a flash shot under the seats, a reflex action from being in battle. This caused some embarrassment and a bit of a titter by the audience.

He took her to meet his family and proudly displayed his new girlfriend.

In all too short a time, Stanley Lawrence's leave expired and he returned to the Point Walter Army Camp. Doreen was head over heels in young love and she constantly talked about him – it was Stanley this and Stanley that. According to her cousin Joy Anderson/Gawned, Doreen talked of nothing else.

Army leave was limited to six hours per week and it is highly likely Stanley Lawrence and Doreen spent that time together.

By the end of May 1942, Stanley Lawrence's unit had been sent to Geraldton to guard the coastline against Japanese attack. They did many route marches and maritime drills and generally kept busy doing nothing that the soldiers thought worthwhile. A general disinterest began to manifest itself, and worse, a feeling that they were not doing anything to help the war effort. They felt abandoned, useless, and disillusioned.

Stanley Lawrence did not go to Geraldton at that time; he stayed at the Melville army camp and did refresher training in signals. He had each weekend off and no doubt spent time with Doreen. Stanley Lawrence was about to be sent to Geraldton to be reunited with his battalion so, within a few days, they became engaged to be married. Again, war changed the psyche of the young people and immediacy was important. You didn't know when you would be parted, sometimes permanently. Young people wanted to live life to the limit and with no restrictions by the previous norms. Stanley Lawrence and Doreen became engaged and made hurried arrangements to be married. Doreen was delighted and her family were happy that she might now settle down.

Stanley Lawrence and Doreen, she is displaying her new engagement ring. (Family photo)

Doreen's fiery nature meant that her engagement ring didn't stay on her finger long. An argument with Stanley Lawrence when they were out in his car made her so furious that she threw the ring out of the car into a vacant block. A later search proved fruitless.

They were married on 20th June 1942, at the Methodist Church in Stirling Highway, Claremont, the same one in which Joan Irene and Francis Peter married.

Methodist Church that Stanley Lawrence and Doreen McGlinn were married on 20th June, 1942 (personal photo)

Doreen's wedding dress was the one Joan Irene wore on her wedding day. Fortunately, the bridesmaids were the same, but Joan Irene and Doreen swapped. The groomsmen in most of the Carroll men's weddings didn't include brothers because this was war and they were stationed away and could not attend.

These wedding dresses were worn again for the marriage of Stanley Lawrence's sister Kathleen Christine to Len Guy. War made people 'make do'.

The wedding party, L-R; Doreen's cousin Ernest McGlinn; Joan Irene Carroll/McGlinn; Stanley Lawrence Carroll; Doreen Carroll/McGlinn; Doreen's father, John McGlinn; Stanley Lawrence's sister, Kathleen Christine Carroll; Signalman friend Reginald Bowen. Front, seated, Doreen's cousin and daughter of John Lannin Gawned now a prisoner of war in Germany, Joy Gawned. (photo – family collection)

Stanley Lawrence Carroll and Doreen McGlinn on their wedding day 20th June, 1942. (photo – family collection)

Their honeymoon was two nights at the Gosnells Hotel. Stanley Lawrence said with a smile that he planned their wedding day to coincide with the longest night of the year!

Stanley Lawrence and Doreen's honeymoon place, the Gosnells Hotel, Albany Highway, Gosnells. (Photo - Bing images, 2022)

Five days after their marriage, Stanley Lawrence's leave was over. He had to return to the army camp and six days later was promoted to Sergeant. He now had the three stripes on his arm, like the ones he faked what seemed like a lifetime ago in the Metropole Café in the Middle East! These were real and another achievement of which he could be very proud, and the bonus of a rise in pay.

He rejoined his unit in Geraldton and went back to route marches and training. He would have felt the disgruntled nature of the group and he soon joined in the 'play' at wargames which for Stanley Lawrence would have been very disheartening, a bit like an elite sports person being sidelined in their sport, and the feeling of – what now? Many of the battle-hardened soldiers could have now been adrenalin junkies and needed excitement. Sandover recognised that the morale of the men was low and was disappointed some of the men requested transfers out of the battalion so that they could go and fight.

Stanley Lawrence, the risk taker, wanted a bit of excitement so, on the 16th August 1942, he took a spin on a military motorbike while he was a bit 'under the weather'. The drink made him a bit more of a risk taker and, as he sped along, he didn't negotiate the road properly and hit a telegraph pole and broke his fibula, the thinner of the lower leg bones. He was evacuated to hospital in Northam and was there for a couple of weeks. While there, he had his ears seen to. The bomb blast in Greece had caused a lot of problems, pain, and deafness.

There had been very little leave so Doreen took this opportunity to go to see Stanley Lawrence in hospital. Because she was a little uncertain about the visit, she took her young cousin Joy Gawned with her. She took any opportunity she could to see her new husband. There were times that she must have felt frustrated and angry when Stanley Lawrence brought a mate with him when he had leave. She would have wanted him to herself, but such is the very tight bond between mates at war. They had seen the horrors and friends killed so there was a very special relationship between them. Civilians just couldn't have understood this tight bond. In some photographs during that time, Doreen looked absolutely miserable – and very thin.

While Stanley Lawrence was away, Doreen was harangued by her mother, Gladys Catherine, to stay home and be the dutiful wife, even though she rarely saw her husband. Boredom would have driven her to distraction. Doreen couldn't just turn away from her friends and her social life – she was just nineteen years old and there was a war on – life was to be lived! She wanted to continue her life as it was before she was married. Doreen and Gladys Catherine constantly bickered. Why could Joan Irene stay home and be dutiful but not Doreen? Because they had very different personalities and Gladys Catherine just didn't 'get it'.

On leave - Stanley Lawrence, an unhappy Doreen, and Reginald Bowen (family photo)

Each period of leave lasted just six days and in one year there were only three periods of leave! Prior to their marriage, they had spent perhaps ten days together. So, during their first year of marriage, they had only spent about one month together. This is an almost impossible period of time to bond and get to know each other; it was still just a period of "in lust". They had no time to bond, plan and do things together, nor to discuss their future. No time to cement their relationship. This was how it was in war – everything was done immediately – just in case!

Training for war continues for Stanley Lawrence

In September, leave was granted for six days at the end of which was a march through Perth with crowds of admiring people cheering and waving, which gave the men a boost. There was still no indication that the men were to go to war and boredom was at a premium. In January 1943, their officers thought the men needed some serious training to get them up to speed for battle fitness. The men were trucked to Yanchep for a long march which started at 9.00 am and was to go to Toodyay. It was very hot, 104 degrees F, and the men had to carry everything needed for the front line, including shovels and weapons. The men struggled through the soft sand and up and over steep rocky hills. They camped at a small creek at 4 am where men just fell to the ground and slept. They were up at 6 am and continued the march to Toodyay, where they arrived at 3 pm – a thirty-hour march with only two hours sleep! Training was a tough business!

Training continued in this hard manner and in March the battalion moved to Chidlow. While camped there a huge storm blew through and several large trees fell onto Headquarters where Stanley Lawrence was stationed. One of his fellow signallers was killed and one seriously injured, and two of his commanding officers were hurt. Later, there was praise from the hierarchy that the essential services performed well in a crisis and signal wires were run out quickly in spite of the pitch darkness and the raging storm and falling branches.

Full and hard training continued. Sandover left the battalion and Colonel Binks took charge. He, no doubt, had been informed of Stanley Lawrence's courage and that he had been awarded the Military Medal. Stanley Lawrence was at Headquarters Company and would now be a signalman for Binks.

Japan had invaded New Guinea and the 2/11th Battalion was to go and defend there, but it was to be some time yet before they would go. The training continued and the men were impatient.

"The 2/11th landed at Aitape in New Guinea on 13 November 1944 to undertake its only campaign against the Japanese. Patrolling, often arduous in nature, constituted the bulk of its operations." (www.awm.gov.au/collection/U56054) Several men were killed during the patrols.

Stanley Lawrence would not go to New Guinea …

Francis Peter leaves the Middle East and goes home to Australia and on to New Guinea

Francis Peter and William Kevin stayed in the Middle East doing their postal duties and, during their remaining time, there were several severe and serious battles. Fortunately, both were still in the Postal Corps so did not participate in the battles. Francis Peter's unit was sent forward to the battle for El Alamein against the famous German commander, Field Marshall Erwin Rommel. The battle was furious and one of the turning points of the war in the Middle East.

Even though Francis Peter was behind the lines, he would have seen the multitude of killed and wounded return from the battle fields. It would have been horrific. There were approximately 13,500 allied casualties. There were two battles for El Alamein, one during July 1942 and the other more brutal battle during October/November 1942. Sadly, for a short time Francis Peter was to be part of the temporary reception group for the soldiers killed in the battle. He told his son-in-law many years later how terrible it was. The dead men were returned in mattress covers to a temporary cemetery. He said that body fluids leaked from the bags and he was traumatised by it all. Perhaps this was a contributing factor to his mental health problems after the war.

The time came for Australia to be ready to defend its shores. The war was on our doorstep and for the first time Australia had to defend itself rather than go and fight for other nations. Now the Australian soldiers were urgently required in New Guinea to fight the Japanese.

Francis Peter left the Middle East on 29th January 1943, and sailed to Fremantle where he had leave and spent some time with Joan Irene. He was promoted to Sergeant in July 1943, and because he was having health issues, he was in Western Australia for six months before being shipped out. He arrived in Queensland on 7th August 1943, and only three days later he had arrived at the RAAF base in Milne Bay, Papua, New Guinea. Milne Bay is on the eastern side of Papua. Here he continued in the Postal Corps of the 2/4th Australian Light Anti-Aircraft Regiment, but was not involved in gun crew activities. The battle for Milne Bay had already been fought by the Americans and Australians against the Japanese during August and September 1942, and was now a major allied air base.

Only one month later, in September 1943, Francis Peter's regiment was mobilized to Lae in northern New Guinea to care-take the Airbase there. The battle for Lae had already taken place during the previous April and the Japanese had been driven back into the highlands of New Guinea and south to Kokoda where fierce battles took place under severe mountainous tropical conditions. Not long after he had arrived at Lae, he was moved with his regiment, along with some AIF troops to Scarlet Beach, and then south to help capture Finschhafen.

At that time, Finschhafen was occupied by the Japanese who had landed there in March 1942 and had set up a base. The newly arrived reinforcements strengthened the battle-weary soldiers there and helped in the fight to capture Finschhafen and were successful by October 1943. Even though Francis Peter was behind the front lines, he wasn't far from the front and would have experienced some of the battles that were very close at hand. It is unclear whether Francis Peter remained with the garrison force in Finschhafen after the battles had finished. Movement in the area would have been extremely difficult during the "wet" so his unit may have stayed to defend. The conditions would have been extremely uncomfortable and disease was prevalent amongst the men. In December 1943, his daughter Kaye was born, a nice Christmas present for him.

Landing at Scarlet Beach, New Guinea 1943 (Photo Australian War Memorial 057470)

Conditions in the "Wet" – this is at Milne Bay (Photo wikipedia.org/wiki/Battle_of_Milne_Bay)

Francis Peter heads home

After six months in the tropics, from January through to September 1944, he became very sick with various problems and diseases. Diagnosis seemed difficult. Suspected were malaria, dengue fever, hook worm, and there were multiple urinary tract infections, including epididymo-orchitis. Eventually, after being in and out of hospital many times during the next six months, he was evacuated to Queensland and sent back to Western Australia. It was his first meeting with his little daughter, Kaye, who was now about ten months old. He remained in Western Australia until the war ended and he was discharged from the army on 25th January 1946.

No one can imagine the mental anguish of war, and Francis Peter was no exception; he suffered with mental illness after the war and may have had a nervous breakdown, probably due to Post Traumatic Stress Disorder, and was hospitalised in Heathcote Mental Hospital for a short time. Mental illness was not really recognised properly by the authorities and these poor men weren't treated with the respect they deserved. Soon after the war, Francis Peter was diagnosed with tuberculosis. Perhaps this was a chronic condition that hadn't been diagnosed earlier and perhaps the cause of some of his illnesses.

William Kevin leaves the Middle East and heads for New Guinea

William Kevin was the last of the brothers to leave the Middle East. He left at the end of May 1942, and sailed to Brisbane, Australia; he didn't get home to see his family. He disembarked there on 10th August, 1942 and was there for a week before sailing to New Guinea. It is not clear what he did in New Guinea for the first year but it is known he was still in the Postal Corps so fortunately wasn't at the front line. He was now only eighteen years old and it is suspected that the hierarchy knew he was very young so they sent him to Headquarters New Guinea Force in July 1943, where he remained in the Postal Corps for almost a year. *"New Guinea Force was a military command unit for Australian, United States and native troops from the Territories of Papua and New Guinea serving in the New Guinea campaign during World War II. Formed in April 1942, when the Australian First Army was formed ... after it returned from the Middle East, it was responsible for planning and directing all operations within the territory up until October 1944.* (Here) *General Douglas MacArthur, placed all Australian and US Army, Air Force and Navy Forces in the Port Moresby Area under the control of New Guinea Force. Over the course of its existence, New Guinea Force was commanded by some of the Australian Army's most notable commanders, including Sydney*

Rowell, Sir Edmund Herring and Sir Leslie Morshead. General Sir Thomas Blamey also commanded the force in 1942 while based in Port Moresby."
(wikipedia.org/wiki/New_Guinea_Force)

Young William Kevin was right at the pointy end among the hierarchy of some of the most famous men in WWII history.

In August 1943, he was transferred to the 2/16th Battalion, but remained behind the lines in the Postal Corps for that unit. The 2/16th had fought in some horrendous battles since arriving in New Guinea. They fought on the Kokoda Track; had very heavy casualties at Mission Ridge and, after the battle of Gona, there were only fifty-six men left in the unit. William Kevin would have been a much-needed reinforcement for this depleted unit. In September 1943, the battalion moved to Lae where Francis Peter was stationed. It is highly possible that William Kevin and Francis Peter had a reunion but they would have only been together for a very short period, because the 2/16th was moved by air to the Ramu Valley on 29th September. William Kevin would have gone along.

It was here that he became very ill with Scrub Typhus and was evacuated to the 2/11th Battalion hospital in October 1943. It is just as well because he did not have to endure the absolutely horrific battle for Shaggy Ridge where the 2/16th fought soon after.

Scrub Typhus is a deadly tropical disease caused by the bite of a mite infected with a form of Rickettsia, now known as Orentia, and causes significant morbidity and mortality. It was a significant disease among allied troops operating in the south west Pacific region during World War II. In Papua New Guinea there were approximately 2,840 cases reported in the Australian Army, with a case mortality rate of 9%. (https://Rickettsial Diseases of Military Importance: An Australian Perspective) Often this disease can have lifelong debilitating conditions.

After several moves to various military hospitals over the next four months, young William Kevin was evacuated to Brisbane, Australia in February 1944. Folklaw has it that he was so ill a priest was called and he had his last rites read to him but he rallied and said that he wasn't ready to go to his maker and that they could all buggar off! As his health improved, he was transferred to Perth for rehabilitation. He was in Perth for the marriage of his sister Kathleen Christine, to Len Guy on the 1st April 1944, and was a groomsman in the wedding party. He stayed in Perth for several months and, as his health gradually returned and he got stronger, he was re-instated to a training unit to get him back to fighting fitness and was then transferred back to Queensland, Australia for several months.

Kathleen Christine's wedding. L-R Arthur Henry's wife Thelma, William Kevin, Len Guy, Kathleen Christine, George Thomas Carroll, Unknown sailor, Mary Ellen (Molly) (Photo Kaye McCallum/Carroll)

The wedding and bridesmaids' dresses were Joan Irene and Doreen's dresses that were adapted by Mary Ellen (Molly).

During this time, he had other visits to hospital for other problems including a suspected broken leg and severe left maxillary sinusitis which was difficult to get rid of. He was attached to the Air Crew Reception Centre in Queensland in April 1945, where he rejoined the depleted 2/16th Battalion and was re-called to war, for the front line. The unit left Townsville, Queensland in June 1945 and sailed to the island of Morotai, Indonesia, in north-west Papua, and arrived there on the 18th June 1945. William Kevin was promoted to Lance Corporal in mid-July.

The battle of Morotai began in September 1944 and the fighting continued until August 1945 when the atom bombs were dropped and the war in the Pacific ended. William Kevin went to Morotai with the 2/16th Battalion in a fighting capacity and would have seen first-hand fighting at the front line. He would have been well aware of what to expect. However, it wasn't to be. After only eight days his unit was re-called to go into battle at Balikpapan, East Kalimantan, south eastern Borneo, where fierce fighting was still raging. The Battle of Balikpapan was a campaign to liberate the Japanese-held British and Dutch Borneo. The

Americans wouldn't send their men into battle until they had almost wiped out the area with artillery. After the bombardment, the allies successfully secured the town and hinterland and the battle concluded in late July 1945. Once the area had been secured, the 2/16th Battalion carried out patrol operations, which were sometimes tedious in the extreme, but there may have been small pockets of resistance by the Japanese, making some patrols very dangerous. William Kevin stayed in this patrol capacity until the war ended. The Australian troops remained in the area until early 1946. (en.wikipedia.org/wiki/Battle_of_Balikpapan (1945)

Australian troops heading into Balikpapan after the American artillery attack in 1945
(Photo Bing images)

WWII ends

Young William Kevin was at Balikpapan when the atomic bombs fell on Hiroshima and Nagasaki, Japan on the 6th and 9th August, 1945. The Japanese surrendered on the 14th August, and World War II officially ended on 2nd September, 1945.

From October 1945 to late January 1946, William Kevin's unit was sent to Indonesia and formed part of the occupation force there. He was stationed at Makassar, southern Indonesia, where he reverted to Private and was assigned to clerical duties until he left for home. Below is a letter William Kevin wrote home to his parents in late 1945 while stationed there. There was no date on the letter which was provided by Lesley Watson/Carroll, William Kevin's daughter.

"WX13227
Pte Carroll WK   (Private Carroll, William Kevin)
BHQ 2/16 Btn   (Battalion Head Quarters 2/16th Battalion)
A.I.F.   (Australian Imperial Forces)

Dear Mum and Dad,

I suppose it is about time that I stopped my galavanting [sic] around and settled down and wrote you a letter. I have been having rather a gay time since I have been in this place, it serves to break down the monotony and by so doing I can look at life in a bit better light. When I was in Borneo I had nothing to do and no where to go, and as a result got very homesick, but since I have been here I have been able to have my little drink and can go out for an evening to some people's place. I can tell you -- it makes a lot of difference to be able to go to a civvy home again after being cooped up in an army camp for months on end. This place I have been going to is quite a nice joint, and the people treat us extra well. It serves the purpose to keep one off the local grog, although I have rolled around there a few times with a few more than the eight under my belt. One night I went round there pretty blind and they got me singing, the chap that was with me was in much the same state as I was, so between the two of us we just about kept going all night. Last night when I went around there they tried to get me going again, but they must have forgotten that I hadn't had one drink.

I went to a party there last Friday night, and I can tell you I had a bit of a battle to get sober so as I could go, I had about three cold baths and about a dozen cups of black coffee before I looked like even seeing the light. Later on in the night when I started to get a bit merry again I tried to get the housekeeper on the slops and I got roared up by the sheilas so I told them that I believed in drinking with anyone and did not consider that anyone was below me. I suppose they are quite right in not letting the black Bs have a drink but I don't believe in this class distinction.

In one way I don't blame these poor cows for putting on a show here, but if they would go about it in a different way it may be O.K. This sneaking into a house of a night and cutting some ones throat is definitely with me. If I ever catch any of them sneaking around the street of a night with a knife in his belt, I will cut him up with an owen (Owen gun) instead of him doing the cutting work. I would not be in any strife if I did do it as we are ordered to shoot to kill any one carrying a weapon, no matter what it is. Things have been rather quiet here the last few days, I think the little doing over the strife makers got the other day has made them think twice about having another go. One of the other Btns here bowled over about sixteen of them so it has taught them a lesson. I suppose you think we are siding with the Dutch, well I suppose, to some extent, we are. I wouldn't care if they had a go at any Dutch joker, but if they harm any of the women and kids well it will be on for mine. It's not in our natures to stand by and see white women and children done over.

We have had double guards of a night for the last week and so far I have copped two of them. One night when I was on I was armed with a bren gun and rifle and was watching for some wog to come sneaking around as I was crooked on them because they were the cause of me being put on the guard.

I have made a bit on dough since I have been here but it goes pretty fast. I have not had to touch the pay book for a month and seeing I have a bit more stuff to send off I will most probably leave my book alone for quite a while. You have no idea of the cost of living here, most of the stuff is black market so it must cost the civilian population a lot to keep going. An ordinary bottle of lemon cordial sell for 8/2 (eight shillings and two pence) so I don't know what the people pay for it. A chocolate is worth 5/- (five shillings) for us to sell, so you see we can make a few deeners now and again. I guarantie [sic] some of the jokers who can obtain plenty of stuff are making hundreds.

I am going to get some of this filigree work soon so let's hope it doesn't run out. I had a pair of earings [sic] and a filigree rose, but the other night one clumsy cow knocked the tin off my table and no one noticed it. The result was that someone's put their great number eight on the rose and finished that, now I have only the earings [sic]. I am going to try and get some of my cats eyes made up here so they will do for Xmas presents. I've put in for the Xmas book today, one for you one for each of the girls and one for Max, so I hope they all manage to get home by Xmas.

The weather over here the last couple of days has been abominable, I have never seen rain like it, it just keeps on pouring for hours on end. The civvies reckon it hasn't started properly yet and when it does it is liable to rain continually for about a fortnight or even a month. The wet season lasts for about four or five months, so it will be lovely if we get flooded out.

By the way do you think you could get me some films, I would like to get a few snaps of the place, and if I get the films I can soon borrow a camera. The size of most of the boy's cameras is 6.20 if you can manage to get me film I will be very grateful.

I am very doubtful whether I will be able to make home for Xmas, though of course one never knows. Latest furphy is February, so looks like another Xmas in a foreign land. If I am here it won't be so bad as in N.G. (New Guinea) I will sling my legs under a table with a cloth and crockery instead of having it in an army mess hut. At the party the other night they were ramming stuff into me at supper time and in the end I had to tell them to ease up, they must think that us Australians can eat like horses.

Has Mrs Tillett heard from Bill lately, I have been on him to write but I suppose he is like me, kept going pretty well all the time.

I have not had a decent sleep for about a fortnight now, if I am not on guard or piquet I am generally out or sitting up here in the barracks having a quiet little party. Last night I managed to get to bed at eleven PM so I got a fair amount of sleep.

Well folks as I have to have my shower before tea I will say cheerio for now, and hope to see you soon. Once again Solong and love to you both.

Your fond son

Bill."

William Kevin Carroll returns to Australia

On the 2nd February, 1946 William Kevin left Indonesia and arrived in Brisbane, Australia on 13th February. In early March, the 2/16th Battalion was demobilised and William Kevin was sent back home to Western Australia and discharged from the armed forces on 24th April, 1946.

Stanley Lawrence's older brothers, Norman George, John Raymond, and Arthur Henry and their wartime experiences

Norman George Carroll

Norman George, Stanley Lawrence's eldest brother, had tried several times to enlist but his trade as a Fitter and Turner and his amazing mechanical skills forced him into the 'Manpowered/Essential' specialist workforce at home and was probably appointed a position in munitions or manufacturing war equipment. Very few tradesmen were sent to war to fight and he was disappointed and unhappy about the fact he could not go and serve with his brothers.

Norman George Carroll 'Manpowered' (Photo Max Carroll)

John Raymond and Arthur Henry Carroll go to war

John Raymond, and Arthur Henry enlisted in the army on the same day, the 20th August 1941. Neither were sent overseas at that time because they had specialist skills that prevented them leaving Australia. They too were Manpowered, but within the armed forces.

John Raymond Carroll WX15910, 1941 (Photo Levene Allen /Carroll)

Arthur Henry Carroll WX15914, 1941 (photo Jacqueline Carroll)

At the age of thirty, John Raymond was living in Greenbushes, Western Australia, and enlisted in the Armed Forces on the 20th August 1941. He, along with Arthur Henry, aged twenty-eight, who was also living in Greenbushes went off to the enlistment office together and enlisted on the same day. Their Army identification numbers are within four numbers of each other. They were both stationed at Western Command General Details Camp in Claremont, Western Australia and attached to General Reinforcements – Signals. They weren't in Claremont long before being sent, at the end of August, to the Northam Army Camp for general military training.

He and Arthur Henry were transferred to Signals in the 1st Armoured Division at the end of October then both were stationed back in Perth in mid-November, 1941.

Even though they were attached to Signals, the same as Stanley Lawrence, they did not have to learn telegraphy nor Morse-code and were commandeered as "Linesmen", which was their particular skillset on joining the war. They were both Linesmen with the Post Master General (PMG) in Bridgetown, Greenbushes, and that general area, however, they still had to go through the general training for war that all soldiers had to do.

On 16th November 1941, they were entrained to Victoria and initially sent to Puckapunyal Army Base, then on to various army bases in Victoria, including Seymour, a major army base that housed many American soldiers, and then on to New South Wales. While stationed at Seymour, Victoria, they both went Absent Without Leave (AWL) on Christmas day 1941, and each fined 10/- and forfeited one day's pay. Then, not long after, on 13th January 1942, they went AWL again, this time they were fined £1.0.0 and lost two day's pay!

These misdemeanours were caused by getting back to base an hour or so late! There was no forgiveness in the military for bad punctuality! However, the reason for going AWL was a good one: their wives had caught the train over from Western Australia to see them. Something that these men would have appreciated tremendously. John Raymond's wife, Audrey, had relatives close by so they stayed with them. Arthur Henry's wife Thelma was pregnant with their first child Beverley, and because she was quite advanced in her pregnancy she stayed on until their baby was born. No one wanted her to return to Western Australia in an advanced state of pregnancy on a troop train!

In late January 1942, they were sent to the PMG Linesman School, presumably to teach other recruits to be linesmen. They then rejoined their unit, Signals, 1st Armoured Division, before being moved to New South Wales where they were out in the field working as linesmen to upgrade and install new lines in the area. Military communications needed to be maintained and new lines installed ready for defence in the case of invasion. While out in the field, John Raymond had a bout of dysentery and had to go to hospital for about ten days. Trench toilets were very unhygienic and disease carrying flies were a real problem.

Arthur Henry was sent back to Perth on the ship *Marella* and sailed from Sydney in late 1942, and arrived in Perth, early January 1943.

John Raymond was sent by train a short time later and arrived in Perth in March 1943. They were both attached to a line building party with the 3rd Australia Corps but soon after, Arthur Henry was transferred back to 1st Australian Armoured Division, Signals.

They were attached to various linesmen tasks while in WA then, at the end of March 1944, they were sent by train back to Victoria for further line work before being sent on to Queensland for acclimatisation and training for tropical situations in New Guinea. In April, John Raymond was promoted to Corporal then in July he became a Sergeant. While stationed in Queensland, his wife, Audrey, a very tenacious and determined woman, went to visit him shortly before he was sent overseas and, as a consequence, she became pregnant and had a daughter, Charmion, on Remembrance Day, 11th November 1945. He left Australia for Morotai in May 1945 and wouldn't meet his daughter for some time.

It is hoped they were able to catch up with young William Kevin while they were in Queensland.

John Raymond and Arthur Henry go to Indonesia and Borneo

Arthur Henry was sent for service in April 1945, and sailed to Morotai in time to see the battles there that lasted until August 1945. He was there to help rebuild the telecommunications infrastructure but did not enter any battles. A month later, John Raymond arrived in Morotai. Their skills were sorely needed and linesmen were required to quickly repair the smashed civilian and military communication lines. William Kevin arrived a bit later, in June 1945 but he was sent into battle for the short period remaining until all the battles ended. It is not known whether they all had a reunion but it is suspected they would have.

After the battles were over, there was a big push to repair those area's infrastructure and John Raymond and Arthur Henry would have been extremely busy carrying out this important and very difficult work in arduous tropical conditions. They were there when the atomic bombs were dropped and the war ended.

Return to civilian life for Arthur Henry but not John Raymond

In August 1945, Arthur Henry was promoted to Corporal then very soon afterwards to Sergeant. In September, he was transferred to Labuan, an island off the coast of north-western Malaysian Borneo, to carry out further vital infrastructure repair work. He continued his work there for over a year, until December 1946 when his work concluded and he was sent back to Brisbane, Australia. He then went on to Western Australia, hopefully in time to spend Christmas with his wife and daughter, Beverley.

On the 18th January 1946, Arthur Henry was discharged from the army; his war years were over and he was, once again, a civilian.

John Raymond worked on in Morotai until the end of October 1945, when he developed a medical problem. There is no mention on his war records what he was ailing from but it must have been very serious. It was so bad he was evacuated to a hospital in Brisbane in mid-November, and was hospitalised for about three weeks before being evacuated by an Ambulance train to a military hospital in Victoria then on to Western Australia where he was able to meet his baby daughter, Charmion. He was discharged from medical care and returned to duty in mid-January 1946. It is possible he may have had a serious infection or had burns to his forearms because it is known that he suffered skin problems on his arms for most of his life.

Unlike Arthur Henry, John Raymond was not discharged from the army after he returned to WA. He was sent to the southwest to a Prisoner of War Camp at Marrinup, just north-west of Dwellingup.

This prison was mainly for Italian and German prisoners of war and many came from the battlefields in the Middle East, probably from some of the battles in which Stanley Lawrence participated. The camp held up to 1,200 men. The Germans who were not trusted were sent out to work cutting wood in the forest. The Italians were tasked with doing farm labour on the local farms – the Italians were not considered a high security risk. (https://dwellingup.destinationmurray.com.au)

At the end of the war, there were no ships available to send the prisoners home so John Raymond, who was good at supervising groups of men, was sent to Marrinup to look after the prisoners until they were able to be sent home.

John Raymond finally discharged from the army

On 31st January 1947, John Raymond was discharged from duty, a long time since the end of the war.

Later in John Raymond's life, he was awarded the British Empire Medal (BEM) for services to the outback of Western Australia, supervising the erecting of telephone lines throughout the area.

War and continuing health problems

The brothers who had gone to war but not experienced the stress of danger in battle would have still seen the horrors of it just by being there, seeing the dead, the maimed, and the exhausted men return from the front line. A sight never to be forgotten. They would have been in areas where the released Japanese Prisoners of War had passed through and seen the pitiful broken men who were just shadows of their former selves. A shock to say the least. The disgusting cruelty and demeaning treatment of the Prisoners of War by the Japanese should never be forgotten.

It is interesting to note that John Raymond, Francis Peter, and William Kevin had skin complaints after serving in the tropics. John Raymond had problems with the skin on his forearms when he arrived back and it was an ongoing problem. Both Francis Peter and Kevin William probably had 'nervous' complaints of the skin. Francis Peter had severe dermatitis and William Kevin had psoriasis. Both can be autoimmune diseases brought on by extreme stress. It must be remembered that the brothers had to work in "*such adverse conditions, often in torrential rain and mud, at all times in dissipating heat, against a myriad of physical deterrents*" to provide the services required to those at the frontline. These services "*put up heroic efforts*" that were highly appreciated by the fighting men. WILLIAMS, L.J. *New Guinea: the Aitape-Wewak Campaign*. In The 2/11th (City of Perth) Australian Infantry Battalion 1939-45. John Burridge Military Antiques, 2000. p. 135.

This would have been the case for all behind-the-lines service providers; they were vital for keeping the fighting soldiers at the front lines.

No doubt war will come again. It is a natural phenomenon that happens across many species, even ants! There is a quote by Plato from over 400 BCE ago! "*Only the dead have seen the end of war*". (Tobruk War Memorial, Kings Park)

Doreen's war
The Americans arrive in Perth

In March 1942, the United States Navy arrived in Perth and were based at Crawley on the Swan River where a Catalina Flying Boat base was established. This was a big deal for the people of Perth, especially those in the suburbs close to the base.

"For young people in particular, Americans represented wealth, glamour and modernity. In some ways, these soldiers matched the Hollywood image: their manners impressed Australian women (calling women 'Ma'am' and men 'sir') and their uniforms were better looking than the baggy uniforms of the Australian soldiers. They were also much better paid than the Australians, and they were ready to spend their money in search of a good time. Their own guidebooks emphasised that they were to be on their best behaviour…" (www.slv.vic.gov.au)

"…Australian women were encouraged to dance with the servicemen who were far from their homes, families and friends. In fulfilling this wartime obligation, these women often became the romantic targets of attentive, lonely young American servicemen looking for companionship in a foreign city.

The men filled the streets, pubs, dance halls and cinemas of Australia's major cities. Young, handsome and fit, these Americans were initially welcomed as "heroes and saviours" to a country with the frontline of World War II not far from its shores". (www.smh.com.au)

"American soldiers in the lower ranks earned twice the amount of their Australian counterparts and in the higher ranks the disparity was even more pronounced. These differences in pay scales, their stylish uniforms, and custom of tipping earned them a reputation as "big spenders". Disagreements between Australian and American forces over rates of pay, food rations, women, race relations, and fighting skill caused major confrontations" (www.awm.gov.au/articles)

Doreen would surely have been impressed with these men who most likely went to the local dances that she attended with her girlfriends and who could expertly dance the jitterbug and other lively dances that Doreen loved. They were handsome and dashing in their uniforms and bore gifts that couldn't be obtained by the public. Rationing had begun in Perth for such things as clothing, tea, sugar, butter, and meat and, from time to time, eggs and milk. The Americans had all of these things and could also give the girls gifts like silk stockings and chocolates, and they had vehicles in which to get around. They had access to petrol that was also heavily rationed to civilians. Not many people could use their vehicles except for absolute necessities and now the girls could be driven all over the place – a real treat. The girls fell hard for these luxuries after having been deprived of most things, including staples like food! The Americans could get them small luxuries they had gone without and many were lonely with their men away and craved some fun and excitement.

On the other hand, the Australian soldiers had a festering hatred for these men and it was well known that they had the saying the 'Americans were – over paid, over sexed, and over here!' They were jealous of their women being taken in by these 'Yanks'. When Australian soldiers were on leave there was often friction and fights ensued.

Doreen was only nineteen years old and still loved the social life. Stanley Lawrence was in Western Australia but she hardly ever saw him, and when she did it was for just a few days at a time. Surely, she still liked to go out with her girlfriends to keep occupied. She had moved out of her family home and gone to live with her mother's sister, Aunty Alma Irene to keep her company and to make room for Joan Irene's baby daughter. Alma Irene's son, Leonard Ernest Cavanagh had enlisted in the Australian Airforce and was away in England on service. Doreen was still working at The Central Provisions Store and went socialising with the girls from there and her old girlfriends from school.

No doubt Stanley Lawrence would have been aware of this and may have been annoyed at his new wife going out with her friends – but, he would have been furious to know she may have been fraternising with these American servicemen, and probably imagined this was the case! The following is highly likely to be true in most respects. Some of the smaller details may be incorrect but, on the whole, the main story is true. The dates of the events add up and Stanley Lawrence's character was true to form, as was Doreen's.

Trauma and marriage breakup for Stanley Lawrence and Doreen

Stanley Lawrence, along with many of his army comrades, would have been very jealous of the American Military personnel and there would have been a huge grudge against them. He was on leave and he and Doreen went to a dance together on the night of 16th May 1943, a Saturday night. It is highly likely the dance was in the Swan Barracks in Francis Street, the current "Mess Hall", where dances were regularly held. The American servicemen also frequented the dances and were out for a good time. It is likely some showed an interest in the very pretty Doreen who was an excellent dancer and she may have flirted with them. No doubt Stanley Lawrence had had a few drinks and became aggressive towards the Americans, and probably accused them of fraternising with the Australian soldiers' women and making big fellas of themselves.

An argument started and then, after some push and shove, a fist fight ensued and little Stanley Lawrence belted one of the Americans (an officer apparently) in the face, breaking his nose and his glasses. All the pent-up jealousy towards the Americans, in general, broke loose. This assault was an offence that could have seen Stanley Lawrence court-martialled and sent to prison. After everything this little hero had been through, it would have been an absolute insult to him to face the consequences. Such a big psychological hit for him. Doreen was probably horrified and very embarrassed by the fight, and knowing Doreen's impetuousness she would have walked off in a huff.

Public transport had finished some hours before so now she had no transport home. She left with another girl and some Australian servicemen, possibly Stanley Lawrence's mates, who offered her a ride home. Stanley Lawrence was held by his mates and ushered out of there in a hurry; they didn't want him nabbed by the much-hated Military Police. Stanley Lawrence was in big trouble and he had to be protected by his mates.

When Doreen and the group left, they found there was little room in the car for them all. Doreen squeezed between the driver and his side door. The driver sped onto the Horseshoe Bridge, lost control, swerved and hit a power pole. It was a bad crash and all were injured and had to be taken to hospital. The soldiers were taken to a military hospital and the girls to Royal Perth Hospital. Doreen sustained a bad concussion and the other girl had facial injuries. Doreen was unconscious and ended up in a coma for two weeks. She was not aware of the events that followed.

Stanley Lawrence transferred to the Navy

Very quickly, Stanley Lawrence's Commanding Officers heard what had happened – army folk-law has it that, before the Military Police could find him, his superiors had closed ranks around him to protect him. Sandover and Binks were both very aware of his contribution to saving Sandover and many of their men from Crete, his astonishing bravery, his very impressive war record, that he was a brilliant signalman and a very gutsy and brave 'runner'.

On the 18th May, they held him at Army Headquarters and swung into action. By the 20th May 1943, they discharged him from the Army and arranged for him to enlist in the Australian Navy the same day. The Navy was desperately in need of a skilled telegraphist. He immediately went through the enlistment process and was in the Naval Base at HMAS Leeuwin by 3rd June 1943. On his Navy record, it is noted that his services were <u>required</u> by the Navy.

Doreen was still in a coma when he went into the Navy and he had been unable to see her. When she came round and was finally released from hospital, things had changed dramatically in her life. Poor Doreen suffered amnesia for a short time after the accident and didn't know of Stanley Lawrence's existence. However, with time, her memory returned. She was met with hostility from her mother, Gladys Catherine, for bringing shame on the family. Doreen's name had been in the newspaper – a big scandal!

All the blame had been put on her for everything that had happened that night. In those times, women often got the blame for 'encouraging' men. She was a beautiful and vivacious young woman – this alone would have attracted the attention of these men who were lonely and away from home, and it was wartime.

Stanley Lawrence would have been highly embarrassed at his wife's name being in the newspaper that stated she was in the car with servicemen. He would have found it difficult to face his mates and the ribbing he would have got from them. His ego would have been trashed and his confidence shattered. He would have been so very angry at his wife for bringing this on to him.

After being discharged from hospital, Doreen went back to live with Alma Irene and was ostracised by many in the family, including Stanley Lawrence's family, especially his mother, Maria Ellen, who seemed to hold a life-long grudge.

Both Stanley Lawrence and Doreen must each have been very upset and had a difficult time coming to terms with their sudden split and there was no opportunity to 'make up'. They continued their separation until the end of the war. They were now physically separated and there had been no opportunity to talk to each other. It was all left in limbo.

Both got on with their respective lives, thinking the marriage was over. They had not quite reached their first wedding anniversary

Doreen's much-loved cousin, Leonard Ernest Cavanagh, is killed

Doreen had only just recovered from her concussion and was home with Alma Irene when, towards the end of June 1943, terrible news arrived. Her favourite cousin, Alma Irene's only child, Leonard Ernest Cavanagh, whom Doreen had had so much fun with as a child, had been shot down over Belgium and was killed on the 23rd June 1943. He had enlisted in the Royal Australian Air Force (RAAF) on the 9th October 1941 – his Service Number was 415377 – and his Unit was the 158th Squadron. He was eighteen years old and had been sent to England to be a bomber pilot with the Royal Air Force (RAF). He flew a Halifax 11 JD 259 'R' Bomber.

1941 - Flight Sergeant Leonard Ernest Cavanagh – No. 415377; 158th Squadron, RAAF (Killed 23rd June, 1943, aged 20) (Photo – Kaye McCallum/Carroll)

The attrition rate of airmen during WWII was extremely high; it is sobering just how many lost their lives, particularly those in the slow bombers which were a prime target of the enemy. Doreen and Alma Irene would have been devastated by this terrible news. For years after the war, Alma Irene would go to the King's Park War Memorial to see her son's name on the wall – there was no grave for her to visit. She would come away sobbing every time. Doreen's mother, Gladys Catherine, would go with her sister to comfort her.

Alma Irene eventually went to Belgium to be close to her boy and sit by his grave. He was the Flight Sergeant and pilot and was killed just before his 21st birthday. His crew of six was also killed.

Later in life - Alma Irene Gawned/Cavanagh/Stamp (Family photo)

Alma Irene's first husband, Leonard's father, James Cavanagh, died in 1930 and her second husband, Edwin J. Stamp survived WWII, came home and was killed when he rode his motorcycle into the back of a bus in 1945. Suicide? She had a most unfortunate and lonely time until her mother, Elizabeth Jane's nephew, Brian Burgess, came to Western Australia and lived with Alma Irene. He kept her company until her death.

Doreen moves on after tragedy and the end of her marriage

Now Doreen had to deal with Leonard Ernest's tragic death, plus the end of her marriage – such a sad and terrible time for her and it is suspected she may have had some sort of minor mental breakdown. She often joked that she and Francis Peter got on so well together because they understood each other – in their madness!

She tried to move on and reconcile that her marriage was over. After a while, she began to go out with her friends again. Now that she was 'single', many men tried to court her, including her womanising brother-in-law Ken Thorley, Stanley Lawrence's sister, Mary Ellen's (Molly) husband, who was very persistent and, rumour has it, she may have gone out with him for a while. She was, after all, a beautiful and vulnerable young woman.

Stanley Lawrence was stationed near Melbourne and, therefore, had no contact with Doreen. He changed his home address in WA from his parents' to Mary Ellen's (Molly) place in Claremont but did not change Doreen as his next of kin.

After Doreen split with Stanley Lawrence, she continued working at The Central Provision Stores. Then in April 1945, she moved jobs and went to work for Selfridges (WA), a large department store in Hay Street, Perth. There were *"three main entrances from Hay-street, with attractive showcases, and also an entrance from the Central Arcade. The whole of the ground floor, (comprised of) 43 different departments"* The West Australian. Sat 28 Aug 1937, p. 4.

This Selfridges was not affiliated with the famous London store.

A very sophisticated looking Doreen when she worked for Selfridges in Perth City, 1945
(Family photo)

Stanley Lawrence in the Navy

A tired looking Stanley Lawrence Carroll – his official war portrait, taken a few days after enlistment. Royal Australian Navy; No. F/V223. June, 1943 (Family photo)

Stanley Lawrence was sent immediately to Victoria, Australia to serve at the Naval Base HMAS Cerberus, situated approximately 70 kilometres from Melbourne. He was stationed there as a telegraphist using mainly Morse-Code, but was competent in most signalling equipment. While there, he contracted mumps and was very ill. He was there until February 1944, until he had finished all his naval training and then transferred to Cape Otway, Victoria, of which he always spoke with great affection. This must have been his favourite place. He met a girl there and they had a short romance. He was stationed there for four months. It was obvious to the hierarchy he was a highly skilled operator and very experienced in signals of all sorts in difficult war situations and, because of this, was chosen for a very important position. They needed only the best telegraphists for Cape Otway which was a top-secret base for the Australian Airforce radar section. *"Data collected from these stations was sent by wireless telegraphy to the top-secret Air Defence Headquarters at 7FS Preston, Melbourne. Cape Otway, the first radar station on the southern coast, transmitted its 'secret' information to Headquarters..."*

(https://www.lightstation.com/explore-cape-otway/radar-bunker)

After leaving this important work, every couple of months he went on naval patrols of the Southern Ocean along the coast of Australia and was stationed between HMAS Lonsdale, Port Melbourne, and HMAS Leeuwin Naval Base in WA.

One night while on shore leave, Stanley Lawrence went out with his mates to Melbourne. They went to a hotel that had booths with privacy curtains for people to sit in. He was outside one of the curtains when he heard someone on the other side make a comment that Stanley Lawrence didn't like. He flung the curtain open and put his head inside and demanded, "Who said that?"

Immediately a fist slammed into his face and his nose was badly broken. When he spoke of the incident, he said he saw stars and reeled backwards and that there was blood everywhere. He said there were bones poking through and he had bone fragments coming out of his nose for ages afterwards. His nice straight nose now looked like the nose of a prize fighter!

In May 1945, he was sent for service on the ship *HMAS Olive Cam*, a mine sweeper, in which he did Naval patrols in the Pacific. He then continued Naval patrols between HMAS Leeuwin and HMAS Monterey, NSW, until the end of the war in September 1945. His final posting was at HMAS Leeuwin Naval Base in October 1945.

Stanley Lawrence and Doreen reconcile

While in Perth, he would have had leave and it was during this time he and Doreen arranged to meet and discuss their separation. Both probably had thought their marriage was over, so the meeting would have been very difficult for both of them. Doreen's family, now reconciled with her, and very concerned about her welfare and the outcome of the meeting, went along with her for moral support. The meeting was held at The Captain Stirling Hotel in Claremont. It is probable they both went into the meeting with great trepidation and wondered what the outcome would be. Both probably expected the worst, with the scandal of divorce on their minds. She went inside alone and met Stanley Lawrence while her family waited outside. The discussion took some time and after a long wait Doreen's family saw them emerge hand in hand from the hotel door, and according to Joy Anderson/Gawned, who was at the hotel with Doreen's family, both looked very happy. Their love had endured through this very trying time and they were reconciled.

On the 18th January 1946, Stanley Lawrence was demobilised from the Navy and could go home. He was officially discharged on 1st February 1946. He was now a civilian once more.

The end of WWII
and getting back to a 'normal' life

The war was finally over and people had to try and get back to some sort of normalcy. Things were still in short supply, especially petrol. Stanley Lawrence had bought a car before the end of the war, a Wolseley Hornet. Cars then had no self-starters – that is, they didn't start by using a key or pressing a button – they had to be started with a long crank handle that was inserted through the front of the car below the radiator and the engine turned by hand until it started. When he could get petrol, he would drive the 'Hornet' with great care so as not to use too much fuel. He would turn the car off at the top of a hill and coast down to do a clutch start at the beginning of the next hill. This frugal procedure was continued all his driving life until he bought an automatic car that had power steering. These cars could not be steered properly if the car was turned off and could not be clutch started.

He and Doreen would go all over the place in the two-seater Hornet. He also had a BSA motorbike with a sidecar that Doreen hated. She would be the passenger in the sidecar and was always petrified that she would go into the back of anything he passed. Stanley Lawrence often put 'letters' as in a degree, at the end of his name. He would say his name and add 'BSA and sidecar'!

Doreen was pregnant soon after they had reconciled. Their first child was a son, Lindsay. During the birthing process, it was discovered that Doreen wasn't like most people – she had an adverse reaction to the relaxing nitrous oxide (laughing gas) normally given for pain relief. She got up from the bed when Lindsay's head was presenting, ran down the corridor and pulled items off the surgical trolley and threw them around! When her next baby was born, she wasn't given gas!

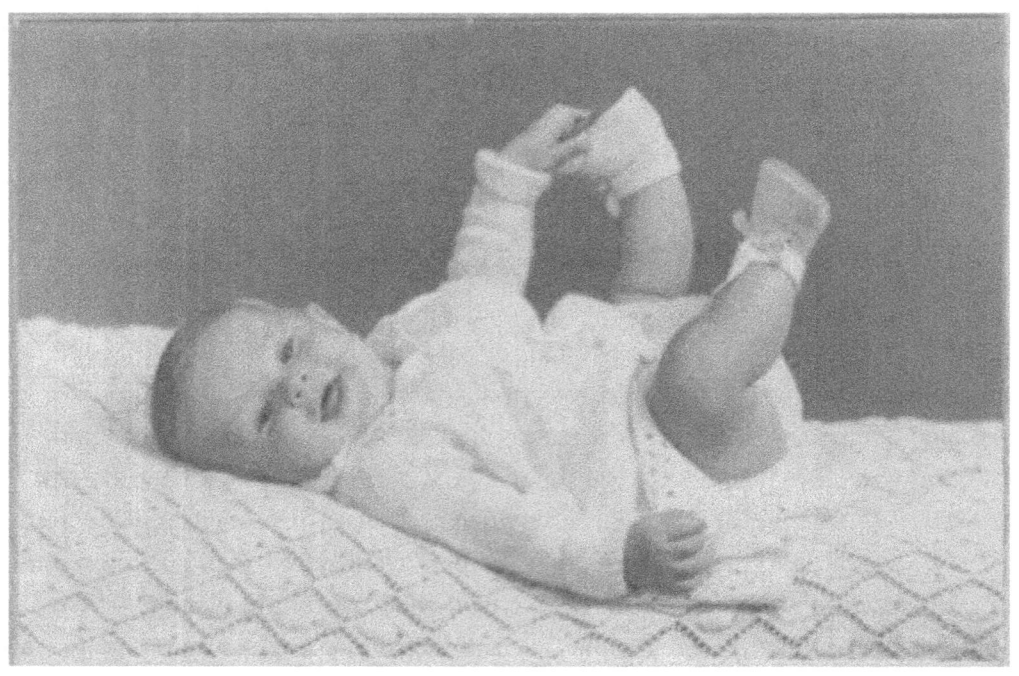

Lindsay, born 1946 (Family photo)

Sometimes the new family would go visiting family in the Hornet and take Doreen's mother, Gladys Catherine, along. It is difficult to believe that Gladys Catherine would sit on the back of the front seat and hold the pram which was perched on the boot! Of course, Lindsay was on Doreen's lap.

The Wolseley Hornet, Lindsay's 1st birthday (at the McGlinn's house in Waroonga Road) 1947 (Photo Kaye McCallum/Carroll)

The Wolseley Hornet 1947. (Photo Kaye McCallum/Carroll)

Their first home together, a rented one

Shortly after the war ended, they rented a house on a hill at 13 Melville Street, Claremont. It was an old weatherboard house with a verandah at the front and a long flight of stairs at the back as the block sloped steeply away at the back. On occasions, Stanley Lawrence had to jack the floor up so the outside walls and floors met. Amazingly, this house is still standing today.

The Melville Street house today, the verandah has been enclosed. Stanley Lawrence's and Doreen's 1st home together, 1946 to 1952 (Personal photo 2021)

At this house, many parties and celebrations were held. The parties were often impromptu and were very common post war. Stanley Lawrence's army mates would turn up at all hours and roll a keg of beer down the path ready for a party. Doreen said that often they would be in bed asleep and be woken by the sound of the beer keg rolling down the path!

Many of these men would have found it difficult to adjust back to civilian life and their camaraderie would have kept them close friends for years. They needed the familiar friendships formed during very difficult and dangerous times. It would have taken a while to adjust to a life where they didn't live cheek by jowl and had to trust implicitly the man next to him. Many men drank alone or together, perhaps to forget the horrors they had experienced. Adjustment must have been very difficult.

Doreen continued to work at Selfridges until January 1946, when she and Stanley Lawrence were reunited.

Back to civilian life and a job

Now it was time for Stanley Lawrence to go back into the workforce. The military had repatriation vocational schemes where training was provided to returned soldiers so they could get meaningful employment. Prior to the war, the depression had left many of these men with no skills because there had been no work. Stanley Lawrence decided that Meat Inspection would be a good career so went into training for that. In order to get Repatriation training, a psychological report had to be done. On the 4th February 1946, the psychological report stated that Stanley Lawrence had a "very high average intellectual capacity, with superior discrimination of size and shape, and very high mechanical comprehension…" He was recommended to the position of Meat Inspector by the Royal Australian Navy Educational Services. It would seem that if he took this career he would have to go and live and work in the country, probably not what Doreen would prefer. He had learnt quite a lot but decided that perhaps a different occupation might be better. He thought that being a school teacher would be a good option and was accepted into the repatriation Teacher's Training course and finished his 'degree' in that profession.

The rented house, family move in

Doreen's sister, Joan Irene and Stanley Lawrence's brother Francis Peter and their daughter, Kaye, had been living in Hastings Street, Scarborough. They left that house and moved into the Melville Street house with Stanley Lawrence, Doreen and Lindsay. The house was affectionately known as "The Ranch". It was all very cosy in that small house, four adults and two, then three, then four children! It was a social hub for friends and ex-soldiers and sailors.

Joan Irene, Francis Peter, and baby, Kaye (Photo Kaye McCallum/Carroll)

The next child born was Russell, a brother to Kaye. He was born in November 1947.

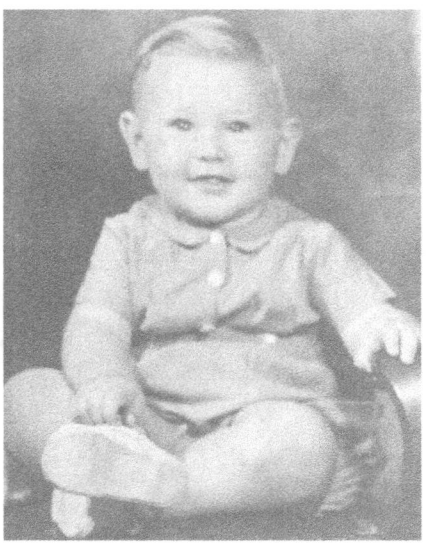

Russell Carroll, born 1947. (Photo Kaye McCallum/Carroll)
(Russell died, aged 74, during the writing of this book. 8th July, 2022)

Stanley Lawrence and Doreen then had a daughter, Maureen, born in January 1950.

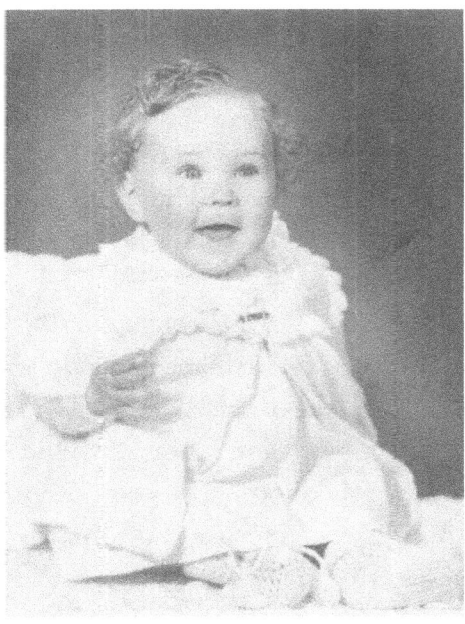

Maureen, born, 1950 (Family photo)

Doreen was very happy in this house, being surrounded by family, and she could walk to her parents' home in Waroonga Road, about one kilometre away. Walking distances was no problem – everyone walked most places – and because there were no refrigerators, a walk to the corner grocery shop nearly every day was necessary, especially in summer. Ice was delivered in big blocks to the home to fill the icebox, which was like a big esky on legs, to keep food cold but it didn't last long.

The Ice-man delivering ice to households for the ice boxes
(photo - State Library of Western Australia)

War Service Home loans and new houses for the brothers who served

Eventually, war service housing grants were made to retuned service personnel. Francis Peter got a block at 47 Banksia Street, in the new suburb of Joondanna. He built a temporary little house from bricks and tiles he had made himself while living at the 'Shack' in Claremont. It was a cosy little house with a laundry and bath in an area made of tin out the back. They lived in this until they self-built their new home on the same block. The older house was then used as a storage area and shed. Francis Peter and William Kevin built a woodwork shed next to this little house and they used it as a carpentry 'factory'.

Francis Peter used the repatriation scheme to study accountancy and became an accountant with the Department of Social Services WA.

William Kevin used his repatriation training to become a carpenter. His woodworking skills from his childhood was now his profession. Later, he did further studies and got his Builders' License and went on to manage the Building Section of the State Housing Commission of Western Australia.

William Kevin married Patricia O'Donnell in 1949 and purchased a house at 175 Daglish Street, Wembley.

William Kevin and Patricia on their wedding day (photo Lesley Watson/Carroll)

All the Carroll brothers who went to war ended up in good government positions. John Raymond and Arthur Henry did not move to Perth to live – Arthur Henry and Thelma remained in Bridgetown at 6 McAlinden Street, and he continued his pre-war work with the PMG – John Raymond also worked for the PMG but moved out to the Eastern Goldfields, and was initially based in Kalgoorlie and Leonora, where he supervised telecommunications line building out into the greater outback. He and Audrey eventually moved to live south of the Swan River at number 8 Corinthian Street, in the new Perth suburb of Rossmoyne.

Mary Ellen (Molly) continued to live in her home in Claremont before moving to the northern part of Floreat Park. Kathleen Christine and her husband Len, moved to the new suburb of south City Beach to live.

Norman George and his wife Dorothy lived in Edinboro Street, Joondanna, not far from Francis Peter and Joan Irene.

Stanley Lawrence and Doreen decided that a house in the very new suburb of Floreat Park would suit them. They got a War Service loan and purchased a ready-made new house at 16 Arbordale Street and moved there in 1952. The house cost approximately £3,000.

Parts of the bush were left intact on these large blocks so there were trees and native shrubs already there to make up part of the garden. Floreat Park was still wild. There was a lot of bushland that was mainly Jarrah, Marri, Banksia and Casuarina and the occasional large Tuart. There was an understory of beautiful wildflowers and shrubs. Perry Lakes was originally swampland surrounded by Flooded Gums and there was a farm to the west of the lakes that had cattle. The house on Perry Drive that houses the Wildflower Society was the original farmhouse. A little further south was an Aboriginal camp/meeting place. Quite near to that was a 'speedway', a circular limestone track that was used by the locals for fun. The now Oceanic Drive was a plank road that was upgraded to a limestone 'road' and was later bituminized, but it was a narrow road with crumbling limestone edging. The quarry amphitheatre was a wild quarry and a dangerous place, but a great attraction for the local kids.

City Beach Road 1955 (photo Perth Reflects; Facebook. 2023)

Floreat Park Primary School was built around the time Stanley Lawrence and Doreen moved into Floreat Park. He had already graduated and was teaching at West Leederville Primary School so he requested a transfer to Floreat Primary. This was granted and he became a teacher there.

The sports ovals and the tennis courts were built a few years later. There was bush where Floreat Forum now stands, and the school was surrounded by bushland.

Stanley Lawrence's and Doreen's new home at 16 Arbordale Street, Floreat Park (Family photo)

In 1953, their third child was born – a boy, Glentyn.

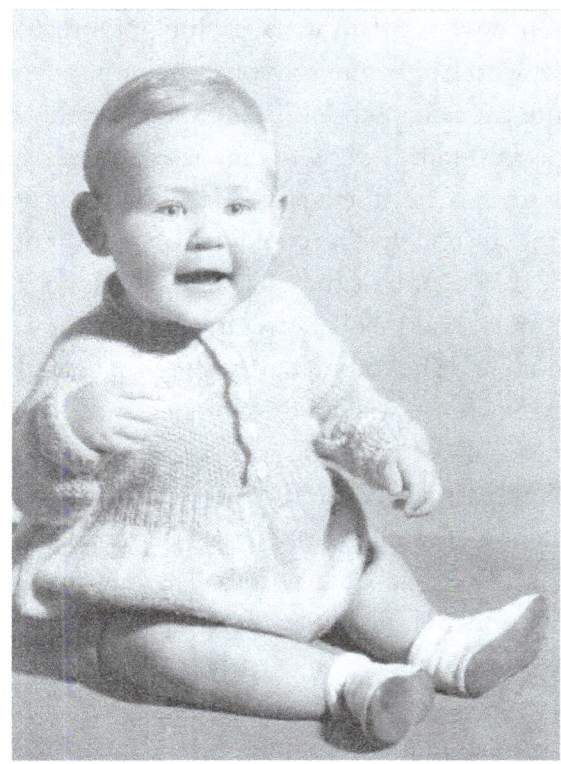

Glentyn, born 1953 (Family photo)

It was time to upgrade their car after Maureen was born, the two-seater Wolseley Hornet was no longer appropriate for a growing family so they purchased a brand-new green Morris Minor.

The new Morris Minor with Maureen (Family photo)

Domesticity

When Stanley Lawrence went off to work each day Doreen was left to care for the children. Lindsay, who had begun school at the same school Doreen attended as a child, Claremont Practicing School (Prac), was now enrolled to go to Floreat Park Primary. He was in Grade Two when he began there. Maureen and Glentyn were cared for by Doreen. After they moved into the Floreat house, Doreen was quite isolated and probably lonely. She could no longer visit her parents whenever she liked. The hustle and bustle of the busy little house in Melville Street was a stark contrast to the quiet and lonely house in Floreat. She couldn't visit her old friends from Claremont and she found it difficult to mix with her new neighbours. Even though Stanley Lawrence walked to school each day, the new car was of no use to Doreen – she could not drive and was stuck.

She was an absolutely dedicated mother and very strict with her children and took on Gladys Catherine's model of bringing up her children. They got away with nothing. There was a great deal of love in the family but it was not displayed openly, which was normal in those times. There was no hugging nor demonstrative behaviour but there was security and love, good food on the table and clean clothes. She was a good mother.

Doreen joined the local tennis club and played once a week. She would walk and take her two small children. Even though this was a social event, she never joined in on the chit chat after the games and did not socialise with the women away from the courts. She did not socialise well and, even though she enjoyed a quick chat and found no difficulty with short conversations, she never became close to any of these women. Her short conversations were probably a skill she built up during her work at the big store in Perth. This was her 'work' personality.

Every Sunday the family would go to visit her parents and have Sunday lunch, a delicious and special meal that was served up by Gladys Catherine. A very pleasant afternoon was then had.

If Doreen wanted a social outing, she would take the children and catch the Trolley Bus to Perth to meet up with Gladys Catherine, Joan Irene and her children, and they would have lunch in the cafeteria in Coles or Boans Department Store. They all enjoyed the outing, including the children. Window shopping was always enjoyed by all. The shop windows were decorated and artistically designed and were a delight to see. Many people enjoyed window shopping without ever buying anything.

For a short time after they moved into the new house, the parties still continued and they would invite their friends and Stanley Lawrence's army and navy mates.

People in the street would also be invited. The men in the street were returned servicemen so there was a bond between them all and they had a lot in common. Several four-gallon drums were set out with a plank across them and a rug thrown over: perfect seating for a lot of people. The beer flowed and the nights were a roaring success and hangovers were common. In the morning, the kids would drink the leftover dregs from the glasses of stale beer and smoke the butts of the finished cigarettes, then everyone felt sick, parents and kids! At those times, with a few drinks under their belts, both Stanley Lawrence and Doreen were the life of the party and could hold their own in the drinking stakes. They were very popular and perfect hosts.

During his meat inspection classes, Stanley Lawrence had learnt that a sheep's tongue when turned inside out looks just like a man's penis. At one particular party he prepared a sheep's tongue and strapped the tongue to his waist, let it hang from the leg of his shorts then walk around in front of the guests. He would put his leg up on a chair and chat to the person. They tried desperately to ignore the sight before their eyes. He laughed and laughed later when telling of their reactions, trying not to look or looking everywhere else! He eventually confessed to the guests who all thought it a great joke and many of the men were interested to know how to prepare the tongue for future events.

Drinking and smoking were popular post-war pastimes. Stanley Lawrence was still a bit of a party animal and if he heard a party going on near their house he would crash it and become the life of the party; he'd drink and smoke and get drunk, sing at the top of his voice, and then go home very satisfied – that is until he encountered Doreen waiting for him to give him a piece of her mind. She would let fly, her fiery side giving him both barrels. They'd argue for a while then all was sweet. It may have been that after being at war, life was a bit too mundane in the suburbs and he needed a bit of excitement. It all would have been a release for Post Traumatic Stress Syndrome that many of these men suffered.

Later, as the children got a bit older, there would be Friday nights with the Carrolls. Usually Francis Peter, Joan Irene, William Kevin and Patricia who would take turns at going to each other's house. The kids would be taken along and this was great for the cousins to play and get up to mischief. The adults would get a skinful of beer and had endless arguments and debates with raised voices and plenty of table thumping. The women were always very animated and were keen to get their point over. At the end of the night, the sleeping children would be gathered up and put in the car and driven home. It is fortunate that drink driving wasn't a problem then and there were very few cars on the road. The next weekend it would all be repeated.

Doreen gets her Driver's License

In about 1958, Doreen decided that she needed to learn to drive. They had bought a new car, a Holden FJ sedan, and Stanley Lawrence gave her lessons. The kids would go in the back of the car and Doreen would nervously drive slowly around the streets. When it came time to reverse park, she would refuse to do it and 'do her block' and tell Stanley Lawrence to go to hell; she's not doing it, even though he warned her in order to pass her license she must.

At last, it was time to go for her driver's licence. The policeman sat next to her and off they went. When it was time to do the reverse parking, she told the policeman to go to buggery she's not doing it and would never do it! She passed! How things have changed! Now Doreen was free to go and visit her mum and Joan Irene whenever she wanted and she was much more content. The Floreat Forum had been built and, along with the grocery stores, there was Moore's Department Store that had everything required for the household. It was the first shopping centre outside of Perth city.

Doreen returns to work

Doreen decided she would go to work while the children were at school. Prior to this, wives of government workers were not allowed to work but the government ban had been lifted so she got a part time job in a green grocer shop on Stirling Highway, Claremont. This is when her ability with mental arithmetic came to the fore. She had no problems calculating the weight in stones, pounds, and ounces and work out the cost in pounds, shillings, and pence. There are fourteen pounds in a stone, and sixteen ounces in a pound, then calculate that into monetary value, there are twenty shillings in a pound and twelve pence in a shilling. There were ten and twenty pound notes, five pound notes, one pound notes and ten shilling notes. In coins, there were two shillings, one shilling, sixpence, threepence, penny, and halfpennies. There were no calculators! She did it in her head, as many shop assistants could do. A pencil was held behind the ear and the workings were done on the piece of paper in which the items were wrapped. No plastic bags then, you always took a basket. The money till only had buttons for the amount paid. Then the change would be given by working out the balance in her head. Amazing stuff. She may not have excelled in written English, but she excelled in arithmetic.

Doreen has health problems

Before Doreen became pregnant with Glentyn, she had problems with her reproductive system and there were worrying signs of some problems that she nor the medical profession could fathom. These problems caused her great stress. During that stressful time, she became pregnant. She didn't feel she could cope with another child while she felt so off but of course when he was born she loved him and cared for him. However, there was a dark side. She fell into depression and her mind was not in a good place. She told Stanley Lawrence to hide all the knives in the house because she felt she wanted to kill the children. She was frightened to the point of insanity. She went further afield about her medical problems and it was soon discovered that, at the age of twenty-nine, she had entered menopause. Her mental state was caused by hormonal imbalance. After some time, the problem was resolved and she was soon back to normal. It is thought her concussion and head injury from the car accident, may have been the cause of all this and she had had a brain injury. She suffered with what she called a 'bad head' all her life.

A life settled into suburbia

A happier Doreen and Glentyn, London Court Perth. 1954 (Family photo)

In the photo above, it can be seen that Doreen had slightly buck teeth. Dentists were very expensive (as they are today!) Most people could not afford to have their teeth filled – fillings were extremely expensive at that time. Any toothache or decay was fixed by removing the tooth. Doreen's teeth had a few problems with decay and because of the cost she had all her teeth removed and a full set of dentures fitted. In both the McGlinn and Carroll families, most of them had had their teeth removed early and dentures fitted – it was a trend of the day. Stanley Lawrence resisted and kept most of his teeth until his death.

Life settled to a routine of work and child rearing.

Doreen was in control of the money and paid all the bills etc. She took control of her children as well and, as it was with her mother, she ruled with her version of child rearing. The new mores of the day were not really to her liking, as it had been with each generation past. This was nothing new but now the concept of 'teenagers' began. Prior to now, there were no 'teenagers' as such. The young people before the war and earlier did not have free time to be 'teenagers', they had to go to work and help the family. Now teenagers had plenty of free time and could stay at school longer. World information became easy with the advent of television and they soon became aware of the new social trends and formed their own opinions about the issues of the day. They found new freedoms and attended protests and street marches against the Vietnam War, the damage to the environment, and they discovered the hippy movement and 'free love' and drugs. The boundaries teenagers pushed were many but they were held back by this generation of strong mothers. Many parents despaired.

Doreen was very strict and ruled with the rod and her children were punished or smacked for misdemeanours but she loved them dearly. None of them could leave to go to school or work without a kiss goodbye and a kiss hello when they got home. She and Stanley Lawrence tucked the children into bed each night and gave them a kiss goodnight. The children were loved and they knew it. Stanley Lawrence and Doreen were a united front and neither went against each other when the children tried to play one parent against the other, the kids soon learnt that it didn't work. They were totally dedicated to their children.

Doreen had no tact in her conversations and you got exactly what she meant whether you liked it or not, but you knew exactly where you stood. She just wanted her children to be good citizens and to follow her rules of correctness.

The family. Lindsay, Stanley Lawrence, Glentyn, Doreen, and Maureen. About 1960. (Family photo)

Doreen, like most women in those days, had to cook all the family's food. She built up an impressive recipe collection for all sorts of culinary delights, especially puddings and sweets. The main meal mostly consisted of meat and a variety of vegetables then a pudding of some sort. Shop bought biscuits and cakes were mostly not available or weren't bought. Even ice-cream was made at home. Restaurants were for rich people and they were few and far between. The proliferation of restaurants and take-a-ways came much later. Doreen had many recipes that were passed on to her from her mother and grandmother who were wonderful cooks, and recipes were shared among family and friends. Bread was about the only thing that was pre-made and was purchased from the baker who brought his freshly baked bread around the streets in a horse and cart. The bread smelt wonderful and tasted very different from today's bread. The baker would take his bread in his cart up and down all the suburb's streets and women would meet him to buy the bread or he would leave it on the front verandah. Milk was delivered in a similar way as the horse slowly moved along the street and the milkman would take the milk to the front of the house and leave it. Money was left out for these items, dishonesty was not a problem, and nobody stole the money that was left in full view. Occasionally the butcher and green grocer would deliver fresh produce from a van that he drove to a street corner and people would shop from them.

Food was supplemented with home grown vegetables and chickens both for eggs and to eat. Every afternoon you could hear the square-mouthed shovel being scraped by Stanley Lawrence over the cement floor of the chicken coop. He used this manure for his vegetable patch. Occasionally, if a chicken had stopped laying eggs, he would chop its head off for the Sunday roast. He let it flap around the yard seemingly to chase the kids who would all squeal in excitement and terror if the chicken flapped, with its blood spurting, towards them. The chicken was then hung on the clothes line to 'set' before being plunged into hot water then plucked and dressed for the table.

Stanley Lawrence was a good and keen fisherman and went to City Beach to fish from the southern rock groyne which had a galvanised wire fence around the perimeter with a pipe along the top. The northern groyne had not yet been built. Many men lined up and leaned on the fence and fished from there. At times, there were arguments about fishing lines getting crossed in the casting process. They used long fishing rods and space was at a premium. Good hauls of fish, both herring and whiting, were caught. Then, when Stanley Lawrence got home, he skilfully cleaned and filleted the fish so there was not a bone in sight, a lovely meal of fresh fish and fresh crusty bread was served up by Doreen. Stanley Lawrence bred 'wogs' (maggots) to use as bait. He would put meat or fish heads down the backyard for the blowflies to blow the meat (lay maggots). After the maggots reached a substantial size, he would transfer them to a jar that contained pollard. He let them clear their intestines of the meat then cleaned out the jar and put the maggots in fresh bran and put them in the fridge to keep them alive until he needed them. He was certainly successful in his fish haul so maggots must be wonderful bait! Before the maggots were put on the hook, he would put them in his mouth and roll them so they would be straight, then they could be threaded onto the hook properly. It seems there are not the numbers of fish along the beaches these days and fewer fisher-people attempt it.

A sporting life for the children

Both Stanley Lawrence and Doreen had been very active sportspeople in their youth and they thought it was time for their children to enter into a sporting life. Stanley Lawrence was instrumental in forming the under-age Australian Rules football in Floreat Park. He ran several of the teams, including those in which his boys played. Doreen helped by washing and drying the team's jumpers and getting things ready for the next match. Lindsay and Glentyn were very good players but Lindsay went on to excel in the sport, eventually playing in the Western Australian Football League (WAFL) for Claremont. He also played in the State team. His number was 24 and he was often best player.

The family was very proud of him and Stanley Lawrence and Doreen attended most of his games, along with Gladys Catherine and John McGlinn. The Friday night 'Carroll get together' had to stop. Lindsay had to go to bed early to be fit for the game next day and couldn't be disturbed. Football was now a big part of life. After the game there was often a party at the Carroll house for the players. Doreen was not keen on Lindsay going out where she didn't know where he was and not knowing what he was up to so they opened their house to the team of players and celebrations or commiserations were spent at home. Doreen's door was always open and she welcomed the young players. Many of them would drop in for a visit and a cuppa and chat with her. She was the number one interrogator and asked many questions of the boys and they loved it and they loved her. She never passed judgement but gave them stern advice if they needed it, she was always direct and honest and she had no 'frills' in her behaviour. She was like a mother to some of them and she always made them feel welcome and always gave them something to eat.

One day, after a few of those parties, the 'bottle-o' – the man who collected glass bottles from the neighbourhood – was carrying the bottles past the window and was muttering "What the fuck do these people do with the bloody beer, bathe in it?" It was no wonder he thought that – on that occasion there were 72 dozen (864) bottles!

During the summer, when the children were younger, the Carrolls would meet at the Wembley Hotel beer garden. There was a carpark by the side of the beer garden and a wire fence between them. The kids had to wait in the car outside the fence while the adults enjoyed a cold drink on the other side of the fence. Occasionally, a raspberry fizzy drink would be given to the kids who were hot and bored witless!

Both Stanley Lawrence and Doreen were keen to ensure their children could swim. They enjoyed swimming and the family often went to the beach in the summer. They bought the kids rubber 'Lilo' surf shooters and everyone loved the excitement of shooting the big dumpers that occurred at City Beach. Stanley Lawrence and Doreen had enjoyed swimming in their youth and Stanley Lawrence probably felt that learning to swim proficiently may someday save their children's lives as it had him during his escape from Crete. They enrolled their children in the City Swimming Club at Crawley Baths where lessons were given by Mr Smith, the club's coach. Stanley Lawrence would take his children to the 'City Baths' every Tuesday and Thursday afternoons for swimming training. Every Sunday morning during the swimming season the children participated in the races.

Francis Peter and William Kevin soon took their children to the 'baths' and they too participated in the races. It wasn't long before the Carroll brothers were officials in the club. They were either organisers, time keepers, or judges, depending on what was required on the day. The women went and watched the races and were very encouraging. They were very dedicated parents.

Later, when the children were in their early teens, Stanley Lawrence decided he would enter in the three mile 'Swim Through Perth'. His only problems were, he didn't have the time to do the training for long distance racing, and his ear problems from the war (damaged eardrums) meant he had to wear ear plugs made of paraffin wax. This seemed no problem to overcome but any water entering his ear would cause severe dizziness, a dangerous situation out in the middle of the river. On the day of the race, he took off first: it was a handicap race. He swam well for the first two miles but then extreme tiredness set in. He plugged on slowly. A boat that was there to follow the swimmers encouraged Stanley Lawrence to give up and get into the boat. No, he wasn't going to give up. His tenacity and determination hadn't left him. The man in the boat yelled out to him that he'd need a calendar, not a stop watch! Still Stanley Lawrence continued on and eventually made it to the WA Rowing Club in Perth and struggled up onto the launch area. Everyone clapped and cheered the little bloke who had a bloody good go at it. His ears only gave him a problem right near the end of the race and he breast-stroked for the last part of the race. He came last.

Holidays at the Cunningham's farm

Every school holidays while the children were still small and during their primary school years, the family, along with Russell, Francis Peter and Joan Irene's son, and Lesley, William Kevin and Patricia's daughter would go to Doreen's aunty's farm in Kirup, Western Australia. The farm belonged to John McGlinn's sister Sarah Ruby and her husband Cecil Cunningham. Their son Tom and his wife Verna lived in a separate house on the farm. The farm was a dairy farm that produced cream for the market. They had Jersey cows, a breed that produces very rich milk with a high cream content. The skimmed off milk was fed to the pigs that were also grown for the market.

Every school holidays, the family went to the farm and helped out in the antiquated dairy. At first, the family stayed with Sarah Ruby and Cecil in their little 'groupie' house but this got to be too small for the growing crowd. Tom and Verna made their house a welcome change and the family stayed with them and their small children. Stanley Lawrence still had his rabbit traps from before the war and he would go trapping rabbits to supplement the meat for the table.

Sarah Ruby and Cecil decided they wanted to leave the farm and retire to Perth. The farm was sold and Tom and Verna moved to a farm in Wilga, Western Australia. This farm was a sheep farm. Stanley Lawrence and Doreen helped with the farm work, either out in the paddocks or in the house. This farm still had the old plank and bucket toilet that had to be emptied. It seems Tom wasn't keen on the job of emptying the smelly pan and it was always full when the Carrolls arrived. Poor Stanley Lawrence would have to dig the pit and empty the pan.

Those times were happy times for the Carroll family and the holidays were always enjoyed. Stanley Lawrence continued trapping rabbits which were abundant. He set traps in the bushland and paddock edges and always got a good haul. He would gut them and skin them and hang them on a broom handle by linking their legs together so they hung in pairs. The broom handle was placed between the front seat and back seat of the car and the rabbits were taken to the town of Boyup Brook where the butcher bought the rabbits to sell to his customers. Much to their delight, the children were given the money. Myxomatosis had not arrived in south-west Western Australia at that time and the rabbits were in plague proportion and very healthy.

The holidays at the Cunningham farm lasted until the children became teenagers, left school, and went to work. Stanley Lawrence and Doreen's son, Lindsay couldn't get the farm life out of his blood and, after his football career and a few varied jobs, went on to manage a few farms. He loved the farm life so much he bought a farm in Manjimup and eventually became a dairy farmer, helped by his wife Maureen (the same name as his sister). Both Stanley Lawrence and Doreen enjoyed helping out whenever they could and Stanley Lawrence would wander over the farm where he enjoyed his own company and grubbed out weeds.

Family holidays with the grandchildren and back to Nannine for Stanley Lawrence

After Stanley Lawrence and Doreen's daughter Maureen had married and had two children, it was decided in 1973 that there should be a visit to Stanley Lawrence's childhood home town of Nannine in the Murchison. While there, Stanley Lawrence wandered around the demolished townsite and found where his house once stood. He probably hadn't been back since he was nine years old and it must have been quite a shock to see the utter devastation of the place. They all visited the grave of his little sister, Eileen Agnes, and he carved her name in the wood at the foot of her grave fence. He would probably have liked to spend some time alone to gather his thoughts and think about what had been, but no, there were impatient grandchildren to see to…

On this trip, they all continued on to the Hamersley Ranges, including Wittenoom Gorge. There were no facilities and there was no one there. The roads in were like goat tracks on very steep inclines that made Doreen screech with fright. They visited the pastoral station, Mulga Downs, which was owned by Lang Hancock, a mining magnate, and were made welcome by the station manager Mr Houston and were directed to the shearers' quarters so they could use the facilities. Mr Houston knew that Stanley Lawrence's brother Norman George had worked on this station for many years, mainly doing mechanical duties. He had scattered Norman George's ashes over the area from their small plane. Norman George invented all sorts of things that were used on the station or in the asbestos mine. He simply drew the plans on his shed floor and made the objects in there. One was the self-closing gate that used weights to close it. This was taken up by many other stations and farms but Norman George didn't care – he wasn't interested in the glory nor the money. He also invented a type of carriage/cart that ran on tracks down into a mine shaft. This was taken and used by the mining industry, especially by Hancock and Wright at their asbestos mine in Wittenoom. Norman George would pay for this: he died of lung problems, aged only sixty-five years.

In 1974, the family re-visited Nannine and Stanley Lawrence visited the only stone ruin of a building still standing, the Post Office, and wrote his name and birthdate and that he was born in Nannine.

1974 - Stanley Lawrence, David, and Amanda – Nannine Post Office (family photo)

Now school holidays could once again be enjoyed away from the city – this trip was the first of many. The red dirt was certainly still in Stanley Lawrence's veins and many holidays out into the goldfields with Doreen, their daughter, son in-law and their small children David and Amanda were had. Stanley Lawrence's and Doreen's son Lindsay had a daughter, Vicki, who was the same age as Amanda. Vicki and Amanda were the best of friends as well as cousins and subsequently Vicki joined the travelling group. Only once did Renny, their son, go.

A Cargill's Caravanette was purchased for more comfortable trips and longer stays. The preferred place to stay was *The Twelve Mile* or *Yaloginda*, as it was known in the old days, between Nannine and Meekatharra. This was a stage coach stopover in the past and was now just broken glass and rubbish. Stanley Lawrence's father George Thomas probably took his Mail Coaches through there.

The old directional sign for when these places were thriving (personal photo)

Across the usually dry creek was a nice campsite that was flat and clear and near some water, if there had been rain. The first time at this camp the station owner came along and Stanley Lawrence asked him if he knew his old school friend, Jack Bell. Stanley Lawrence was delighted that this man was indeed Jack Bell and the camp was on Norrie Station, which he owned. They hadn't seen each other since they were nine years old and with each year that went by after that a visit to the Bells was had.

Stanley Lawrence and Doreen decided that a better car for travelling should be bought so they bought a blue Volkswagen Kombi with a white roof and an annex. Perfect! There was now more room and more comfort and the poor old Kombi went everywhere and was loaded to the gunnels. On one trip even a doll's house was attached to the roof to house a few chickens and a rooster. When they were parked in Meekatharra, the rooster stuck its head out of the window and began to crow. A drunk Aboriginal man took exception to the crowing and abused Stanley Lawrence, who calmly pointed to the rooster. There were chuckles all round.

Stanley Lawrence and grandson David were not just grandfather and grandson, they were the best of mates, and from the time David could talk he called Stanley Lawrence 'Stan'. It was 'Davy' and 'Stan', together in a beautiful relationship that lasted until Stanley Lawrence's death.

A swim in a dam 'Stan and Davy' – 1973 (Family photo)

'Stan and Davy' rabbiting with David's toy rifle 1973 (Family photo)

Stanley Lawrence's teaching skills and his interest in natural history were a boon to his grandchildren. He taught them about the bush and the animals, birds, and insects, and a bit of geology by encouraging them to search for special rocks, including quartz crystals. He told them to be on the lookout for bits of gold and made them a small 'billy' can with a wire handle to collect their treasures. Everyone would wander the bush for hours, looking at all the wonderful things that were there. Stanley Lawrence was a wonderful amateur naturalist with an interest in all things. His enquiring mind meant his knowledge was vast on many topics.

Stanley Lawrence teaching Vicki and Amanda (right) about 1978 (Family photo)

Stanley Lawrence – school teacher

At school, his teaching skills and interesting methods meant that while teaching his pupils he would take them on bush rambles around the nearby bushland. A student, very many years later, reminisced about her time in Mr Carroll's class and his passing on his love of the bush to her. She remembered the bush walks around the school and his enthusiasm. She had had a teacher the year before who had made her feel unworthy and she went down in her grades and became less confident. However, she loved Mr Carroll's teaching style and felt he was the type of teacher who made her feel worthwhile and important and, because of this, she excelled in her school work. She said he seemed to know she had a problem and he provided support and encouragement. (Personal comment: Julie Johns, 2022).

He encouraged the pupils by using novel teaching methods. For example, part of the curriculum was to learn about imports and exports between Commonwealth countries – a boring subject at the best of times! To make it interesting, he would go out into the playground and draw a map of the world on the ground. The pupils were allocated an item that represented a product and the amount of that product. He would get these children to stand in the country of origin and that was 'their' country. Each child, or group of children, had a country. Then they would take the item and 'export it' to the receiving country. Imports into and out of Australia were done similarly. This made the children easily remember and they excelled. He did other inventive teaching methods and was also very much involved in the sporting activities of his pupils. The children loved him even though he was very strict and didn't allow them to play up. Any chatting would result in an aluminium rod being brought down on the desk of the offending child, making a very loud bang. This would shock the children into line!

Eventually, he found that his hearing was failing, caused by the bombs during the war, and pain from his war injuries meant he had to give up front of class teaching. He went to Applecross Primary School to do administration for a while then he was posted to the Correspondence School near Perth Modern School to teach children in Distance Education. He thoroughly enjoyed this work and was able to visit some of his pupils in the outback. While at the Correspondence School, he began to teach on School of the Air on 6WU, a country version of ABC radio. He could relate to the children of the bush and could talk about the bush with them. His grandson, David 'Davy', excelled in reading aloud from a very early age. David would go into the radio studio and read to the children over the radio; he was very impressive for such a young child.

Time ticked by and his grandchildren got older and were no longer able to go on holidays to the bush so in time only his daughter and son-in-law went with him. Doreen had decided that she didn't want to go any more.

Just after his retirement from work in 1977, aged sixty-two (war veterans could retire at 60), he began guitar lessons. His love of music was still with him and he became quite a good player. He went out to aged care homes to entertain the residents.

Gold fever

Then the love of his life developed – gold prospecting! He had Gold Fever! The new metal detectors had recently come on the market and from then on he was out prospecting every chance he could get, alone or with someone else. He found a considerable amount of gold and as a result all of his brothers, (excluding Norman George), and his sister, Kathleen Christine's husband Len Guy, decided to give it a go and they went along with him. Between them they got quite a good haul.

Camp at Nannine Siding. Stanley Lawrence at his Kombi and John Raymond with his caravan (Family photo)

Camp at Murrin-Murrin, L-R William Kevin, John Raymond, Arthur Henry. (Family photo) Stanley Lawrence went out in his Kombi and the other brothers had, or shared caravans.

Meat was always available if you had the stomach to live off the land. Unfortunately, the brothers weren't that keen, particularly Francis Peter who flatly refused to eat anything Stanley Lawrence brought in.

Stanley Lawrence with a dead kangaroo he had shot, ready for the next meal (Family photo)

Stanley Lawrence had roughed it in the bush during the depression and among his bush skills was the ability to make an earth oven in which to cook. This oven was very efficient and sometimes he would make bread or scones for the group. None of his brothers had had to experience the harshness of the depression years in the bush as Stanley Lawrence had, and therefore had not built up these bush skills.

Stanley Lawrence with scones at his in-ground oven (Family photo)

They all enjoyed their time out in the bush roughing it but in time they too tired of the bush and the tedium of prospecting. Not Stanley Lawrence: he continued for many years. His favourite place to go was Tampa, near Kookynie, but he went out well beyond there to the historical goldfields to try his luck. He would go rabbit trapping so meat was always available – there were no car refrigerators so fresh meat couldn't be kept. The rabbits were cooked in a camp oven with potatoes and root vegetables and were delicious.

The poor old VW Kombi had had a very hard life and had to have a few new motors. A couple of times it broke down on his way back to Perth and he had to ring home for assistance. On occasions, his son-in-law John went to his rescue by taking a spare part or once, a full motor, out to Stanley Lawrence and together they would fix the problem. It was fortunate that they both had excellent mechanical skills.

Stanley Lawrence often took a push bike out with him and would go looking for likely spots to prospect or get water. He would ride the same track each day, out and back. Once, a visitor came to his camp and said he had seen a million bike tracks and wondered why there were so many cyclists way to buggery out there! Unfortunately, Stanley Lawrence came a cropper and fell heavily from his bike and injured his arm and shoulder and had to return home early.

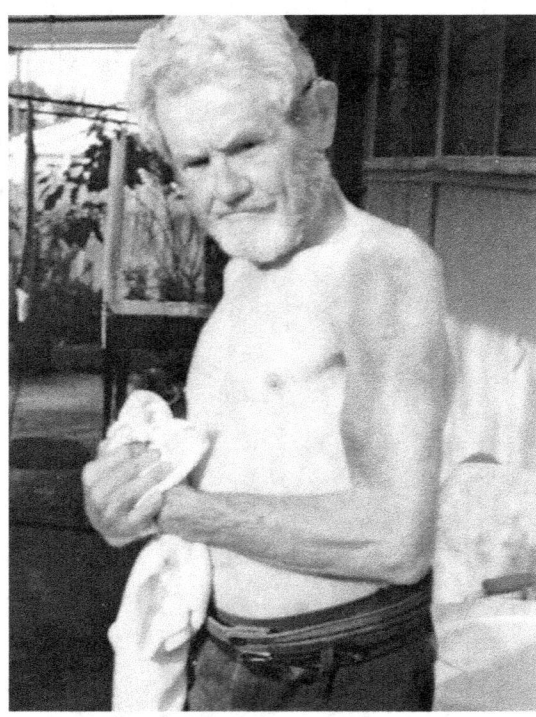

Stanley Lawrence and his injured arm and shoulder (Family photo)

After several years, eventually, only his daughter went with him; she had got the red dust in her veins and had developed a love of natural history and together they enjoyed the bush.

Doreen was a timid woman in as much as she didn't like being alone and was frightened of being in the house alone at night. Fortunately, their son Glentyn had moved back into the family home so was there when Stanley Lawrence went away, sometimes for three or four weeks at a time.

Pain and suffering for Stanley Lawrence

Stanley Lawrence's insatiable desire for adventure and love of the bush came to an abrupt end. In 1988, on the last trip of his prospecting career, he came back wracked with pain. He went to Hollywood Hospital, a hospital for war veterans, and after tests they found he had rheumatoid arthritis. He must have had it for several years but he took the medication, Indocid, a nonsteroidal anti-inflammatory medication and it masked the pain until now. Because he had a bad stomach and suffered with acid, he took this medication by suppository. Once, he gave Lindsay, his son, one which he took by mouth, it made him woozy and light headed. He never took another one! The rheumatoid arthritis curtailed Stanley Lawrence's activities properly. He had to stop doing many physical activities.

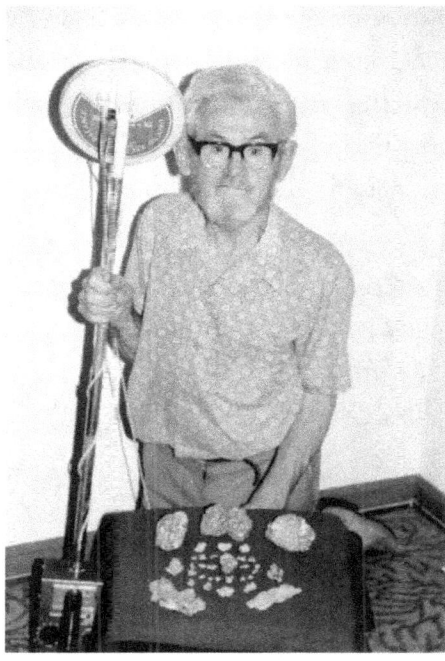

Stanley Lawrence pre diagnosis of Rheumatoid Arthritis with his haul of gold he had found. (Family photo)

Stanley Lawrence, John McGlinn and Doreen a few days before Stanley Lawrence's bleed (family photo)

In late 1991, Stanley Lawrence went to Hollywood Repatriation Hospital for some tests. He had complained of breathlessness and pain. From then on it seems the medical profession failed him badly. He went into hospital for tests and ended up having part of one lung removed. When his daughter Maureen visited him, he was crying and asking why they did this to him. It was very distressing for him (and her). Stanley Lawrence had recently applied for an increase to his military pension for war-caused injuries. A portion of a letter, below, written by Maureen explains in part what transpired.

Letter dated 3rd July 1992, to the Commonwealth Department of Veterans Affairs

> *" At that time and up until recently he has constantly refused to apply for an increase in his pension because of his patriotism and the urge to always do the right thing', also he is very proud man and did not want anyone thinking he was 'weak' for seeking help.*
>
> *He retired from his job, which he loved, earlier than necessary because of his war caused disabilities. Had he applied then chances are he would have received the T&PI* (totally and permanently incapacitated) *pension like so many others less deserving.*
>
> *As it is he did not apply but did seek medical treatment for the pain in his back and shoulders and for the stomach upset and was prescribed Indocid an anti-inflammatory drug which as we have now been told*

he took for too many years (approx 18 years). Initially he took the Indocid orally but this caused stomach bleeding so he was told by the Doctors to take it in the form of suppositories. He was never told to stop taking the drugs which were constantly prescribed to him until he was admitted to Hollywood Hospital last year with his lung complaint. The Doctors immediately stopped the Indocid and told us he had been on them for far too long. It is now well known that Indocid has very severe side effects if taken over a long period. This has been common knowledge for some time now and we would like to know why he was constantly prescribed these drugs when problems were known.

I find it particularly distressing and rather amazing that you can categorically state that his lung problems are due to interstitial lung disease related to his arthritis. We were constantly told by his Doctors at Hollywood Hospital that they did not know the cause of his lung problem nor could they identify anything from the large lung sample they took to test. They also said in hindsight after the operation that they possibly should not have done the operation when he was in such a weakened state, especially since they discovered no cause. Following the operation, because of his severely depressed state of health, he needed special care to get him back to a satisfactory weight.

The Doctors suggested to us that his problems were probably drug based; drugs which he had been prescribed for war caused problems. How do you get different information from that given to us?

(As a side issue my Mother was very shocked when she went to the hospital for a visit to find that he had been operated on and was in intensive care, she, nor any of his family, had been notified that an operation was to be done. This issue in itself needs to be addressed at some time.)

On the understanding that his lung problems were due to the body breaking down from drug taking it is easy to relate his current problems back to war caused injuries. You state in your letter that these injuries have taken a back seat' to his other medical problems, arthritis. This is not so, the arthritis is 'in the back seat' compared with what he has had to deal with over the years and his current problems, all stemming from medical treatment and prescribed drugs for war caused injuries.

To make matters worse he is now in a stage of rehabilitation from a stroke' not bleeding into the brain but into the ventricles of the brain, and bleeding into the bladder and possibly other areas that the capillaries lead to. His mental state has been one of no memory for some time, approx 6 weeks, and is now in a state of confusion. He is gradually getting better but there are no guarantees on him returning to normal.

The stroke was caused by the high level of Warferin, a blood thinning agent, in his blood. The Warferin was administered by Doctors from Hollywood after a blood clot was found in his leg after the lung operation. On his admittance to the Queen Elizabeth Medical Centre the Doctors advised us that the Warferin levels were far too high Why?

Mr Carroll has been under the Repatriation Doctors for many years and with events from last year, all medically caused, we feel the Repatriation Department has a lot to answer for. Mr Carroll has always suffered in silence and his sense of duty to his country seems to have cost him dearly"

An advocate to the Veterans Review Board, Mr G.W. Clark-Hall stated on 4th June 1996 – *"Part of his wartime service, particularly in Greece and Crete and the well documented escape from Crete, were stressful to the extreme limits of human endurance"*

Still, he did not get any satisfaction from the Veterans Affairs!

Sadly, Stanley Lawrence did not get better and suffered mental disability for the rest of his short life. He went from a mentally vital man with an indomitable spirit of adventure to a man who spent most of the rest of his life in bed. Before he was discharged from hospital, the doctors suggested to Doreen that she put Stanley Lawrence in a home but she refused.

Stanley Lawrence after his 'stroke' (Family photo)

A few months before he died, the media still had an interest in his war heroism and printed an article about him.

Stanley Lawrence
Once again his heroism was recognised
(Sunday Times April 23rd 1995. p. 44)

Death of Stanley Lawrence

He died at home in his own bed during the night of October 15th 1995. He had been in a mental fog of mild confusion for three years. His last week or so was that of a state where he didn't recognise anyone. However, the day before he died, his daughter Maureen went into his room; he turned his head and gave her the most beautiful smile before returning to a non-responsive state.

Maureen tried to get answers from Hollywood Hospital and had meetings with doctors there, only to be met with what she felt was a cover up and no explanations – frustrating in the extreme. Eventually, they sent her his medical records.

Stanley Lawrence was cremated and his ashes scattered at Nannine Cemetery. His son, Lindsay, organised the memorial plaque that sits on top of the hill under the old *Hakea* shrub and overlooks the usually dry Lake Annean. His ashes were scattered there: once again he was home in the bush. Some of his family members also have plaques near the grave of his little sister Eileen Agnes who had died there so many years ago.

The plaque at Nannine Cemetery – back to the bush he loved so much (Photo. by Maureen)

Finally, it was recognised by Veterans Affairs that he had died of war caused afflictions and a plaque was inserted in the remembrance wall at the War Cemetery next to Karrakatta Cemetery, in Smythe Road, Hollywood, and is placed near his brothers, Francis Peter and William Kevin, who were also considered to have died of war causes.

Stanley Lawrence Carroll

Francis Peter Carroll

William Kevin Carroll

Stanley Lawrence Carroll – his place in the bush.
Born 6th January, 1915 - died 15th October, 1995 (photo John Francesconi)

Doreen

Life without Stanley Lawrence

Doreen now had to get on in life without Stanley Lawrence. She had looked after him, sometimes with great frustration and impatience as it would be for anyone who has to deal with someone with reduced mental abilities. She kept him clean and fed him well and her part in his care should not be underestimated.

With all that had happened and the stonewalling of bureaucracy, Doreen fought on with the Department of Veterans Affairs so that she could have Stanley Lawrence's service to his country and war caused death recognised and for her to receive the War Widows' Pension. If a man was a Prisoner of War, it is an automatic right.

After many meetings with officials, Maureen was sick of the stalling and fobbing off and said sternly to the meeting that if Stanley Lawrence had stayed with those who were captured, his wife would have got the pension, but because he risked his life and saved many men, she got nothing and what a sad state of affairs it was that his service was not recognised. Not long afterwards, Doreen was awarded a War Widows Pension. Someone must have looked at Stanley Lawrence's war record – at last! … and his medical records that showed the neglect of his war injuries and their treatment. Doreen could now live a little more comfortably in her old age.

Doreen's life continues

Doreen still needed to be entertained, and boredom was something she tried to avoid. On occasions, she went away on holidays with her daughter, Maureen. One included a trip on the paddle steamer *Murray Princess* along the Murray River in South Australia. Doreen absolutely loved this trip. She loved to travel and was good company. She joined in on all the activities and didn't want to miss a thing. Many years earlier, she went to Singapore on the ship *Centaur* with her sister in-law Patricia, William Kevin's wife. They had a wonderful time and subsequently had a few holidays to Rottnest Island together. She and Stanley Lawrence went on the cruise ship *Achille-Lauro* to Sydney. Doreen loved the trip but Stanley

Lawrence was a bit quiet about the whole thing. Cruises were not to his liking – perhaps it brought too many memories back to haunt him. Then, in later years, she and her sister Joan Irene went to Sydney and had a great time. If Doreen had the opportunity, she may have become an intrepid traveller but it was not to be.

In 2002, her sister Joan Irene died of breast cancer at the age of eighty.

Glentyn had taken Doreen to visit Joan Irene quite often in their later years. They had always been very close but as sisters do, they squabbled on occasions. Doreen was the only one in her family left and she mourned for her loved sister.

For years, Maureen took Doreen on outings every Sunday either to Kings Park or Point Resolution. Doreen would make a flask of coffee and take a cake and they would sit together and chat and watch the ever-changing views. Later, Glentyn went along but the venue changed to the Southport Ferry Terminal where it was easier for Doreen to walk to the coffee shop.

Doreen on her Sunday outing to Kings Park (photo Maureen)

2003 - Doreen on her 80th birthday at her favourite coffee shop, Southport Ferry Terminal, then owned by John Moreno (photo Maureen)

Doreen loved going out but having to wait until Sunday was a bit too long, so she joined Mercy Care who picked her up once a week and took her on an outing with other people in a small bus. She enjoyed going but again was not really good at mixing. It's strange that she was very good at fleeting meetings with people but if they were going to be seen for a longer period she withdrew into herself. Even with her neighbours through the years she didn't mix with nor chat often. She divulged nothing of her life to them. However, she did spend a bit of time with one of her neighbours, Paula Halliday, whose husband Ian died young after being a prisoner of war in a Japanese prison camp and had left Paula with two young children, John and Judith. Paula was the only person outside the family that Doreen spent time with, but Paula too died reasonably young from a rare blood complaint.

Doreen becomes frailer

As she aged, Doreen stayed home with Glentyn and did everything for him. Then, as time moved on, she became more fragile and less able to walk with any strength. She became more unsteady on her feet and in 2008, at the age of eighty-five, disaster struck. She fell and was badly bruised around her hip area and she got a black eye, among other bruising. Glentyn couldn't get her up and she was taken to hospital by ambulance and then moved to Hollywood Hospital for recovery. Her recovery was good and she attended all the safety courses set up by the Occupational Therapist.

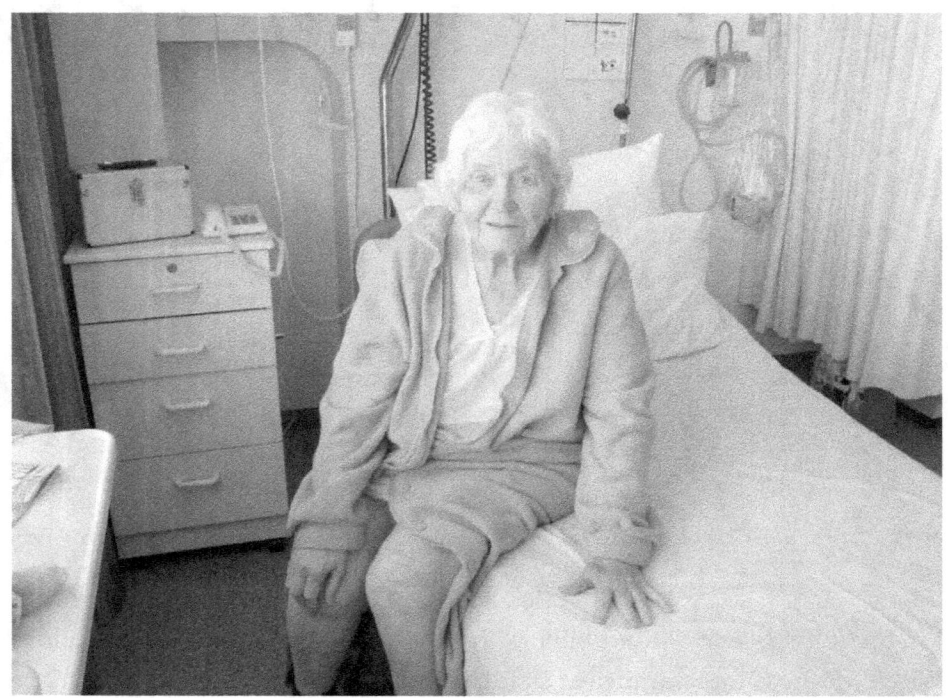

Doreen badly bruised and sporting a black eye – in Hollywood Hospital, 2008. (Family photo)

Doreen became frailer but she was still strong and her personality was still a force to be reckoned with. She did all the things she had done prior to the fall and still went out on her Sunday outings with Maureen and with the group from Mercy Care.

On the 25th April, ANZAC Day, 2012, at the age of eighty-eight, Doreen fell over the mat in the hallway of her house. She was quite a big woman and she fell heavily onto the floor. This time it was serious. Glentyn couldn't move her and she was in severe pain so he called an ambulance and she was taken to Sir Charles Gairdner Hospital emergency department. X-rays proved she had broken her hip. This is often a death sentence to the elderly, and everyone was very worried. She was operated on and, much to the relief of the family, she survived. After a short recovery, she was sent to Osborne Park Hospital for rehabilitation where they made her walk. This was painful in the extreme and she cried out when they made her walk quite long distances but they told her if she didn't do this rehabilitation she would be in a wheelchair. Doreen complained that the nurses were cruel and unhelpful and that she wanted a transfer to Hollywood Hospital which was approved. Hollywood Hospital made life easier for Doreen and didn't insist on the more difficult rehabilitation. Doreen was happier, but the consequences were she now had to use a walking frame and if she went on outings she had to be in a wheelchair.

It was now Glentyn's turn to look after Doreen, which he did well. He didn't have to do too much because Veterans Affairs went through the house and put in aids to help Doreen get around the house more easily. There had been many aids already there that were done to help Stanley Lawrence when he was ill. They supplied a house cleaner and a gardener and the Silver Chain visited to shower Doreen. For Glentyn, it was mostly doing the cooking and seeing that Doreen got to bed okay and empty her commode each morning. Much to her distain, she went into respite care for a week or so to give Glentyn a break.

Sadly, she couldn't go on her outings with Mercy Care but could go to their day care centre which she enjoyed. Maureen still took her out each Sunday, and she always looked forward to this outing and sometimes other members of the family would join them.

Then the family dynamics changed. Doreen changed her will and, sadly, whenever money is involved, there is often conflict. The family unit was now fractured.

Doreen grew weaker and over time she found it more difficult to go anywhere. She sank into a depression but she was stoic and didn't show her feelings. She was the master of cover-up, as she always had been, probably since her youth when she had suffered so much. She never cried! The family didn't realize, her cover up was complete, and they just thought she was tough! We just didn't ask. Sad.

Doreen dies

In about May 2013, Doreen was out to lunch with the family when she felt faint. Subsequent medical check-ups revealed that she was suffering left side heart failure. Again she was hospitalised in Hollywood Hospital. She spoke to the doctors and between them they agreed that no treatment would be given. It was a difficult decision for her because she wanted to stay and not miss anything but she wanted go as well; she was confused and frightened but very brave. Eventually, she decided she had had enough and she went into palliative care.

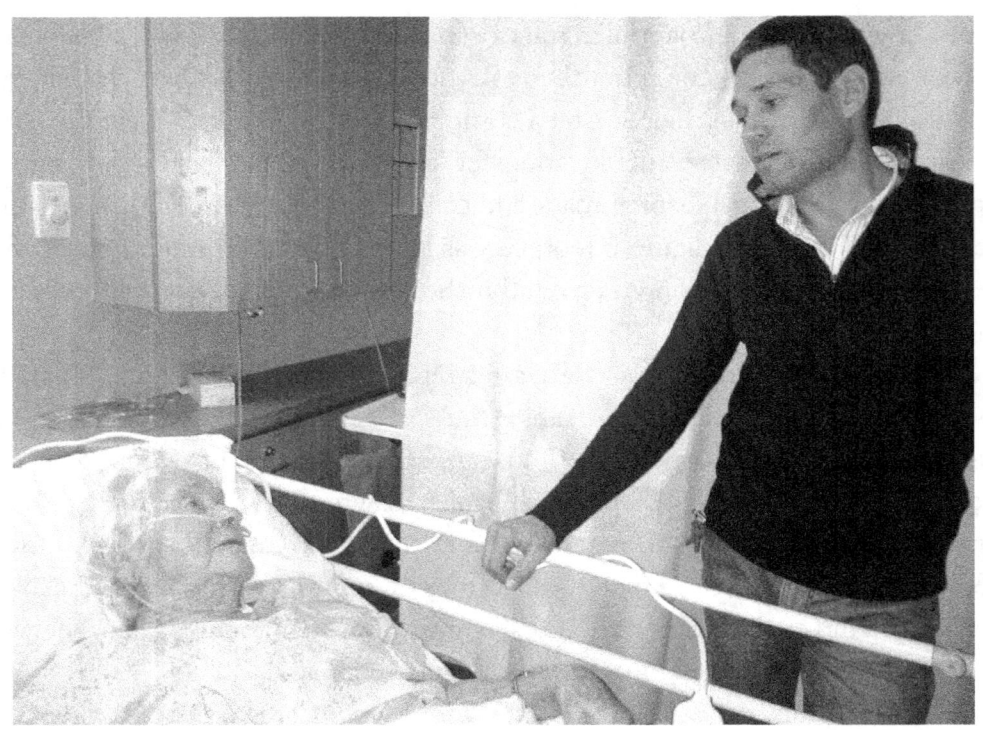

Doreen and 'Davy' a few days prior to her death (Photo – Maureen)

All of her grandchildren visited her at once; she was delighted to see them all there together and laughed and joked with them. It was a sad but beautiful farewell.

Maureen stayed with her until she died during the night of 16th June 2013. She was eighty-nine years old.

Doreen McGlinn/Carroll - born 1st December, 1923, died 16th June, 2013.

Kevin Williams' wife Patricia died in 2020. She was the last of the Carroll gang.

The Carroll gang was an amazingly resourceful group who had experienced privations, danger, and plenty of suffering. Their type will probably never be seen again: they had a toughness and a resilience to be proud of. They were all very kind and wonderful people and all are sadly missed.

Stanley Lawrence and Doreen had had a solid relationship and a good life. They had seen very tough times and were stoic to the end. Because of the hardships they experienced, they knew they didn't want their children to ever suffer the way they had. They dedicated their lives to the care of their family and helped to ensure they became good and responsible adults. Stanley Lawrence always strove to better himself throughout his life. They could look back over the years and know that they did their best – not much else could be asked of them.

The end of an era.

About the Author

Maureen Francesconi (nee Carroll) was brought up in a war service housing area in the western suburbs of Perth, Western Australia during the 1950s and 60s. She went on to become a qualified ladies' hairdresser before marrying and having two children. Later, she went to university and was awarded a Bachelor of Applied Science in librarianship followed by a Post Graduate Diploma in business. Her employment included Head Librarian in various public libraries and Manager of a newly formed computer service in local government. Throughout her life, she was intensely keen on natural history with a particular interest in birds and their behaviour. A chance encounter led to professional work in this area for over 25 years.

Throughout her life, she always had an interest in Western Australian history. When Covid 19 brought lockdowns, this interest flourished and an underlying curiosity in family history was satisfied. Research led to more and deeper knowledge of her past relatives and she felt this information should be shared. The product is this book.

www.ingramcontent.com/pod-product-compliance
Lightning Source LLC
Chambersburg PA
CBHW081613100526
44590CB00021B/3426